When *the* Rivers Flowed

AN AMBITIOUS HILLBILLY AND A SOUTHERN FLAPPER DISCOVER KNOXVILLE, TENNESSEE

BY MARILYN LAYMAN MASCARO

First Edition

ISBN: 978-1-960146-16-8 (hard cover)
978-1-960146-17-5 (soft cover)

Editor: Melisa Graham

Warren publishing

Published by Warren Publishing
Charlotte, NC
www.warrenpublishing.net
Printed in the United States

This work is dedicated to Marie who battled dementia in her later years. I couldn't let that be the end of her story.

AUTHOR'S NOTE

My interest in writing this book sparked as a child listening to my grandmother's stories of her early life. In many ways, Marie Little Layman and Earl Layman, my grandparents, led ordinary lives as they came of age in the Southeast, then raised a family in Knoxville, Tennessee. But history has a way of enveloping us all. The couple lived through major regional and national events while their decisions reflected the societal standards of their time. In this work, I've documented those events and attitudes through sources ranging from academic histories and newspaper accounts to interviews and personal letters. A few of my choices, mainly about character or motive, stem from my experiences as their granddaughter. In any case, *When the Rivers Flowed* places Earl and Marie in their time and town as they veer between exuberance and hardship while facing the sweeping challenges of their generation.

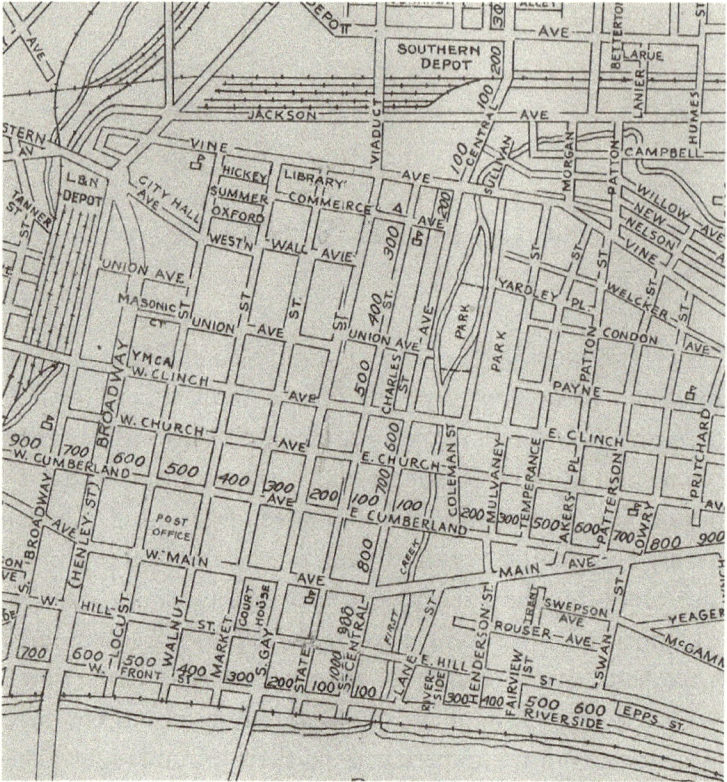

Map of Knoxville

PART I: *Around Appalachia*

CHAPTER 1

Aspirations

COLD RULED THE MORNING, spot-freezing Earl Layman's bare fingers to the silo's metal ladder. Climbing to its highest point, the seventeen-year-old linked his elbow around an iron rung and looked around. Above him, sparks of light punctured the black thickness of sky. To the east, beyond the horizon, a faint glow emanated from Knoxville, Tennessee. A farmhand who didn't particularly enjoy agriculture, Earl pictured the town as radiating with excitement, full of vaudeville shows and bowling alleys, cafeterias and automobiles.

Because the Great War spurred the national economy, well-paying jobs could be found in town, as well as on farms. War-related inflation cut into paychecks, though, while shortages disrupted daily life. So did the weather. The winter of 1918 brutalized all East Tennesseans, not just Earl. During the first weeks of January, the daily lows hovered near zero degrees Fahrenheit. In the terrible cold, residents struggled to heat their homes. Coal was the preferred fuel because it burned efficiently and produced sufficient heat, but it was expensive and rationed. Firewood was more commonly used, but by midwinter, the region's stockpiles of this staple were nearly depleted. The weather even rivaled the war for awful news. One Knoxville paper reported that area songbirds would starve in these conditions while another promoted "seven ways to increase winter comfort on the farm."[1]

Earl threw feed to the twenty cattle snorting below him, mist streaming from their nostrils. A functioning silo would have increased his winter comfort. So would a thick pair of gloves. He worked for an uncle, but Jack Shultz refused to give him special treatment. Earl couldn't afford to buy gloves himself and refused to ask his mother for money. Besides, more than his hands needed protection from the cold. Frost would be clinging to his underwear by the time he descended the silo.[2]

* * *

One man in a long-running, mass migration out of the Appalachian Mountains, Earl had left his home in East Tennessee's Sevier County. This large district began a few miles east of Knoxville and stretched to North Carolina. It had rolling hills closest to the city which escalated into foothills and then mountains that included the highest point in Tennessee. While beautiful, Sevier County's steep terrain made building roads expensive and difficult. Its communities tended to be small and had to be self-sufficient. Earl came from Eldee, which in 1917 contained a country store, several churches, and an elementary school. From there it took a full day to travel eight miles across winding, unpaved roads to the county seat in Sevierville, conduct business, and return home. Everyone, including Earl, knew the frustration of miring a wagon in a road-devouring mud pit.

Of all the problems caused by poor roads, Sevier County's lack of a high school most affected Earl. Slow travel made it impossible for its far-flung students to commute, and the scattered communities couldn't afford a secondary school on their own. To access a high school education, a few determined scholars boarded with relatives who lived in town. Earl left home to stay with, and work for, his Uncle Jack Shultz because it allowed him to attend Knox County's Farragut High School, which had a good reputation for academic and agricultural studies. He never graduated though.

Instead, a few months after climbing his uncle's grain silo in the frigid cold, the seventeen-year-old moved to the city. In doing so, he abandoned not just farm work but also his only chance for a high school education. The risky decision narrowed his options but put him in the location he craved.

Earl gambled his future on Knoxville, Tennessee.

The city had long attracted Appalachian in-migrants such as the teenager. They moved out of the Smoky Mountains to its east and the Cumberland Plateau to its west, geography that made Knoxville an obvious destination. Those two highlands framed the Tennessee Valley, and the city sat in its center. Railroads rebuilt after the Civil War radiated from town, following the valley north to Virginia and south to Georgia. For several decades, Knoxville prospered as a wholesaling center because of those railroads. Sensing opportunity, mountain residents left their overworked farms for jobs in its railroad yards, warehouses, and factories. Appalachian workers also fueled the region's lumber and coal industries that accessed widespread markets through the railroads. Marble, another East Tennessee product, became especially profitable, drawing acclaim for its pinkish coloring and helping to fuel America's late nineteenth century building boom. Knoxville's fortunes intertwined so closely with the highlands, its workers, and the extraction industries they fueled that it dubbed itself "Queen City of the Mountains."[3]

Having begun life as a riverside fort on the frontier, by the late nineteenth century Knoxville started gaining modern conveniences. In 1876, it adopted an early streetcar system. In 1880, it added a telephone service, then running water three years later, and electricity two years after that.[4] Not everyone could afford such luxuries, which were only available in the town's most prosperous areas, but they gave the affluent a higher quality of life and reinforced positive attitudes toward the city's future. Businesses flourished on Gay Street, Knoxville's main thoroughfare, while meat, fish, produce, and baked goods were sold at the downtown Market House.

*** *

Earl arrived into town a few decades later in 1918. His sisters, Ola and Mae, already lived there, and he first arranged to board with Ola and her husband. She had apprenticed with a Knoxville dressmaker, then briefly lived in California. Now, the couple resided on Luttrell Avenue in a brick, craftsman-style home.

If Earl wanted to stay in the city, though, he needed a job. His search for employment began on one of the streetcars that ferried residents into the city center. The short journey from Ola's neighborhood proved uneventful until the streetcar reached a bridge that crossed the Southern Railroad yards. There, it joined the carriages, wagons, and occasional automobile that crammed onto an awkwardly designed overpass.[5] Under the bridge, long lines of train tracks stretched across the city and rounded a bend in the distance. The railroad yards occupied a huge chunk of town and formed the boundary between Knoxville's main business district and its northern neighborhoods.

Abandoning the streetcar, Earl walked south on Gay Street, past buildings that had names such as "Emporium" and "Phoenix" chiseled into the marble above their doorways. In this summer of 1918, the armed forces had siphoned off much of the city's work force, so every business seemed to be hiring. Earl could choose among job openings. A few blocks past the traffic jam, two department stores faced each other across the road. Their display windows dazzled the city with fashionable merchandise, including women's skirts so short that they revealed the wearer's ankles, along with spiffy men's suits that looked far more professional than Earl's best clothes. As he lingered in front of the displays, shoppers, businessmen, and farmers-come-to-town hustled by him. Here in the heart of the city, telephone poles led the eye upward to signs that advertised billiard rooms, barbershops, eateries, and hotels. A profusion of wires crisscrossed above the road, announcing the telephones and electricity that made city life alluring. Aside from the occasional one-story structure or half-filled construction site, multiple-story buildings lined both sides of Gay Street. Two structures towered above the others, one housing the Southern Railway ticket office and another the Holston National Bank.

After walking several blocks farther south, Earl passed a theater and an opera house, which stood amid more businesses, but the red brick Knox County courthouse dominated this part of the city. A little farther south, Gay Street crossed the Tennessee River, the only road in Knoxville to do so. Earl watched as several wagons and carriages crossed the bridge and made their way out of town. He had seen automobiles on his walk, but horse or mule-driven transportation dominated city traffic. Reaching the bridge, he looked down to the river, a still-vital component of town commerce. Rickety wharves cut across its muddy floodplain while the ever-present odor of river sludge drifted upward.

In spite of that smell, Earl's journey had highlighted the city's vitality and its possibilities. Energized in a way that he had never felt on the farm, he returned to the center of town. The department stores beckoned with "help wanted" signs, as did a nearby hardware store that had "Woodruff's" carved into the marble above its doorway. Earl didn't want to earn his living using hammers and plows, or even selling them, but he knew their value.

By the time he contemplated applying at Woodruff's Hardware, the company had served Knoxville for fifty years and was led by a second generation of the Woodruff family. Originally a wholesaling business, the company had persevered through several challenges. When its headquarters burned during Knoxville's great fire of 1897, the owners had rebuilt. A few years later, an unfortunate experience with dynamite decimated that store. Era businesses often stocked the explosive, sometimes with disastrous consequences. The family had rebuilt again, adding an automatic sprinkler system. As the city's wholesaling economy faltered, Woodruff's started selling directly to the public. Now, its sales floor overflowed with the goods that East Tennesseans needed: pots, pans, rifles, knives, plows, and even automobile paint.

In the summer of 1918, Woodruff's hired Earl as an office boy.[6] Considering no task too menial, he ran errands, took messages, and fetched items for the staff. He adjusted to modern conveniences not found at his Sevier County homeplace, such as a telephone. Two companies served the Knoxville area, so a successful enterprise like Woodruff's kept a line from both of them. First in town to sign up with one of the companies, the store's owners and employees took great pride that their telephone number was "1." Earl and his employer came to appreciate each other. The hardware store gained a reliable worker in a time of labor shortages; Earl found a steady job in the city that he was determined to make his home.

CHAPTER 2
Tenant Farming

MARY LITTLE LIFTED THE HOE TO HER KNEES, then plunged it into the ground near a mound of yellow blooms. She chopped several times, working her way to the weed's roots. After annihilating the dandelion, she attacked a clump of Johnson grass, her wide-brimmed bonnet flopping vigorously. It shaded her face and theoretically kept the sun from sowing freckles across her cheeks. At age thirteen, Mary didn't mind hoeing, even though the muscles in her arms and back protested against it. Country girls such as herself often worked outside for hours a day. This made it especially unfair that in 1917, when she toiled diligently, most people considered tans and freckles unattractive.

Mary lived among the fields of North Alabama's hill country, which contains the southernmost tail of the same Appalachian Mountains that dominate Sevier County, Tennessee. Her parents, Fayette and Minnie Little, headed a typically sized farming family for their generation, meaning a large one. Mary had two older brothers, as well as three older and three younger sisters. Because the vegetable patch supplied their summer meals and the produce they canned for winter, gardening dominated Mary's schedule from spring through fall. Her efforts reflected a blunt reality: in order to survive, each member of her family had to contribute, with no exceptions made for young girls.

The Littles rented their home and cultivated someone else's land. This circumstance relegated them to the category of "poor Whites," a stereotype denoting ignorance and lack of ambition. In rural America during the early twentieth century, owning land provided financial security and social standing. Fayette Little's family had once enjoyed this protection, but his father gambled by buying several acres near Alabama's Coosa River. The family tilled rich, productive soil until an unusually high flood ruined the harvest. After several more destructive floods, they couldn't make their mortgage payments, and the bank claimed the farm. Devastated, the Littles had become tenants, forced to rent a house and farm. Only sharecroppers, who paid rent out of their future profits instead of with cash, had lower status and fewer prospects. This small difference resulted in a highly protected line of demarcation between the two groups, although both systems favored the landlords. Tenant and sharecropper farming dominated North Alabama's economy.

After the family land was lost, Fayette's plight worsened. With no chance of an inheritance, as a nineteen-year-old he worked as a laborer on a local estate. While working the harvest, a mechanical thresher drew in his left hand, ripping it from his arm.[7] The terror and pain that came with this tragedy deeply affected him. He spent months recuperating, trying to adjust to his disability. Fayette's ability to make a living as a farm laborer had been crushed along with his limb, which probably explains why he didn't marry for over a decade. The tragedy affected him emotionally as well. The family sometimes decided to "let Fayette worry" about a problem because they knew he would be fretting over it anyway. In spite of this spiral of poverty and misfortune, Fayette eventually married Minnie McGriff, and the couple started a family.

Their lives hinged on Fayette finding work. In 1900, he was employed on the Coosa River locks,[8] doing as much as any human could do to control the river. During the next decade, the family moved among three Alabama counties, beginning with Talladega and then St. Clair, where Mary was born.[9] Somewhere along the way, they transitioned into being tenant farmers. Tenants had little control over their lives, but relocating provided some autotomy and occurred within communities as well as across counties. The practice was so common that children such as Mary learned to greet each other by asking, "Where are you livin' now?"

By 1910, the Littles had moved to Etowah County into a rural neighborhood called Smokeneck. Fayette's brother Abe, who possessed a positive outlook on life that eluded Fayette, lived nearby with his family. As much as possible, considering they rented various farms, the Littles put down roots in Smokeneck. Here, the one-armed Fayette worked as a laborer, Minnie bore several children, and Mary began her career of garden-hoeing. She considered Smokeneck to be her home.

The houses rented by tenants typically perched atop short, stone pylons that lifted the floor about a foot off the ground. Dogs usually roamed underneath. Inside, the house's unpainted plank walls and flooring showed heavy use, as did the simple furnishings. With their transitory lifestyle, the family had few possessions to enliven these rooms. The accommodations usually included a cast-iron stove for cooking and winter heat and a wide porch for summer shade. Water came from an outdoor well, and a privy sat behind the house. Small shacks might dot the landscape: a chicken coop, a hog pen, a rickety barn. No plants survived in the barren yard, not even near the front steps. The family's constant foot traffic, combined with the intense summer heat, ensured that dust or mud prevailed, not grass.

As Fayette's injury suggests, accidents plagued tenant farmers. As a child, Mary fell into a large bin of harvested cotton. Unable to find a handhold amid the loose balls, she struggled, then passed out while suspended head-down. Her brother Jim eventually discovered her feet sticking out of the fluffy whiteness and hauled her out of the vat. As Mary lay sprawled and unconscious on the ground, her parents and siblings gathered around, horrified at the pooled blood that colored her face and upper body. A distraught Jim forever endeared himself to his sister by crying, "Oh, if Mary dies, I want to die too!"

Mary did recover, and her siblings teased Jim for his outburst. His concern wasn't overblown, though. She could have died in the cotton bin.

Disease also threatened their lives. Mary contracted malaria in childhood, probably through a mosquito bite. She shivered and sweat through a severe fever, along with joint pain, headaches, and vomiting. Mary gradually recovered, but not all her siblings were as lucky. Before she was born, her brother Clarence had succumbed to an undiagnosed illness. He suffered for ten months, his entire life, before dying. Fayette and Minnie altered a family photograph in remembrance of Clarence, sketching a portrait of the deceased infant into the picture so that he seemed to sit on his mother's lap in the midst of his father and siblings. Although sentimental, this gesture was less gruesome than the common practice of photographing the dead and displaying that picture in the parlor.

Without land, the Little family's chances for social mobility were virtually nonexistent. Alabama's tenants and sharecroppers rarely married into landowning families, and they almost never became public leaders.[10] Thus, these groups couldn't challenge the status quo that kept them from advancing. Their offspring received substandard educations, partly because the state only provided a five-month school year in the rural areas where most of them lived.[11] The children's status as farmworkers and the families' frequent relocations magnified their poor schooling, with stark results. Over several decades, one typical North Alabama high school graduated 50 percent of landowners' offspring but only 10 percent of those from non-landowning households.[12] Black children went to segregated schools and fared even worse.

With so few opportunities, factories lured some farmers into town. Textile mills paid in cash but kept wages so low that entire families had to work in order to survive. For parents who considered their children's factory jobs to be on the same level as farm chores, it was a fine system, especially since the mills paid these adults for their offspring's work.[13] As a result, so many children labored in the mills or fields instead of attending school that the state's literacy rate suffered.[14] There was one crucial difference between farm and factory labor. Farming required intense activity twice a year during the spring planting and fall harvest, but the long days of mill work were rarely broken, even by holidays.

Despite their circumstances, Fayette and Minnie Little created a home that centered around family. They kept their children out of the factories and took them to church. Fayette faithfully read the local newspaper, the *Gadsden Daily Times-News*, and taught Mary to as well. He knew the editor, who once wrote that Mary's father might have "lost one of his arms in a threshing machine, but he continues to farm and makes a good living. In fact, he does a great deal better than a lot of farmers who have two arms."[15] While a nice sentiment, this claim ignores the extensive efforts of Fayette's children, most of whom were girls. Still, Mary attended school as much as possible because her parents valued education and she enjoyed learning. She also excelled at socializing and loved school because she could see her friends there.

Since the school term only lasted a few months, Mary's siblings were her main companions. Her half dozen sisters stirred her with joy and irritation. Sometimes Mary laughed so hard at her sisters' antics during games of tag or crack-the-whip that she would lose the competition. On other days, she stomped her feet when tormented by the older girls or yelled in frustration when pestered by the younger ones. She did admire her older sister Martha, who kept track of fashion as best she could, dressing in the Gibson Girl style, with tiered skirts and hair piled high.

Mary's sister Grace, the older by two years, was her closest friend and most intense rival. The younger sister viewed Grace as possessing many advantages, such as a fair complexion that lacked blemishes and hair that naturally formed ringlets. Other circumstances made Mary feel unappreciated. Since both girls had birthdays in mid-August, with Grace's first, of course, their mother combined celebrations. As the younger girl, Mary was expected to wear Grace's hand-me-down clothing. Mary found this practice particularly galling when it involved an Easter hat. After Grace had worn the accessory to church for a year, the older sister received a new, stylish version for Easter service. This left Mary to wear Grace's used hat on the most important and well-attended day of worship. Temperament also figured into Mary's resentment. Grace's poise highlighted the older sister's triumphs while the younger sister's impetuousness often revealed her flaws. Even if Mary could obliterate her freckles and tame her red hair, she still needed confidence in order to equal Grace.

Feelings of inferiority sometimes compelled Mary into unwise choices. One took place during the sweltering and exhausting task of harvesting cotton. Fayette and Minnie tried to turn the family chore into a game among the children: whoever picked the most cotton would win.

Apparently, this lackluster challenge engaged Mary's competitive nature. Knowing she couldn't out-pick her older siblings, she decided to cheat. Since the winning amount of cotton would be measured by weight, Mary knew she needed to make her bag of pickings heavier than the others' bags. She had to be sneaky about it, though, since her parents would notice dirt or rocks among the crop. Inspiration came through one of her chores: carrying buckets of water from the outside pump to the kitchen. Knowing that liquid had weight and that it sloshed around instead of clumping, Mary sprinkled water, lots of it, over the cotton bolls in her sack. She weighed down her pickings enough to win the contest and, for a few moments, reveled in her success. Unfortunately, the water spoiled the cotton, which her parents soon noticed. Mary found herself in real trouble for ruining the precious cash crop ... and for lying ... and for cheating.

CHAPTER 3
Appalachians in Town

BY THE TIME EARL ARRIVED IN KNOXVILLE, instead of celebrating its connection to the nearby mountains, the city planned on prospering in the New South.[16] Economic troubles had increased the migration of Appalachia's poor until they flooded the town, stressing its resources and its patience. During the Great War, however, this population proved to be advantageous. America's cities scrambled to benefit from the booming economy as their industries outfitted the troops and local farmers fed them. With the armed forces an eager buyer, an industrial town only needed two components in order to be successful: workers to make goods and a way to transport the finished products. Knoxville, of course, sat amid an extensive railroad network.

A large workforce willing to accept relatively low wages proved elusive for many towns. So many men joined the war effort that everyone, including women and minorities, could find jobs. Before the conflict, immigrants had provided America's entry-level workforce, but wartime policies prohibited new arrivals from overseas. One underused labor force willingly moved across country in order to fill the available factory jobs. In fact, White and Black Southerners migrated northward for decades. When they didn't leave the region, Black migrants moved into nearby cities. In Knoxville, they joined an existing Black population and a Jewish community as well as enclaves of Italians, Germans, and Greeks. All these groups contributed to the city's work force, but they didn't dominate it. That role belonged to another source of low-wage laborers: the mostly White East Tennesseans who, like Earl, came from the region's foothills and mountains.

These in-migrants lived in the city and walked to work at factories rimming its center. They spoke with sharp mountain twangs that contrasted with the Southern-influenced drawls of wealthier Knoxvillians. Their neighborhoods overflowed with shacks and tenements but lacked electricity, running water, and sewage systems.[17] Foul smells emanated from area outhouses, and the inhabitants bought drinking water from horse-drawn wagons, a practice held over from the previous century. Typical businesses included a junkyard, livery, and feed store while sheep and pig pens filled in the lots between buildings.[18] These shantytowns brought rural living into the city.

Knoxville's poorest neighborhoods had originally huddled near the Tennessee River, in the oldest part of town. As Appalachian migrants moved to town across the decades, however, their communities expanded, overlapping with each other. They also intertwined with an infamous section of town known as the Bowery. Those looking for a good time in Knoxville went there to play cards, shoot pool, and throw dice.[19] But the Bowery's allure went beyond gambling. Bordellos, drinking establishments, and drug havens had long flourished in its enclaves,[20] attracting travelers as well as locals. Naturally, the city's hotspot for illicit trades was also the center of its violence. The area appalled wealthier citizens who blamed its existence on the poor,[21] whose homes sat alongside the disreputable establishments.

As the shantytowns grew, they eventually collided with the town's upscale neighborhoods. Knox County's red brick courthouse, for example, sat at the intersection of Gay and Main streets. One block to the west, a lovely neighborhood thrived amid clipped lawns, spreading shade trees, and gracious homes. Here, women strolled at their leisure, wearing elegant ensembles topped by wide-brimmed hats. Families such as these could take advantage of the city's infrastructure, using electricity, owning telephones, and increasingly, driving automobiles. On the other side of the courthouse, several more elaborate homes honored Gay Street with stately columns and Victorian turrets. Both neighborhoods reflected Knoxville's long-term prosperity. Downhill and a few blocks east of the Gay Street homes, however, a crowded shantytown teemed with activity. This close proximity contributed to animosity between Knoxville's elite and its Appalachian lower class.

As the city's main labor force, these in-migrants didn't always function as their employers wished. Appalachian people often had less education than town-raised employees, and they possessed a sense of independence that veered toward a distrust of those in power.[22] Some bristled at contact with the city's poor Black citizens who had also flocked to town and who worked the same low-wage jobs. The workers also had legitimate complaints. Just as in America's Southern sharecropping agreements and Northern factories, the economic system kept them from prospering. In previous economic downturns, animosity toward the workers hardened when they weren't needed as laborers,[23] proving that the city tolerated them according to their usefulness. The shantytowns' poverty appalled wealthier Knoxvillians, and those who lived there likely found it frustrating as well. Even with the workforce's large and growing numbers, their grievances went unheard. City leaders colluded in order to restrict the lower classes' political power.[24]

For years, Knoxville's elite had been moving north and west out of the city, fleeing the workers with their mountain ways as well as the town's industrial pollution. Developments such as Sequoyah Hills beckoned the wealthy with wide boulevards and spacious parks. Then middle-class residents started leaving the central city, moving north into neighborhoods such as the one Earl lived in with his sister Ola and her husband. These outlying communities expanded so quickly that Knoxville annexed them in 1917, greatly increasing its size but doing nothing to solve the city's fundamental housing problems.

As low-wage workers moved into the city and those who could afford it moved out, the character of downtown Knoxville evolved, becoming more congested and less desirable.

* * *

Prejudice against Southern Appalachian people settled deeply into the American mindset during the nineteenth and twentieth centuries. The early causes of this disdain vary. Civil War soldiers from the North returned home with stories of violent, poverty-stricken communities, perhaps without acknowledging the conflict's destructive influence. Newspaper accounts of the post-war Hatfield/McCoy feud were exaggerated and biased. However, the popular literature of the late nineteenth century, called "local color" writing, bears much of the blame.[25]

Local color writers aimed to depict the oddities of specific American regions, and some did so without being prejudiced and inflammatory. The western United States benefitted from having Mark Twain use it as a setting, and Kate Chopin explored Louisiana culture in her works. These gifted writers could be critical, but they tried to avoid stereotyping. Both ultimately surpassed their regional origins and gained literary acclaim.

The local colorists who wrote about Southern Appalachia lacked the talents of Twain and Chopin. One, Mary Murfree, hailed from a wealthy Middle Tennessee family. As a child, she spent summer vacations in the Cumberland Mountains. She used the area as the primary setting for her novels, gaining an avid, national readership. Murfree's disparaging attitude toward mountain people can be seen in descriptions of middle-aged women written by her and Twain. Both characters have minor importance in works published in the mid-1880s, Twain's *Huckleberry Finn* and Murfree's *In the Tennessee Mountains*. Humorous but succinct, Twain describes Miss Watson with appropriate depth considering her slight role as "a tolerable slim old maid, with goggles on."[26] Murfree, on the other hand, lavishes disdain on her minor character, the heroine's mother: "So gaunt she was, so toothless, haggard and disheveled, that but for her lazy step and languid interest she might have suggested one of Macbeth's witches."[27]

Thus are stereotypes born.

Early film adapted the local colorists' attitudes, depicting hillbillies as rotten-toothed, filthy, and menacing. In fact, storylines about mountain bootleggers and vendettas had been popular since the early nickelodeons.[28] Mary Pickford's fame solidified in 1914 after she appeared in *The Eagle's Mate*, in which uncouth mountaineers kidnap her character and force her to marry.[29] When sound technology developed enough to allow it, movies would gleefully disparage Appalachian accents.

Certainly most Americans, including many Knoxvillians, accepted these stereotypes as valid. Prejudices of all types were openly expressed during the early twentieth century, including bigotry against Appalachian people. In 1918, a sixteen-year-old named Cora Ogle moved with her family from Sevier County to Knoxville. In town, they were ridiculed as being "hillbillies" and "mountain hoosers."[30] Her experience was so common that it often led to defensiveness. Cora commented that, "Some people tried to hide that they were from the mountains." Successful East Tennesseans who tried to fit into the larger society by disparaging or hiding their rural roots also perpetuated the idea of an inferior Appalachia.[31]

Earl's home county of Sevier, which shares a long border with southeastern Knox County, was classically Appalachian. By his youth, logging dominated the rural county's economy. Overpopulated compared to its relatively few acres of farmable land, poverty thrived in Sevier County. Residents experienced low life expectancy and a high number of infant deaths.[32] Adult males suffered such ill health that over 57 percent of the county's Great War conscripts were rejected.[33]

Earl's background, however, revealed the region's economic variety. Arriving in Sevier County around 1800, his family settled on fertile, if hilly, land. A branch of the Little Pigeon River formed one of their property lines. It provided cool waters during the summer and fish for dinner. By the time Earl was born, outbuildings dotted the farm and sheltered livestock, tools, and large equipment. The house was modest, but its two porches and two fireplaces ensured summer and winter comfort. During the nineteenth century, which measured prosperity in land and productivity instead of cash, this farm provided a decent life, and most family members gained the respect of their community. After the Civil War, Earl's father served a term in the state legislature.[34]

But if Knoxvillians looked down upon most of rural Appalachia, they definitely considered Sevier County to be full of backward ruffians. This opinion solidified in the 1890s when even New York City newspapers reported on the county's troubles.[35] Local authorities had failed to curtail prostitution and violence in the Emert's Cove community. After several months, the area's law-abiding citizens grew impatient. They organized a group of vigilantes called the White Caps in order to address the crime and immoral behavior. These men hid their identities by covering their faces and making nighttime raids. While Whitecapping occurred throughout the rural United States and was sometimes racially motivated, these White Caps did not target any particular ethnic or minority group. Because they targeted criminals, however, Sevier County residents initially supported them.[36]

White Cap activity soon increased in scope, frequency, and brutality. As the organization grew, some members didn't participate in the raids but provided money and other support. Eventually, the White Caps became no better than criminals themselves, but they gained power until they controlled much of Sevier County. For years they plagued innocent citizens as well as those who tried to curtail them. After one young woman testified against the group in court, she and her husband were murdered.[37]

Sevier Countians attempted to counter the vigilante organization in several ways. When gang members were arrested, the county tried to prosecute them but was unsuccessful because Whitecappers who had infiltrated the legal system voted them "not guilty" as jurors.[38] A competing group called the Blue Bills physically confronted the White Caps but had little success. Finally, the state of Tennessee passed an anti-Whitecapping bill that took control of local courts and placed them under the jurisdiction of a Knoxville judge. Most Sevier County residents felt genuinely embarrassed over the episode. They also resented Knox County's oversight of their judicial system, especially since the prostitutes who first caused the problems had come from Knoxville.[39]

Earl Layman, born two years after Whitecapping ended, never knew the extent of his family's involvement in the saga. His relatives could have ridden as White Caps or as Blue Bills. His mother was born in Emert's Cove, where the movement started, and her parents moved from there to Pigeon Forge, another hotspot. His family could also have been victims of the era's collateral violence.

Whether the Laymans took part in the county's vigilante justice or the struggle against it didn't really matter in town. Knoxvillians associated Sevier Countians with the sordid episode, considering them violent and unruly. This attitude could have thwarted the aspirations of Earl and his sisters, Ola and Mae, despite their comfortable family farm. Ironically, the trio's world views extended well beyond East Tennessee. Ola met her husband in California while Mae married a native of Connecticut. To prosper in the city, the siblings emphasized their town-oriented, middle-class traits and downplayed their most obvious Appalachian ones, such as their accents. When the sisters first moved to Knoxville, both worked in the city's textile mills, but they lived in its northern suburbs, away from the poverty-stricken neighborhoods that housed many of their co-workers.

As the Layman family circumstances reveal, not all of Knoxville's in-migrants were violent, uneducated, and crammed into tenements. Accounts of the city's population frequently ignored their more successful demographic, though, because once the Laymans and others like them appeared more city-like, they weren't considered Appalachian. This benefitted them in town, but their ability to blend into mainstream culture complicated their self-image. These East Tennesseans often occupied a no-man's-land between mountain and city, inherently connected to one but eager to join the other.

These diverse groups of in-migrants influenced Knoxville for decades. They fueled economic booms during the late nineteenth century and the Great War that allowed wealthy Knoxvillians to prosper. Some provided a distinct society of fiddle playing and square dancing that long went unappreciated while others contributed to area commerce. Ultimately dominating Knoxville's culture, they created an Appalachian city.[40]

Since the terms "Appalachian" and "city" were considered to be mutually exclusive, town leaders rarely acknowledged and certainly never appreciated this status. After all, it complicated their desire to gain influence in the South. During Earl's lifetime, however, as Knoxville struggled with changing economics, politics, culture, and self-image, it did so with a core Appalachian population.

CHAPTER 4
Becoming Marie

IN NORTH ALABAMA, Mary Little's loving parents, active siblings, and energetic outlook helped to counteract many effects of her family's poverty. Other influences were her Christian upbringing and a national movement that started before her birth. Her childhood took place during the Progressive Era when Americans worked to transform society by solving problems caused by industrialization. Concerned groups, often led by women, had started locally. Many of them campaigned for temperance, encouraging others to stop drinking, but they had decades of uneven success. In Alabama, activists focused on improving the lives of families, and they unsuccessfully fought to restrict the factories and mills from hiring children. As the nation's scattered groups coalesced into a widespread movement, however, Alabama Progressives joined in a national effort, one that they deemed as essential as ending child labor or securing rights for women.

They sought Prohibition—to outlaw liquor.

Because the experiment of Prohibition ended in failure, Americans often devalue the concerns from which it grew. Women from across the country and from all socioeconomic backgrounds sought to banish alcohol because they lived with its effects. Families usually depended on the husband's wages, and in an economy based on physical labor, overindulgence could cause lost work days, increased injuries, and accidental deaths. Through the traumas of spousal and child abuse, a chronically drunk husband could make home life intolerable. Alcoholism also had other less extreme but still devastating effects. Even if just used as a response to stress, it could lead to economic disaster.[41] Wives, who were forced by law and convention to depend on their husbands, had little power with which to confront these problems.

Many Progressives felt called to action because of religious conviction, believing that women's natural instincts provided them with a moral compass that men lacked. The movement played on this idea, which was emphasized when church groups and individual clergymen joined their ranks. These activists genuinely considered their cause to be a morally correct one, a struggle for the country's soul.

During Mary's childhood, the war over alcohol raged throughout her community and dominated Alabama's state politics. Anti-liquor forces had long been powerful in Etowah County, where Mary lived, including in the county seat of Gadsden. The town founded Alabama's first Woman's Christian Temperance Union (WCTU), one of the era's most powerful groups.[42] The WCTU only allowed women members, and their experiences working for a cause would be profound.[43] The Anti-Saloon League, a group led in Alabama by male clergymen, also joined the fight, although they were more interested in providing a steady workforce than they were sober husbands.[44]

These groups lobbied tirelessly, first winning the right for Alabama's counties to set their own liquor laws. This led to local confrontations but many successes. In 1909, the groups celebrated a great victory when alcohol production and sales were banned across the state. But language in the new law proved problematic, making it unenforceable,[45] which pro-liquor forces soon exploited. Before long, some citizens tried to reinstate legal liquor in Etowah County, using the argument that the loss of tax money from alcohol sales was harming the city.[46] Furthermore, Gadsden was home to a thriving, and completely illegal, saloon. The city's two newspapers took opposing positions on the issue,[47] and a battle over Prohibition raged throughout the county.

The temperance movement had long detested saloons, as shown by activist Carrie Nation who was known to attack them with a hatchet. Alabama's state WCTU leader, Mrs. J. B. Chatfield, claimed that saloons "have robbed us of our husbands, sons, and daughters, destroying both body and souls."[48] Holdovers from the frontier and post-Civil War eras, these rough drinking establishments catered almost exclusively to men. Respectable women, no matter their social class, simply didn't enter them. Temperance leaders viewed saloons as epitomizing the dominance that men wielded over women and hoped that destroying the physical buildings would lessen this authority.[49] Plus, the businesses profited from drunkenness. They were seen as contributing to poverty because some men went there directly after work, especially on payday. Wives complained that the bars devoured their husband's paychecks, leaving no money to pay bills and purchase food. Gadsden's temperance leaders spoke for many women when they identified local saloons as "destroying their homes and bringing so much sorrow into their families."[50]

Since American women couldn't vote, temperance leaders drew attention to their cause through other means, including their role as mothers. They paraded through towns and cities while wearing signature white dresses or ribbons, their innocent children beside them. Members publicly announced that one of their main goals was to prevent their sons from falling into alcohol's clutches. In fact, saving the children became a rallying point. Alabama Progressives convinced state lawmakers to include the damaging physical and mental consequences of drinking liquor into the educational curriculum.[51] Thus, at school, children such as Mary heard lectures about alcohol's crippling effects on the body and mind. While at church, they heard sermons against its soul-crushing evil.

Singing was found to be an especially effective technique in engaging children against liquor. Mary memorized the lyrics of several temperance songs with their mournful emotional appeals.

She especially loved "Little Benny," a ballad with a child narrator whose mother sends him to fetch his drunken father from a saloon. Each stanza portrays another hour as the child returns to the bar and futilely entreats his father to come home. The night is chilly, and the narrator mentions that his brother is ill.

The song's ending lines take place in early morning when the child has made a final trip to the saloon.

He pleads with his father:

Father, dear Father, come home with me now.
The clock in the steeple strikes three.
The house is so lonely, the hours are so long,
For poor weeping Mother and me.
Yes, we are alone; poor Benny is dead
And gone with the angels of light.
And these are the very last words that he said:
"I want to kiss Papa goodnight."[52]

Yes, this song is designed to make listeners cry.

If Mary and her siblings encountered alcoholism at home or within their extended family, such knowledge is lost. Considering its prevalence at the time among her economic class, she likely would have.[53] Liquor was widely available in Alabama, with alcoholism festering among moonshiners and within the textile mill towns and mining camps they supplied.[54] However, well into the twentieth century, social ills flourished in an atmosphere of secrecy. Families rarely discussed alcoholism or depression, anxiety, or violence, even within the homes they affected.

In 1915, Prohibition passed in Alabama, and two years later the state voted to ratify America's constitutional amendment on the issue. Activists celebrated their stunning achievement, and women's groups vowed to advance other Progressive causes. They continued campaigning for literacy, better schools, and a woman's right to vote. These efforts directly improved Mary's situation, increasing her educational opportunities and expanding her life choices. The campaign for Prohibition permanently influenced her. She spent her life convinced of alcohol's inherent dangers, never reconsidering her stance.

Another, less inhibiting, opinion of the Progressive movement was its view of change as positive. This attitude fueled a passion for social improvement and probably spurred one of Mary's crucial childhood decisions. Long before personal reinvention became a mainstream concept, she and her sisters amused themselves by considering alternative names. This bit of fun had long-term consequences when several permanently renamed themselves. Pretty Grace never felt the need for reinvention, but their mother, Minnie, christened herself "Ninevah," which she soon shortened to "Ninnie." Martha Evangeline had the honor of being the namesake of her grandmother McGriff; nevertheless, she became "Patsy."

In the most creative upgrade of all, Mary rejected her plain, respectable name while keeping its Biblical overtones. Perhaps sensing that "Mary Little" evoked an unremarkable girl who was overshadowed by her older sister, she chose a lilting title that fit her lively personality. With this new identity, she would tackle life—as Marie.

CHAPTER 5

Flu and Lawlessness

IN SEPTEMBER OF 1918, a few days after his eighteenth birthday, Earl registered for the draft.[55] He knew how to shoot a gun, having owned one since age seven, but he tended to avoid bloodshed. As a child, in an early sign that he might not have been suited for farming, Earl had fled into the house during the more violent events of late fall's "hog killing day." Four thousand Knox Countians[56] were serving in the Great War, though, and he would join them if called. Most of the men fought with the Army's 30th Division in the 59th Infantry Brigade and would see intense action. After training at Camp Sevier in Greenville, South Carolina, under the command of General Lawrence D. Tyson of Knoxville, they underwent more preparation in England. Once deployed in Europe, they became some of the first American troops to enter Belgium.[57]

The draft had been enacted because large numbers of young men were needed for the war effort. The armed services even accepted minorities although often with restrictions. Immigrants from Italy and elsewhere fought for the United States in order to gain citizenship, and hundreds of Black men from Knoxville served in the conflict.[58] In general, Black soldiers were used for physical labor instead of fighting. The United States government had promised these men increased rights in exchange for service, a promise that it reneged on, but many of them were posted overseas, especially in France. The soldiers' experiences there proved illuminating, and many of them returned home with greater confidence in themselves.

Knoxvillians avidly kept track of wartime events. Newspapers flooded the town with information that included a map of battle locations in France and a report on Belgian royalty visiting the front. Letters from soldiers, sent in by families and the troops themselves, were printed for all to read.[59] Some newspaper articles focused on furthering the war effort, such as those that explained how women could prosper and contribute to victory through employment. When these women dared to ask for equal pay for equal work, however, the Young Women's Christian Association rushed to assure readers that the request would not lead to a war between the sexes.[60]

Reminders of the conflict infused everyday life. From Woodruff's location on Gay Street, Earl watched enormous parades march through town that encouraged the purchase of war bonds. These extravagances always ended with Cal Johnson riding by in a stylish buggy pulled by a flashy racehorse.[61] Born into slavery, Johnson had worked tirelessly, turning himself into a Knoxville entrepreneur and teetotaler whose properties ranged from a thriving bar to a racetrack.[62] His status and popularity likely contributed to Knoxville's view of itself as lacking racial problems, an opinion that would soon be disproven.

Other than buying bonds, ordinary Knoxvillians contributed to the war effort through conservation. The US Navy's steamships ran on coal, gobbling it voraciously and leaving civilians with a short supply. Measures attempting to counter this shortage ranged from the nation's first use of daylight-savings time to the unprecedented step of having East Tennessee miners work on Sundays. Industries closed on "fireless Mondays," a concept designed to save coal. Area department and retail stores, such as Woodruff's Hardware, stayed open by heating their businesses with wood. In order to save gasoline, the relatively few Knoxvillians who owned automobiles were prohibited from driving on Sundays.[63]

Feeding the troops required sacrifices, including dietary restrictions on the public that ranged from suggestions to government-imposed regulations. Local families and restaurants observed meatless days. Earl probably didn't mind "Wheatless Wednesdays," which helped to conserve flour. He had always preferred cornbread over dinner rolls. This East Tennessee staple, still popular today, met the wartime standard because the regional recipe calls for cornmeal but no flour. It also lacks sugar, which met another goal. Early in the war, the federal government started discouraging the use of sugar because three quarters of it entered the country on ships needed by the armed forces.[64] Apparently, this was a tough sell. One local paper ran four articles on one page, all touting the need to conserve the sweetener. The use of sugar was eventually banned in wartime America,[65] forcing cooks to try to compensate with honey and molasses.

Before long, another concern joined the war's disruptions. Doctors had been fighting an epidemic of "grippe" for over a year, but at first the illness remained relatively mild. By late summer 1918, however, it had evolved into a deadly pandemic: Spanish influenza. Health officials understood basic aspects of the disease. The elderly and those in poor health were most susceptible, with many of them dying from complications after the initial illness. Sadly, the disease also killed the young and healthy. Greatly contagious, it flourished at a time when troops gathered in American and European training camps, traveled in groups, and lived together in trenches.

Influenza also hit the home front. One Tennessee official used humor to point out the dangers. Dr. E. L. Bishop of the Tennessee State Board of Health discouraged "promiscuous kissing [...] especially that of the nonessential variety."[66] He then cautioned that a "kiss of infection [...] may truly be the kiss of death."[67] At first, the public was urged to call a physician when needed, but the epidemic spread so quickly that doctors soon stopped making house calls. This left Knoxvillians to take care of each other.

The American Red Cross helped by giving instructions on how to care for the sick. Other, less-valid advice was to stay calm and use Vicks Vaporub on patients. Through advertisements, a variety of goods promised to counter the illness. They joined hundreds of the era's virtually unregulated products that were no more than moneymaking placebos, which claimed to correct ailments ranging from hair loss to a woman's fatigue.

Knoxville's epidemic peaked in October. By the ninth, Dr. Cochrane of the city's board of health had shut down most public events. He ordered the local fair, places of worship, movie houses, and billiard halls to close.[68] A frightened populace started sheltering at home. Those who ventured onto the streets wore masks, and authorities instructed citizens to wash their hands frequently.[69] Officials even made it illegal to sneeze in public without a handkerchief.[70] Unfortunately, a parade designed to sell war bonds was well attended, and soon afterward the amount of influenza cases increased fourfold, overrunning the local hospitals.[71] By the time the epidemic subsided, over seven thousand Knoxvillians had been ill, and 129 of them died.[72] Influenza continued to cycle around the country.

Earl managed to avoid contracting the disease, and no draft notice arrived in the months after he registered. In fact, he thrilled to the constant energy of town life. With an ongoing pandemic, however, many Americans lived with a sense of unease that overshadowed their daily lives and magnified their worry for loved ones in uniform.

* * *

Knoxville also faced issues with illegal alcohol. The city had enacted Prohibition in 1907 and at least on the surface approved of its own decision. When officials announced the ballot results, the town celebrated. Church bells pealed, a parade moved down Gay Street, and at the nearby University of Tennessee, students rallied to show their support. A segment of the population continued this praise. *The Knoxville Independent* featured a long-running column furnished by the National Women's Christian Temperance Union. Named "Temperance Notes," it publicized the group's achievements. A typical article applauded Seattle shipbuilders for becoming more focused by drinking milk instead of beer.[73] This claim subtly equated temperance with patriotism since a steady supply of ships furthered the war effort.

From the beginning, however, the majority of Knoxvillians ignored Prohibition laws, buying illegal liquor at will.[74] In fact, when alcohol was first outlawed across Tennessee in 1909, officials in the four major cities, Knoxville, Nashville, Chattanooga, and Memphis, all neglected to enforce the new law.[75] Seeing an opportunity, East Tennessee entrepreneurs distilled bootleg liquor in the countryside, then transported it into the cities. Considered a natural part of the regional economy, moonshine allowed rural residents to earn cash from their corn crops. Before long, elements of Knoxville society openly mocked the concept of temperance. By January of 1918, a local newspaper named *The Journal and Tribune* announced that "wildcat booze flows freely."[76] Since a grossly inadequate staff of three revenue agents patrolled East Tennessee, area moonshiners had scant chances of getting caught.[77]

A certain amount of pride stemmed from the region's expertise in making hooch. At Camp Sevier in Greenville, South Carolina, soldiers from East Tennessee called themselves the "Moonshine Division," insisting that many of their most capable soldiers hailed from areas that produced bootleg liquor.[78] As for Earl, he understood the product's value to farmers, and he likely enjoyed a nip or two of 'shine himself.

In Knoxville, revelers visited the Bowery to buy liquor, and bootleggers such as Cecil Thompson ran their operations from there.[79] By Earl's arrival in town, the infamous neighborhood began around Vine Street and followed Central Street to the river.[80] It had shrunk from its heyday because temperance activists had targeted its drinking establishments. The most notable saloon, Patrick Sullivan's, had closed and was converted into an ice cream parlor. This transformation surely thrilled temperance advocates but eventually helped the building survive as a reminder of the once-thriving Bowery and its urban saloons.

Prohibition's spotty record of success in Knoxville and elsewhere did not deter a national ban on alcohol. Proponents claimed it would aid the war effort because making liquor used corn and grain needed to feed the troops. While this argument made sense, national Prohibition took effect in early 1920 after the war's end. Most Americans responded to illegal alcohol the same way that Tennesseans had, and the federal government soon implored the nation's governing officials to support a crackdown.[81] East Tennessee moonshiners met the increased demand for their product by expanding operations.

Prohibition had deeply negative repercussions. Because officials weren't enforcing the country's laws, some citizens lost respect for the government. Americans appeared hypocritical by voting in laws, then promptly ignoring them. Since it criminalized liquor, Prohibition increased the risks associated with making and transporting the product. This drove up prices and attracted organized crime to Knoxville, a city with long-running struggles against gambling, prostitution, and violence.[82] Moonshiners paid off officials in order to operate, and even the sheriff's office appeared involved in questionable activities. In September of 1918, over two thousand gallons of confiscated liquor disappeared from the Knox County jail.[83] A newly elected sheriff acknowledged the theft, but the previous official refused to comment on the matter and was never prosecuted for the missing contraband.

Examples of Knoxville's WWI-era crime problem are plentiful. In early 1918, one thief accosted a young woman on the Fifth Avenue Bridge, stealing her purse and jewelry. Masked men committed armed robbery by threatening a grocery store owner with a gun. Another example of local violence occurred that February when Earl was still living with his Uncle Jack Shultz.[84] Shortly after the previously mentioned store robbery, three men accosted another Knox County grocer. This victim owned a store near Bay's Mountain, the main geographical barrier between Sevier and Knox Counties. The road crossed the mountain through a pass called

Shook's Gap, and the grocery store sat on the Knoxville side of that pass.

The business owner was Peter (Pete) Nichols, husband of Earl's Aunt Susie. Earl's mother, Sallie, and his Uncle Jack were Susie's siblings. Aunt Susie was six years younger than Sallie, but the two sisters got along well. Both gave birth to sons in 1900, and both named their sons "Earl." With such close ties to the Nichols family, the Shultz household buzzed with news about the crime while Earl lived there. In fact, Jack Shultz offered a $200 reward for information leading to the murderer's arrest and conviction.

Several armed robbers had ambushed Earl's Uncle Pete Nichols as he walked home after closing his store. One criminal aimed a gun at him, insisting that he raise his hands. Pete complied, but slowly, and the masked gunman shot him in the hand. Apparently realizing that he faced a life-threatening challenge, Pete lunged toward his assailants.[85] The gunman fired again, striking him near the waist. With their victim bleeding from both wounds, the men stole $200 from Pete, money he thought safer at home than left overnight in the store.

The criminals then left Pete to die. He managed to crawl home, however, and stayed conscious long enough to describe the robbery.[86] Family members rushed him to Lincoln Memorial Hospital in Knoxville, where doctors soon operated. His wife and son feared for his life because the second gunshot had entered Pete's intestines and could spread infection throughout his body. Their worry was well founded. After suffering for several days, Earl's uncle died of his wounds.

Soon after the robbery, authorities began a manhunt for the three outlaws, aided by volunteers from Shook's Gap. The sheriff questioned and released one suspect, then offered a fifty-dollar reward for any information helping to apprehend the criminals. Within a week of the robbery, authorities arrested three men: Hobart Suffridge and brothers Ehude Fellows and Harvey Fellows.[87] One newspaper article incorrectly specified that "all the suspects are boys."[88] Ehude Fellows had been featured in a Knoxville newspaper

article the year before, recounting an adventure he had in Europe—
at age twenty-one.[89] Now, a year later, he claimed to be eighteen.[90]

The trial for Pete Nichols's robbery and murder took place in
late April. Susie Nichols testified, recounting how her husband
entered their home after being shot and took a long, shuddering
breath when she went to him. Hobart Suffridge turned state's
evidence, stating that Ehude Fellows had shot Nichols.[91] Near the
crime scene, authorities found a discarded pistol and bits of cloth
caught on barbed wire.[92] This last evidence pointed to Ehude as
part of the gang because he frequently wore a coat made of that
material. Much of the prosecution's case rested on this cloth, but
other circumstantial evidence also implicated the twenty-two-year-
old. He sported a deep gash that several witnesses agreed could
have come from barbed wire.

On the trial's first day, Ehude entered the courtroom wearing a
light-colored overcoat identical to the one he had owned before the
robbery. When he set it aside, the state's attorneys eagerly examined
it for rips or fraying, anything to indicate it had been damaged.[93]
They found nothing. Years later, attorneys learned that Ehude had
cut a swatch of material and the identification tag from his torn
overcoat, traveled to the manufacturer in Cincinnati, Ohio, and
used that information to purchase an identical garment.[94] Then he
wore the new, undamaged coat to trial.

These machinations, which aren't the actions of a young boy out
of his league in a murder case, resulted in a mistrial.[95] Authorities
soon announced that they would retry Harvey and Ehude. The
court set a high bail, so the two remained in jail, at least briefly.

On a Saturday morning in mid-September, five men escaped
from the Knox County jail: a convicted murderer, a convicted
burglar, a bigamist, and Harvey and Ehude Fellows.[96] This jailbreak
occurred during the same month, and possibly at the same time,
as the theft of confiscated liquor. Remarkably, the escapees had
the tools needed to remove a cover that blocked an earlier escape
route.[97] Well-prepared and unsupervised, they quickly fled. Later,
Ehude would deny all responsibility, claiming a cellmate discovered

that the jailer had forgotten to lock their cell door and then had fallen asleep.[98] A more likely scenario, of course, is that a bribed or inebriated jail employee facilitated the men's escape, which was also aided by smuggled tools and perhaps a waiting automobile. The brothers didn't remain free for long, though. By the end of September, two squirrel hunters with the noteworthy last name of "Nichols" found Ehude in nearby Loudon County and tipped off the sheriff.[99]

In April 1919, a second trial began for the murder of Earl's Uncle Pete. Finding jurors for this trial proved difficult, and the court called two hundred men in order to find an unbiased jury.[100] Ehude's lawyer claimed that his client had an alibi, but the jury found it insufficient, pronouncing him guilty of murder in the first degree.[101]

The judge sentenced Ehude to life in prison.

Because of the mistrial and jailbreak, Earl's family had waited over a year for the verdict. The outcome had been in doubt, jeopardized by a well-planned and cleverly executed escape that nearly negated Knoxville's legal system. To Earl and his extended family, it seemed that criminal forces permeated the city to an alarming degree.

The scale of these forces would soon become apparent to everyone.

CHAPTER 6

Adult at Fourteen

BY AGE FOURTEEN, Marie Little's life sparkled with excitement, most of which she created herself. She still lived in Etowah County, Alabama, home of Gadsden, which had the dubious distinction of being the seventh-largest town in the state. Her rural community of Smokeneck lay well outside of town.[102] For the Little family, going to Gadsden involved a wagon ride, then a ferry trip across the Coosa River, then a second stint on the wagon. Tenant and sharecropper farming dominated Smokeneck's economy, with most of the few hundred residents scattered across acres of farmland. The area would eventually be renamed Southside, as it lies on the south bank of the Coosa River.

Smokeneck had a definite sense of community. Most social events centered around its churches, which held potluck suppers, group singings, and youth presentations along with formal religious services. In the fall, the local fair provided entertainment, and Fayette, Marie's father, served on the board that oversaw the cotton competition. Farmers won this coveted prize by producing the most pounds of crop per acre. The *Gadsden Daily Times-News* kept locals updated on national and regional events. It also covered the town's weddings and get-togethers, emulating the society pages of major newspapers that glamorized movie stars and debutantes. The *Times-News* also printed brief columns sent in by members of nearby rural communities. Informative but dull, these columns typically related farming conditions, the health of area citizens, and some church news.

Two adolescent girls decided to enliven these reports. Marie and her sister Grace began submitting news articles from Smokeneck that presented themselves as busy socialites. While these articles never included a byline, the content relentlessly focused on the sisters' activities and inadvertently revealed their sibling rivalry.

An April 1919 column, for example, began by noting that the inhabitants of Ohatchee Route 1, the Little's mailing address, enjoyed the good health needed to plant cotton and corn. Then it got down to business: Miss Grace Little had gone shopping in Gadsden and spent the previous Friday night with a friend. Miss Marie Little and two companions had recently dined with the Harp sisters.[103] This dinner likely consisted of simple fare such as collard greens and cornbread, but the writer omits any such revealing details. The dinner party could be as grand as the reader's imagination allowed it to be. The column does mention that Marie Little spent Sunday afternoon "Kodaking" with friends—ten friends, in fact, all listed by name. Marie documented her life through photography, a rarity in her generation. The article, with its emphasis on both girls, shows cooperation between them that soon ended. Competition often dominated the sisters' interactions, as Marie's outgoing personality conflicted with Grace's poise and conventional beauty.

Fourteen-year-old Marie likely wrote the next submission. After briefly referencing health and farming concerns, it mentioned that Grace had overnighted with a friend and both girls enjoyed an afternoon outing. The column focused on Marie, though, detailing four of her social events. Most importantly, she and Alma Keenum had spent Saturday night with the Hood sisters.[104]

A mere two days later, Grace galvanized her rivalry with Marie by submitting a competing column. It began with some community news: Pilgrim's Rest Church planned a cemetery cleanup, Saturday night's candy drawing raised a respectable amount of money for a veteran's charity, and numerous guests had dined at various households. The next detail revealed Grace as the article's author and launched years of animosity: "Mary Little" and Alma Keenum had spent Saturday night with the Hood sisters. In identifying her sister as "Mary," Marie's plain, discarded name, Grace deliberately and publicly provoked her.

"Mary" continually appeared in Grace's submissions. The writer often used the phrase "the Misses Grace and Mary Little" in case readers mistakenly assumed that Grace referred to someone other than her younger sister. In retaliation, Marie submitted articles that presented her social life as much more active than Grace's. No outing or gathering of friends was too inconsequential to appear in Marie's columns. She proved to be an especially prolific writer and apparently knew *everyone* in Smokeneck.

These articles highlighted the girls' rivalry, but they obscured a fundamental truth. The Little sisters weren't carefree debutantes. A spring 1919 column contained revealing news: Marie and two local boys had taken an examination commonly given to students after they completed the seventh grade. If she earned a successful score and had lived in Gadsden, Attalla, or Glencoe, Marie could have attended one of Etowah County's high schools. But her family, and any relatives she could have boarded with, lived in the country. In any case, a seventh-grade education was standard for poor White people in her region. News soon arrived that she had passed the test, one of seventy-three rural Etowah County students to do so.[105] Marie's public education had ended.

At age fourteen, she faced a crossroads, one dictated by poverty, low social status, and scant formal education. The girl who viewed her activities as social events worthy of countywide attention had encountered reality. Her culture considered fourteen-year-olds to be adults capable of joining the workforce.[106] She had to find a job, and her options were meager.

Marie's most obvious choice meant staying with her parents where she would be expected to take on additional farm chores.

Always a struggle against nature, Southern farming in the early 1900s became even more challenging when a weevil started ruining the cotton crops. This devastated farmers, especially those living on slim margins. Plus, if Marie stayed at home, it might lead to her marrying a farmer and becoming a tenant or sharecropper's wife. For years, she had labored daily to help ensure the family's survival. She had cooked and cleaned, tended the garden, and contributed to the planting and harvesting of crops. With her future at stake, Marie knew that she wanted more out of life than these endless chores.[107]

But manual labor was what North Alabama offered its residents. Men who didn't farm worked in the coal mines, on the railroads, or in the steel mills. Textile factories employed so many children that it perpetuated the idea that fourteen-year-old girls should work as adults. These mills often had absentee owners, Northeasterners who had closed their New England facilities and moved south in search of cheap labor.[108] These owners were typical of their era in considering factory workers as commodities instead of individuals. Marie intended to avoid employment in the dirty, regimented mills.

As the state's poorest region, North Alabama had little power or prestige. Lingering resentments from the Civil War simmered between the sustenance farmers working this hilly, less fertile region and areas further south that had once thrived with slave-dependent plantations. For decades, North Alabama's politicians had clashed with South Alabama lawmakers who dominated the state's politics. Over the years, hill country representatives had advocated raising the minimum age of child laborers and opposed lessening the state taxes that supported public education.[109] They also argued against a plan to give increased power over taxes to the state's wealthier property owners.[110]

North Alabama politicians often lost these power struggles, but the loss was especially devastating in 1901 when state legislators proposed requirements for voting that included owning property, being literate, and paying a tax. If passed, these changes would restrict the voting rights of poor Black and White citizens throughout the state. Hill country politicians aggressively fought the measure's passage, and the region's citizens voted decisively against it.[111] However, White election officials in areas with heavy Black populations stuffed their local ballot boxes, resulting in almost 96 percent of their mostly Black voters supposedly voting in favor of the restrictions.[112] After these requirements became law, not only did the number of Black voters plummet but also "tens of thousands of poor White men" were disenfranchised.[113] Fayette Little lost his ability to vote. A literate man, he could scrape together enough cash to pay the poll tax, but the loss of his family's land continued to haunt him.

Poor Alabamians of both races would spend decades trying to regain their voting rights. The first successful challenge came from Progressive women who were empowered by the temperance movement's success. Anti-liquor organizations such as the Women's Christian Temperance Union had only accepted men as honorary members. This forced the group's women leaders to learn organizational skills and practice public speaking.[114] As a result, even impoverished Southern women had gained confidence and now expected to transcend the role of homemaker.[115] Many of them wanted to vote, and Alabama's Progressives began campaigning for women's suffrage. Considering the extent to which the state restricted voting rights, this was an ambitious goal, and the state legislature continually rejected the women's attempts. However, Progressives across the nation were also campaigning for women's suffrage. Through their efforts, the United States Congress approved the measure in 1919 with Tennessee providing the crucial, final vote that ratified the constitutional amendment.

Women voters in Alabama faced restrictions similar to the men. They had to verify their literacy and, after a few years, pay the poll tax.[116] When these women began voting, they remembered their recent interactions with the political parties. The Republican Party, by far the smaller of the two in Alabama, had courted their votes and stressed the importance of suffrage. Throughout the 1920s, this party would gain support in the South, which was credited to these new voters.[117]

Growing up during the struggle for suffrage greatly influenced Marie, who watched as the conflict played out across the state and the country. During her childhood, women's roles expanded in ways that had previously been unimaginable. Marie never took these advances for granted and would vote throughout life, explaining that every American should exercise this crucial right. She also volunteered for poll duty, helping to ensure that elections remained legitimate. No one would stuff a ballot box and throw an election while Marie was around.

* * *

As the fourteen-year-old searched for an occupation, she considered the choices of her older siblings. Her brothers had chosen an option that was unavailable to her. The Littles were of Scots-Irish descent and had a history of military service in America reaching back to the Revolution.

At age sixteen, Jim enlisted in the National Guard and was stationed at Fort Huachuca, Arizona, fifteen miles north of the Mexican border.[118] This fort served the 10th Calvary, one of the famed units of Buffalo Soldiers comprised entirely of Black men. During Jim's deployment, a Mexican revolutionary named Pancho Villa and his gang repeatedly raided the countryside on both sides of the border. Eventually, a detachment from the fort chased the outlaw out of the US and into Mexico, although they had to follow him there to do so. Jim served as the company bugler and probably didn't engage with Pancho himself, but he did earn an honorable discharge. [119]

Marie's brother John served in the last months of the Great War, starting at age seventeen. Just like in Sevier County, Tennessee, medical issues hampered Alabama's ability to provide healthy soldiers. During the war, local authorities disallowed almost a fourth of eligible recruits for health reasons, but nearly a fifth of the men whom they approved still couldn't meet the national standards, the highest percentage of rejection in the United States.[120] Of the state's National Guard units sent to Arizona with Jim, well over half of the men had hookworm.[121] This parasite lives in the soil and enters the human body through the soles of the feet. During an era when summer shoes were a luxury, they thrived in the South's warm climate, causing severe fatigue, diarrhea, and anemia in the host. A study that explored the health of Alabama citizens revealed additional problems. Tuberculosis, which had no cure, and pellagra, a vitamin deficiency that could lead to dementia and death, festered in the population alongside hookworm.[122] Health services were rare. The state budget provided twice as much money to combat health issues in farm animals as it did for people.[123]

So, Marie resided in the poorest region of a state that faced significant challenges. As a White child forced into full-time labor at age fourteen, however, she had more options than some in her region.

Black Southerners had long endured various forms of prejudice. The worst violation, lynching, prompted outrage across Black communities and activism in groups such as the NAACP. The practice would continue throughout the twenties and beyond. Some White people joined the fight against lynching. In the early 1930s, for example, a group of White Southern women would meet in Atlanta and call on the federal government to work toward "eradicating this evil."[124] A core obstacle to change in Alabama and elsewhere was that few, if any, events compelled the races to work together. The voting restrictions enacted against the poor were not challenged by a united front. Instead, as the races competed economically, animosity grew between them. White landowners preferred to hire Black tenants because they considered them less challenging than the White ones, who often expected better conditions and migrated more frequently between tenant farms.[125] Black children, however, had noticeably fewer educational opportunities than poor White children such as Marie. Of the seventy-three students who passed Etowah County's seventh-grade exam when she did, only two were Black.[126] This number reflected the region's relatively low Black population and its abysmal, segregated schools.

In this climate, Black Southerners moved north in a massive event called the Great Migration. Northern factory owners had long resisted employing Black laborers, but worker shortages during the Great War changed their stance. The owners began hiring Black employees and advertising job openings in the South. During the war years, about eighty-five thousand Black people left Alabama.[127] Early Black migrants knew little about the areas they were entering or how they would be treated there, but migrant "streams" emerged that funneled them into particular cities and neighborhoods.

These cities were not always welcoming. The North held many advantages for Black migrants, but an absence of racism wasn't one of them.[128] At the time, despite some individual voices against bigotry, many Americans viewed prejudice as natural or unchangeable, and even the idealistic Progressives did little to counter racism and the mistrust of immigrants.[129] Events that took place in East St. Louis, Missouri, reveal the employment and racial complications that Black migrants encountered. Between 1915 and 1917, thousands of Black Southerners moved to the city.[130] Meanwhile, the town's unions took advantage of the wartime employee shortage by going on strike in order to win better working conditions. When Black migrants took jobs vacated by the protesting workers, East St. Louis erupted in racial violence. A mob set fire to Black-owned homes and businesses, assaulting and murdering the inhabitants.[131] When Black residents retaliated by shooting two White men, violence erupted that lasted for days. This incident didn't fester in isolation; it foreshadowed similar events that would occur after the war.

Nevertheless, Black Southerners kept moving north. By the early twenties, Gadsden-area factories reported a labor shortage that was specifically blamed on Black migrants and the Northern labor agents who enticed them.[132] Town leaders didn't seem capable of trying to retain these workers. One newspaper article admitted that the workers moved north in order to live in urban areas and earn higher wages, then irritably implied that they just wanted to escape segregation.[133] The many components of systemic racism went unacknowledged.

But the story of Southern migration isn't just a Black one. During the Great War, sixty-five thousand more White people left Alabama than Black people.[134] Southern economic opportunities had weakened so badly that migrants left the region when they didn't necessarily want to.[135] Patsy, Marie's older sister, joined this historic group. She had gained some schooling after the seventh grade, then married a local boy, Jim Robertson. After the war, the couple moved to Washington, DC, seeking career-level jobs. Jim worked for the postal service, and Patsy became a stenographer at the United States Treasury Department. The move required sacrifices, and at first the husband and wife lived in separate boardinghouses.

Fourteen-year-old Marie didn't follow her sister to the north because their mother, who considered Marie too young for such a move, adamantly rejected the idea. But Marie couldn't enter the military, didn't want to work in a mill, and had tired of farming. She had to have a job but was running out of options.

CHAPTER 7
The Red Summer

EARL'S FIRST YEARS OF LIVING IN KNOXVILLE fulfilled every expectation a Sevier County boy could imagine. The eighteen-year-old found the city endlessly fascinating. While rubbernecking from Woodruff's Hardware, he and his coworkers could see a huge swath of Gay Street. This thoroughfare, center of the city's business district, teemed with activity. A block or so to the south, a new hotel grew higher and more substantial each day. Miraculously, Knoxville attracted enough visitors to require its rooms. Even more fun to watch, a few blocks north of Woodruff's, workers labored to elevate Gay Street by fifteen feet. This project aimed to improve the road where it crossed the Southern Railway yards, better connecting North Knoxville to downtown. The construction buried the ground level of several businesses, forcing them to create new entrances from their second floors. Lane closings during work on the congested bridge caused terrible traffic jams. As they endured these inconveniences, Knoxvillians debated the project's worth. Some thought the raised road an unnecessary expense, others a sign of progress.

City life provided enough activities to fill any man's spare time, although Earl didn't have much cash to spare for them. He frequented the city's new Lawson McGhee library on Gay Street, just north of the hardware store. Never an athlete, he enjoyed watching baseball games. Vaudeville shows, nickelodeons, and plays provided the core of the city's entertainment industry and were found at numerous theaters. Silent films, often shorts instead of full-length movies, played between vaudeville acts at the Staub Opera House and the Bijou Theatre.[136] Black Knoxvillians could watch shows at both locations, although from a separate seating area at the Bijou.[137] Soon, the Gem Theatre would open on Vine Street and serve the Black community for decades.

More entertainment venues were just a short trolley ride away. Several years earlier, Chilhowee Park had been built east of town for an exposition on Appalachia. There, Black patrons congregated at a so-called "Negro building," while the White ones enjoyed a pond, bathing beach, and dance floor. Evening square dances were held in the park, but Earl never attended them. He intended to transcend such country pastimes.

* * *

Earl lived with his sister Ola and her husband for less than a year before the couple moved out of state. A gifted and imaginative seamstress, Ola had ambitions that her job with a local dressmaker couldn't fulfill. Once she left, Earl looked for acceptable lodgings in town. Boardinghouses provided most rooms in urban areas, but many of these facilities were considered disreputable. As a flood of young people moved from rural America into the cities, parents worried about threats to their offspring's morals. Urban areas were considered to have looser standards than the countryside, probably because liquor and prostitutes congregated there. This belief spurred states to establish their land-grant universities in midsized towns instead of large ones. Ironically, the presence of a university often increased the city's size, as happened in Knoxville with the University of Tennessee. When Earl found a place to stay, he made a conventional choice, pleasing his mother and establishing his respectability by taking lodgings considered above reproach: at the Young Men's Christian Association (YMCA).

A national organization, the YMCA (or simply "the Y") promoted education and wholesome living among young men. In order to distinguish itself from disreputable boardinghouses, its buildings were called "dormitories," and the organization forbade women from visiting the men's rooms. The Y provided educational lectures, employment aid, and Bible studies. Knoxville's facility contained a swimming pool with lockers and a gymnasium where the men played basketball, volleyball, and horseshoes.[138] During his time in the dorm, Earl entered a handball tournament and participated in informal checkers games. He had learned checkers as a child, then honed his skills playing Sevier County old-timers at the local store. At the YMCA, he discovered those old-timers had taught him well.

The Knoxville YMCA occupied the former Palace Hotel, which featured a four-story turret and large dome. Located at the corner of Commerce Avenue and State Street, it sat halfway between Gay Street and Central Avenue, home of the Bowery. The dormitory's back door opened onto Charles Street amid a thriving Black neighborhood with two-story homes and an African Methodist Church.[139] A block farther north, Charles intersected with Vine Street, center of the city's Black-owned businesses. Knoxvillians of both races patronized the area's attorney, dentist, tailor, photographer, shoemaker, barber, and undertaker.[140] Other Vine Street businesses ranged from restaurants to billiard rooms, a confectionary shop, a fruit stand, and the Colored Men's Business Club.[141]

From his location at the YMCA, Earl could easily walk to any section of Knoxville, including the disreputable ones.

* * *

On November 10, 1918, word came that nations fighting the Great War were attempting to reach an armistice. Americans waited, praying that the conflict would end. Throughout the day, the *Knoxville News Sentinel* published three extra editions to keep citizens informed about the peace talks, but at times, up to two thousand people lingered outside the building, eager for the latest updates.[142] Excitement grew in Knoxville as families and wives, friends and sweethearts of soldiers waited for news that their loved ones in uniform might be spared from more fighting.

Early the next morning, the city exploded with noise. Church bells rang, whistles blew, and a fire engine sped through the streets with its sirens blazing.[143] The day morphed into an impromptu holiday as thrilled Knoxvillians celebrated the signing of an armistice agreement that signaled an end to the chronic worry, daily restrictions, and constant disruptions associated with the war. Revelers swarmed Gay Street in a joyous crush of humanity that prevailed for hours. That night, the University of Tennessee hosted a celebration on its athletic field. Roughly ten thousand Knoxvillians of every age and description paraded through town, delighting tens of thousands of spectators who lined the streets.[144] Everyone waved the Stars and Stripes. Once the partiers reached the university's campus, soldiers entertained the throngs with a "snake dance" around the raging bonfire.[145] The crowd burned effigies of German leaders when they weren't busy kissing in public or drinking on the streets.[146] After a long day of celebrating, some went home, but many festivities lasted well into the evening.

Troops from Knox County had faced heavy fighting in the months leading up to the armistice, and local parents celebrated while still unsure of their sons' safety. They knew that battlefield reports took time to reach the US from overseas. Sure enough, during the next few days, local newspapers carried accounts of several fatalities among Tennessee soldiers. Then on November 13, a local couple announced that they had received a cable from their son, a Lieutenant Wright of the Army's 30th Division. He had written them on November 10, just before the armistice, announcing his safe arrival in Paris.[147] Since most of Knoxville's troops were in that same division and presumably accompanied him, the war's end could now truly be appreciated.

Knoxvillians took great pride in the accomplishments of local troops. As part of the 30th Division of the Army National Guard, Tennesseans received high praise, including that from an Australian officer with whom they fought in France and a British general who they battled alongside in Flanders.[148] The 59th Infantry Brigade, part of the 30th Division, contained most of the troops from Knox County and was one of the first brigades to break through the Hindenburg Line. This major German defensive position had previously been challenged several times but never broken. The 59th withstood heavy fire and captured several small towns in northern France, but it sacrificed heavily while doing so. Over 45 percent of the casualties inflicted beyond the Hindenburg Line occurred in the 59th, which eventually received nine medals of honor, more than any other brigade.[149] No wonder Tennesseans celebrated these men.

* * *

During the spring of 1919, vast numbers of American soldiers returned from overseas. Knoxville feted its veterans with an enormous parade overseen by Brigadier General Lawrence D. Tyson. An influential member of Knoxville's textile industry, Tyson had also supported the city's fledgling public library and served as a state senator. On this day, however, most Knoxvillians knew that little of that mattered. Tyson's only son, Charles McGhee Tyson, died near the war's end while serving as gunner on a four-man flight over the North Sea. Knoxville's Tyson Park and McGhee Tyson Airport would later be established in his honor. Area servicemen honored Knox County's war dead by erecting a statue of an infantryman on the grounds of Knoxville High School. Its inscription partly read: "To our living dead; that company of shining souls who gave their youth, that the world might grow old in peace."

The engraving continued with a poignant assertion that the men's sacrifice would never be forgotten. General Tyson himself oversaw the dedication ceremony.

The Great War had benefitted America's economy through a thriving job market that lured Appalachian people into cities and

Southerners to the North. It spurred innovative technologies and encouraged purchases of products such as automobiles. At its conclusion, however, a harsh reality awaited. The conflict's abrupt end resulted in disrupted industries, laid-off workers, and soon, alienated veterans. Reverberations from these changes would sweep through the country and into Knoxville.

Despite being enthusiastically welcomed home, Great War veterans often had difficulty readjusting to civilian life. Having experienced the horrors of trench warfare, mustard gas, and shell-shocked comrades, they suffered profoundly. As an added insult, the United States government paid them poorly. Upon being discharged from service, veterans received a sixty-dollar bonus and five cents per mile to travel home; only those with disabilities could hope for more.[150] The traumas of war and stresses of returning to civilian life went unacknowledged. No programs were created to provide these men with housing loans or free education. Furthermore, Prohibition had already been voted on and was about to become law, so the cheap escape of liquor would soon become illegal nationwide. Many soldiers resented this restriction.

Veterans also faced a tight job market, especially since the war ended so abruptly. Reeling from the end of lucrative government contracts, industries and farmers laid off workers instead of hiring the newly available veterans. The job prospects of former soldiers lagged so badly that some essentially entered the Great Depression a decade before the rest of the country.[151] They grew resentful of the factory laborers who had often made higher wages during the war than they did. For the first time, many of those industrial workers were Black, triggering the era's racism.

The American public also struggled with the war's aftereffects. Propaganda had helped to strengthen resolve while the conflict raged, but afterward, the public's patriotic anger settled into general anxiety. Russia's communist revolution triggered this angst, and the United States began harboring a fear of radical beliefs that verged on paranoia. Some long-running issues persisted after the war ended.

Flare-ups of influenza and the era's increased crime continued to concern Americans.

As this mixture of paranoia and racism, fear and unemployment simmered, it served as a background for ongoing violence across America's cities. In a period now called the Red Summer, over two dozen significant strikes and race riots occurred in 1919 and 1920. These events started in early summer of 1919, when riots took place in Cleveland, Boston, Charleston, and New York City. In Omaha, Nebraska, the public lynching of a Black man entertained or horrified the many onlookers. Striking unions created flashpoints, such as one in Seattle, because Americans associated unions with communism. The unions often felt animosity toward Black people, especially when they worked during strikes such as they had in East St. Louis during the war. For their part, Black communities remembered the inadequate police protection of that same riot.

These riots and unrest continued throughout 1919. In Washington, DC, weeks of newspaper articles about a Black sexual predator inflamed the city's White population. One night in late July, servicemen drinking in the city's taverns heard that a Black suspect had been detained, then released, for the violation of a Navy man's wife.[152] A mob formed, then entered a poor, mostly Black neighborhood. Although the community provided scant resistance, the men became violent, burning homes and attacking and killing Black residents. The next day, *The Washington Post* ran a front-page story stating that all available soldiers should attend a "clean-up" operation that night.[153] When the mob returned, Black residents retaliated, firing indiscriminately from moving cars and forming an angry gang of their own.[154] The riot lasted four days.

Less than a week later, similar viciousness occurred in Chicago. White beachgoers threw rocks at a Black swimmer who had crossed an invisible line between segregated beaches. The teenager drowned, either from being hit on the head or because he was too afraid to return to shore.[155] This time, there was no day of submission before the Black community fought back. Mobs of men battled each other, leaving fifteen White and twenty-three Black people dead and over five hundred people injured.[156] Arson committed by both groups resulted in the loss of hundreds of homes, the majority in Black neighborhoods.[157]

Soon after the Chicago riot, W.E.B. Du Bois, one of the founders of the NAACP, declared that Black Americans had to go beyond self-defense. He proclaimed, "We have suffered and cowered. [...] When the armed lynchers come, we too must gather armed. When the mob moves, we propose to meet it with bricks and clubs and guns."[158] America's Black communities increasingly agreed, resolving not to be vulnerable when faced with aggression.

Knoxville's local papers reported these events, but the city felt immune to the country's unrest. In early 1918, a local Black leader named Charles Cansler, principal of the city's Black high school, had stated that the town enjoyed racial harmony.[159] On Armistice Day, the races had celebrated the war's ending together, with groups of Black citizens participating in the city's parade and general revelry.[160] Nevertheless, a few weeks after the Chicago violence, in August 1919, the city of Knoxville, its Black community, and Earl Layman found themselves immersed in Red Summer violence.

CHAPTER 8
Normal School

AFTER REJECTING MOST OF NORTH ALABAMA'S employment options, fourteen-year-old Marie struggled to make a decision about her future. Finally, she settled on an occupation, one that could lead to a lifetime of fulfilling employment. It also would take her away from family, test her resolve, and ultimately endanger her health.

Alabama needed teachers. Many communities had a small, neighborhood school with students who walked to class. Most of these facilities had one room and one educator, but so many of them existed that they caused a teacher shortage. Many American states wanted to improve their public education in the early twentieth century, and they all faced challenges. In Alabama, roughly one-fourth of the state's citizens who were old enough to read couldn't do so.[161] Women's clubs had long lobbied for improvements such as increased teacher pay and state-provided instructional materials. Reformers overwhelmingly wanted a longer school term. In 1915, when Marie turned eleven, the state mandated that sixteen weeks of classes be provided to school-aged children *each year*.[162] By the time she finished her schooling, the average yearly term outside of the cities had increased to a paltry twenty-one weeks.[163] Thus, during

Marie's seven-year lifetime of public-school education, she attended classes about four months each year.

Not surprisingly, the state lacked a well-educated pool of applicants for its teaching positions. Men earned most of the four-year teaching degrees, but they gravitated toward higher-paying, administrative jobs. Only two colleges in the state accepted women,[164] so Alabama created educators the way many states did, through special institutions called "normal schools." These facilities tended to have low admission standards, and they often produced young, ill-prepared graduates.[165] Desperate for educators, though, the state provided a rare opportunity to its citizens: they could attend a normal school for free if they agreed to teach in Alabama's public schools for two years after graduation.[166] Rural communities didn't particularly respect these graduates, but out of necessity, they considered them good enough to hire.

Incredibly, Marie Little's seventh-grade education made her eligible for the state's offer. For all the known problems with normal schools, attending one had advantages for her. She would be able to continue her education, which she found appealing. She could gain a profession that would allow her to avoid a life spent in the field or the mills. Through teaching, Marie could provide for herself with her intellect instead of menial work.

In the fall of 1919, just after she turned fifteen, Marie left her home to attend Jacksonville Normal School in Calhoun County, Alabama.[167] The small school employed twelve instructors and four staff members. Marie's coursework would not lead to a college degree. If she took classes for a year and passed a state exam, however, she would earn a certificate that allowed her to teach for twelve months. That accreditation could be extended to four years if she returned the next summer for more classes, then passed another test.[168] Many Alabama teachers followed this path to accreditation, and enrollment in Jacksonville's twelve-week summer program often exceeded the number of traditional, fall-to-spring students.

Marie arrived at Jacksonville in the midst of a determined attempt to improve the state's educational system, especially in rural areas. Remarkably, the legislature increased taxes, with part of the money going to public schools.[169] In order to improve its teacher education programs, a State Board of Education was formed, which took over the normal schools. Under its guidance, courses at Jacksonville ranged from the sociology of education to the practical aspects of grading and making lesson plans.[170] In reality, though, fifteen months of classes for such young and often poorly educated students couldn't provide them with the skills they needed to be successful teachers.

Separated from her family and friends, at first Marie's year in Jacksonville proved challenging. She yearned for the familiarity of home.[171] Writing letters helped, but she constantly ran out of the stamps needed to mail them. Her new circumstances did have advantages, though. In Jacksonville, she could flourish outside of Grace's shadow. Most of the students were women, and a childhood spent with six sisters had prepared her to coexist with them. Marie loved a joke and, lacking all glamour or pretense, would slap her knee or stomp her foot when she laughed. She made friends easily, interacting with others out of a desire to know them. The school offered a wide variety of social activities, which Marie undoubtedly enjoyed. She could join the glee club, watch basketball games, and attend musical recitals, all more glamorous events than the meals with neighbors and nights spent with cousins that she had publicized from home. Her inner society editor had to have loved it.

After twelve months at the Jacksonville Normal School, Marie earned the certificate that qualified her to teach for a year.

In the fall of 1920, the Etowah County Board of Education hired the sixteen-year-old for the upcoming term.[172] She was assigned to teach in Morgan's Cross Roads, a small community on the Gadsden side of the Coosa River. Most of her students walked to school, sometimes long distances. Etowah County had segregated educational systems, so her charges were poor White children, the offspring of tenant farmers and sharecroppers. These students, their parents, and the community would withhold their respect until she earned it. Neither the state nor the college provided Marie with any on-the-job support.[173] Society expected teachers to labor selflessly for little personal gain, so she earned low pay for her eight-hour days, about 80 percent of what other local workers made.[174] Her employer dictated much of her life, believing that restrictions on educators revealed the community's high moral standards. In Etowah County, teachers were forbidden to drink, smoke, or get married.[175] They also had to attend church and live in approved housing.

* * *

On October 4, 1920, Marie stood in front of a classroom for the first time as an educator. Over sixty faces representing seven grade levels looked back at her.[176] She had sole responsibility for their education. Students who had failed the seventh-grade exam but stayed in school might be older than Marie. She taught a wide variety of subjects: arithmetic, penmanship, history, spelling, geography, and the all-important reading. Her employers also expected her to provide moral instruction. Since she was responsible for student safety and behavior, Marie supervised her charges during lunch and recess. She had no scheduled planning time during the school day but had to keep the building clean and maintain a fire in the pot-bellied stove during cold weather.

Facing this massive amount of duties, Marie knew that she had two options: she could try to be an educator in this isolated schoolroom or she could not try. She attempted to stand taller.

"Good morning, students," she began.

* * *

Active children produce a miraculous amount of sound and movement. Loud, demanding, and boisterous, two or three of them can dominate an adult's time. Sixty in one room emit a rumbling, ceaseless energy. Surreptitious pinching and hair-pulling interrupt lessons while name-calling and shoving dominate recess.

Even inexperienced teachers know to check any relentless bad behavior, but they are often unprepared for reality: every distraction interrupts learning, and children are gifted at finding distractions.

Overwhelmed by the workload and level of responsibility, sixteen-year-old Marie had a difficult first year at Morgan's Cross Roads. Convincing sixty youngsters to be productive and well behaved for eight hours a day proved impossible. The energy required to even try eludes most humans. With no mentor to consult or experience to draw upon, isolation and youth compounded Marie's problems. The stress mounted for a day, a week, several weeks. At some point she undoubtedly slipped, regressing to the frustrated sister who yelled at her siblings.

She attempted to improve the situation through exertion. After working all day, in the evening she checked her students' papers, then taught herself to type on a rented typewriter. On Saturdays, she took an extension course from the Jacksonville Normal School. The relentless schedule exhausted her, especially since she slept less in order to work more. She rarely socialized, even though she lived at Gadsden number four, a county-provided boardinghouse for teachers.[177] This living arrangement might have been convenient, but it took her away from the daily support of her family. The relentless pace ultimately caused Marie to become physically ill. Throughout her lifetime, she suffered from migraines, which she described as "sick headaches," that would worsen amid the stress of her first teaching experience.

Marie learned hard lessons while working in that one-room schoolhouse. Some of them had to do with teaching. She discovered the value of keeping the students occupied, and her first success came in a form that fit her natural abilities—community interaction. Under her direction, the children provided an outdoor Christmas tree for Morgan's Cross Roads, complete with a holiday performance at its unveiling. She returned from Christmas break with another idea: the students would host a temperance program. The entertainment included musical salutes to America and to Alabama, a recitation of "The Price of a Drink," and a reading of the federal constitutional amendment that outlawed liquor. A debate on alcohol and health followed these rousing presentations.

By the spring of 1921, Marie acknowledged to herself that overwork can be counterproductive. Articles touting the social events of Morgan's Cross Roads started appearing in the Gadsden newspaper. They had a familiar tone and focused on the activities of a teenaged schoolteacher. Grace visited her sister for a weekend, no doubt checking on Marie's welfare for their mother. Marie accepted several dinner invitations, enjoyed an evening of parlor games, and attended group singings in neighborhood churches and homes. Of her many skills, musical capability ranked decidedly near the bottom, but her friends surely forgave her lack of pitch. Marie had emerged from hiding.

* * *

This dreadful first year of teaching was followed by three more months in summer school. Afterward, Marie took another exam and spent time at home, regrouping and reassessing while she awaited her test results. If she passed this exam, she would earn the four-year teaching certificate that many educators transformed into lifelong employment. Word soon arrived that she had earned the multiyear certificate, a feat that gained her community recognition.[178]

Marie returned to Morgan's Cross Roads in the fall of 1921. This time, she practiced the basic survival techniques of a one-room schoolteacher: disciplining students as soon as they misbehaved or ignored her, planning lessons efficiently, and keeping everyone busy, with older students assisting the younger ones. She also developed a skill that never left her: the ability to sense when children were attempting clandestine mischief. This insight likely had more to do with sudden silence than the proverbial eyes in the back of her head, but her charges didn't know that.

The seventeen-year-old also took better care of herself. Recognizing that her personal strength had limitations, she slept more, accepted the need for diversions such as exercise, and balanced her work duties with weekend socializing. Her family provided support and diversion. When she returned home for the holidays, a cousin, Lorene Gray, honored her with a dinner party. Decorations made of roses and holly sprigs created a festive setting for the guests who dined on a six-course dinner and played parlor games. Even Grace helped to entertain her sister by hosting a well-attended evening of singing.

Marie's second year of teaching met her standards for excellence much more than the first one, a feat that she publicized. In April, an Etowah County newspaper column noted a long list of social events that had occurred in Morgan's Cross Roads. The article began with its crucial information, however, noting that school there had closed for the summer "after being successfully taught by Miss Marie Little."[179]

CHAPTER 9
The Knoxville Riot

ONE LATE SUMMER SATURDAY EVENING IN 1919, Earl had a decision to make. He could stay safely in his rented room at the YMCA, or he could walk a few blocks to watch an angry mob congregate at the county jail. Knoxville had stewed with unrest all day, its citizens speculating ominously about what would happen that night.[180] Eighteen years old, Earl lived on his own in the center of town.

Of course, he went to see the action.

During the Red Summer outbreak, racial unrest became a national trend, causing Americans to fear imminent and widespread conflict between the races.[181] The riots in Washington, DC, Chicago, and elsewhere had revealed fundamental problems in the culture. When Knoxville joined the race-related violence, the causes ranged from the obvious to the underlying: unemployment and overcrowding, lawlessness and racism.

East Tennessee's economy faltered along with the nation's when the war-related spending came to an end. Local farmers suffered as markets contracted and an improved national railroad system increased the scope of their competition. As Knoxville's factories laid off workers, poor White and Black laborers competed for the remaining jobs. Despite the city's positive view of its race relations, tensions had simmered as its Black population multiplied. In the fifty years prior to 1920, Knoxville's Black population increased fourfold.[182] These in-migrants moved into low-rent areas near the city's Appalachian population, forcing the groups to interact.[183] Now, the unemployed of both races idled in cramped neighborhoods without positive outlets for frustration or anger. Emotions flared when the Ku Klux Klan marched through town, even though Knoxville Mayor John McMillian denounced the organization.

Prohibition encouraged a disrespect for the rule of law that also played a role in Knoxville's riot. Several jailbreaks, including Ehude Fellows's escape, made incarceration less threatening. In August 1919, however, when Earl left his room at the YMCA to watch that night's events, Ehude again sat in the Knox County jail, awaiting transfer to prison where he was supposed to serve a lifetime sentence for murdering Peter Nichols.[184]

Among these underlying issues, the murder of a White woman ignited Knoxville's violence. Mrs. Bertie Lindsey was shot during an attempted robbery that followed a pattern familiar to police. A repeat offender, nicknamed "Pants," sneaked into homes as his victims slept, then took money out of their wallets and pants pockets. This time, the burglar threatened Bertie and her cousin, Ora Smith, and warned them not to flee. When Bertie attempted to escape, he shot and killed her. Later that same night, a local policeman named Andy White presented Knoxville native Maurice Mays as a suspect in the crime. There wasn't hard evidence for Mays's guilt, but White and Mays had long disliked each other.[185] White insisted that a gun found in Mays's room had recently been discharged, even though other law enforcement members disagreed.[186] Nevertheless, in the middle of the night, hours after she watched her cousin die, Ora identified Mays as the man who shot Bertie, and authorities arrested him. The next day, the city's *Journal and Tribune* commented on the arrest, pointing out that previous to Mrs. Lindsey's murder, no evidence had pointed to Mays being the "pants" burglar.[187]

Handsome and dapperly attired, the mixed-race Mays commanded attention in town. At one point, he ran a successful nightclub in the Bowery. Since it allowed dancing between the races, it was referred to as a "black and tan," slang for such establishments.[188] Because he was being raised by foster parents, Knoxvillians speculated about Mays's father.[189] Even Earl knew the gossip, saying, "I have heard he was the illegitimate son of a White man ... a banker."[190] Reportedly, John McMillian, local banker and Knoxville mayor, was Mays's father.[191] The two knew each other, and Mays had spent the day of his arrest campaigning in the Black community for McMillian's reelection.[192]

The day after Mays's arrest, rumors began circulating that "there was going to be trouble."[193] Earl remarked that "talk of possible riots and fights" flourished because some townspeople "became inflamed and decided to mob Mays." In other words, they planned to attack the jail, seize Mays, and lynch him. Earl blamed this plan of vigilante justice on "a certain element" of White people, his way of describing the uneducated lower class. The gossip became so widespread that Knox County's Sheriff Cate learned of the plot and transferred Mays to a Chattanooga facility. The Black community also understood the seriousness of the situation. Some left town while others began arming themselves.[194] Anticipating trouble, Knoxvillians spent the day working themselves into a frenzy.

By dusk, a mass of agitators had formed around the jail on Hill Avenue. Beyond this core group, an enormous crowd extended several blocks to Gay Street.[195] These onlookers milled around for hours, many of them drawn by the same perverse excitement found at public hangings. Earl succumbed to an inherently human motive when he joined them. He explained that "out of curiosity, I went ... to see what happened."[196]

At the jail, authorities tried to convince the mob that Mays had been moved. At least three groups of men were allowed into the facility to search for him.[197] Despite there being no evidence that Mays was present, the core mob continued to act as if he was. Family members of men imprisoned in the jail mingled among the crowd,[198] no doubt encouraging the insurgence. They could have been among the twenty-odd men allowed to search the facility, verifying just who was incarcerated inside. One of those prisoners, of course, was Ehude Fellows, convicted killer and practiced jail escapee. If Fellows's cohorts planned to free him from the Knox County jail, the mob's actions made excellent cover.

When Earl arrived at the scene, he worked his way through the outer crowd so he could watch the events. He saw several men "beating in and trying to knock down the jail door" with a log so heavy that it took six of them, three on each side, to carry it. Someone in the jail's upper story tried to calm the horde, assuring them that Mays wasn't present. In response, Earl heard a chant: "We want that nigger." Soon, watchmen from a riverside lumber company entered the fray. Notoriously tough characters, they shot the glass out of the jail windows, convincing the deputies to leave the scene.[199]

Finally, the mob succeeded in breaking down the jailhouse door and swarming into the building. For all their racist comments and fury against Mays, once it became clear that he had been moved, the troublemakers did not harass the Black prisoners.[200] Instead, they ransacked the sheriff's nearby home and plundered the jail's stores of confiscated whiskey. A jailer who watched events from inside the facility reported that its leaders moved directly to the White prisoner's cells in order to free them.[201] These men first destroyed the cell block's outer doors with a battering ram, most likely the same log used to break the main door. Having brought tools, two men worked to open the substantial locks that secured the inner cell doors while another one provided light from a lantern. After laboring for over an hour, the men successfully freed Ehude and Harvey Fellows, as well as most of the other prisoners.[202] Once free, Ehude merged into the crowd that loitered outside the jail. A special deputy saw the felon and moved to arrest him. When he got close, however, the deputy felt a gun being pressed to his side and heard an unfamiliar voice instructing him to stop or "I'll shoot a hole through you."[203] The deputy backed off, allowing Ehude Fellows to make a second escape from the Knox County jail.

Police and deputy sheriffs immediately started searching for Ehude, Harvey, and the other escaped felons. Sheriff Cate, who started the job after the Fellows brothers' first jailbreak, offered a $200 reward for information leading to the capture of these dangerous men.[204] Weeks would pass without news of Ehude and Harvey Fellows. In fact, Earl and his family would spend years waiting for information about the convicted murderer. In retrospect, the freeing of White prisoners, especially "friends in jail charged with high felonies,"[205] was considered the main goal of some mob participants.

* * *

After Earl watched the prisoners escape, he left the scene and returned to his room at the YMCA.[206] He intended to stay there.

On the city's streets, Knoxville's violence intensified, even though Mays had not been found and most of the White prisoners had been freed. Trouble occurred in the Bowery near Vine Street when White and Black citizens fought in hand-to-hand combat.[207] Shots might have been fired. The restless mob heard about the altercation and, fortified by liquor, lurched toward the city's primary Black neighborhood and business district. Along the way, they vandalized stores while looking for weapons. At Woodruff's Hardware, where Earl worked, looters stole over a dozen of the hardware store's best guns, along with ammunition and knives.[208] The night's events descended into anarchy, with its only purpose destruction fueled by racial animosity.[209]

Earl's room at the YMCA sat a block south of Vine Street, between it and the county jail where the riot started. With windows open in the late summer heat, shouts from the approaching mob and sounds of the breaking glass of storefronts would have been unmistakable. Curiosity again prevailed over common sense when the teenager left his room and walked to the intersection of State and Vine Streets. This position placed him ahead of the mob, so he would be able to see events as they unfolded. It also put him in the center of the coming chaos and almost got him killed.

Once he reached Vine Street, Earl could see that Knoxville's Black residents intended to defend their homes and businesses. A fence, or breastwork, made of empty wooden boxes had been constructed across the road at its junction with Central Street. Several Black men crouched behind the barricade. Determined to see what would happen, Earl moved onto Vine Street and stood near the entrance of the Fielden Hardware Company. From here, he could look uphill to Gay Street or downhill to Central.

Soon, the National Guard, who had been training nearby, entered the scene. They set up a machine gun at the intersection of Gay and Vine. Instead of targeting the destructive mob, however, they aimed their guns at the barricade to the Black neighborhood. As Earl watched, the machine gun "cut loose" when the guardsmen fired at the makeshift wooden fence. He saw "boxes fly everywhere" and noticed that bullets hit several men who were crouched behind the breastwork.

From his position between the barricade and the machine gun, Earl found himself in the midst of a war zone. As he put it, "by golly, there was plenty of firing ... most of it was the machine gun." He added, "There were shots fired, I guess, from both sides."

Pinned into the hardware store entranceway by the shots, he hid behind a wall. This action probably saved his life because the militia shot with no regard for safety. Their recklessness resulted in the death of one of their own. As Earl explained the incident, "There was a White officer killed ... that night, right there in that exchange of fire."

When the shooting momentarily stopped, the teenager left the protected enclave and sprinted toward the YMCA. He would never again consider mob violence to be entertaining. Other bystanders also regretted their curiosity. One boy thought he had been shot and asked Earl for help. Earl looked at the boy's bleeding knee, then helped him to the YMCA to receive medical attention. Luckily, the injury had occurred when the boy fell while running for cover from the gunfire, not from a bullet. He soon walked home on his own.[210]

Knoxville suffered through a restless night as racially inspired viciousness cropped up across town. Gunshots attributed to "hoodlumism" disturbed the night air, and racially motivated violence occurred near the University of Tennessee and the Bowery's Jackson Avenue.[211] Authorities placed machine guns within the city and on several trucks that roamed through town. During the next few days, the National Guard confiscated hundreds of weapons from both White and Black citizens,[212] although they harassed only the Black ones, taking money and cigarettes during unnecessarily rough searches. This didn't always go smoothly. When four Black men resisted being searched, guardsmen reportedly shot two of them and bayonetted the other two.[213]

The riot's exact number of casualties has never been determined. Era newspapers reported that many men were wounded but only two killed: the victim of the National Guard's friendly fire and one Black man.[214] Rumors persisted, though, of unmarked graves and bodies dumped in the river. While thousands of spectators had milled about during the events at the jail, few Knoxvillians saw the Vine Street shooting. But Earl did. Having watched men being shot as they crouched behind the wooden barricade, he believed that many Black citizens died in the August heat.[215]

* * *

Even though riots and general unrest occurred throughout America during the summer of 1919 into 1921 and 1922, Knoxville's riot contributed to the city's reputation of being ungovernable and added racial instability to that image. In an article titled "Knoxville in Throes of Serious Race Riots," East Tennessee's *Greeneville Daily Sun* proclaimed that "the presence of troops and machine guns saved Knoxville from a bloody race war."[216] *The Chattanooga News* more accurately reported that "State Guards Turn Machine Guns on Crowd."[217] *The Maryville Times* noted that Knoxville experienced a "sure enough riot."[218]

As for Maurice Mays, his story ended tragically. While he sat in jail awaiting trial, another White woman was attacked in Knoxville in a crime almost identical to the one involving Bertie Lindsey. A mixed-race man entered a woman's bedroom, telling her that if she didn't do as told, he would shoot her. He claimed to have recently shot a young boy and did, in fact, shoot the woman when she resisted him.[219] The timing and details of this crime placed considerable doubt on Mays's guilt, but the judge did not allow witnesses to testify about it during his trial.[220] Knoxvillians hotly debated Mays's possible guilt. Some told Earl that since the Black man was a criminal, it wouldn't be amiss to electrocute him, even if on a false charge.[221]

Earl, however, believed in Mays's innocence, maintaining that the case against him rested on "purely circumstantial evidence" given too much weight because "people were inflamed." To him, the most damning evidence presented against Mays, that mud on his shoes matched mud found in Bertie Lindsey's yard, could be easily disputed. Earl insisted that it could have come from "a hundred different places."

In fact, Earl clearly stated, "I never believed he committed that crime." Nevertheless, Maurice Mays was convicted of murder in Knox County Criminal Court and sentenced to death. He was electrocuted in Nashville.

The events of August 30, 1919, horrified many Knoxvillians. Soon afterward, Judge T.A.R. Nelson presided over a trial of several mob participants. He described their crimes as targeting "the very root of civilization and decent society" and condemned the "criminals of the lowest type" who endangered Sheriff Cate as he attempted to do his job. However, when the nineteen men arrested for participating in the riot were tried locally, fourteen were found not guilty and five more released because of a mistrial.[222]

This failure to convict the riot's participants illuminated the racism that fueled the Vine Street attacks and subsequent treatment of Black citizens.[223] Knoxville, it turned out, wasn't immune to America's racial prejudice or the era's explosive atmosphere.

CHAPTER 10
The More Things Change

TEACHING IN A ONE-ROOM SCHOOLHOUSE had a certain frontier Romanticism to it, but Marie Little craved a more manageable workload. Employment at a larger institution would give her higher prestige, better pay, and colleagues to interact with. After two years of working in Morgan's Cross Roads, she applied to nearby Burns Academy. When the school hired her in the fall of 1922, she returned to the neighborhood near the Coosa River where her family tenant farmed. The community felt great pride in Burns Academy, having built it themselves. A local citizen had provided the land, and area farmers donated timber for the structure and profits from their cotton crops to fund the project. At a time before county governments provided rural schools, families had worked together to construct the building so their children could be educated.

Marie could easily have stayed with her parents while teaching at Burns Academy, but the Etowah County School Board dictated that she live in approved housing, which didn't include parental homes. Instead, she resided at Gadsden number one, a boardinghouse for educators. Housing requirements complicated the lives of teachers and administrators alike. Three days before the 1922 school year began, some county educators still lacked lodging. Even worse, many didn't know where they would be teaching. They gathered in the superintendent's office on a Monday afternoon to learn their final assignments. Classes started Tuesday morning.

Burns Academy employed a principal and two teachers, but even this small faculty provided the eighteen-year-old Marie with much-needed camaraderie. Nellie Cornelius, the other instructor, was several years older than Marie, but the two appear to have worked well together. Marie joked around with the principal, A. H. Hand, by kiddingly and repeatedly asking him for a raise. Finally, he retorted, "Marie, you should be grateful that I took you out of that one-room school!"

She hooted at his reply.

After a dismal start as an educator, Marie had found her footing. Her employment stipulated that she attend church services, an easily fulfilled requirement for Marie. Burns Academy had an affiliated church, Cedar Bend Baptist, where her parents worshiped. She joined the young adult Sunday school class, called the Baptist Young People's Union (BYPU). Other members included Nellie Cornelius and Hazel Myrick, one of Marie's longtime friends.

Since social life in rural areas centered around schools and churches, Marie's days became a whirl of activity. Newspaper columns detailing the dinners and get-togethers of Morgan's Cross Roads, where Marie previously taught, all but disappeared in the fall of 1922.[224] Burns Academy events, however, suddenly started receiving lots of press. In addition to teaching, Marie helped the children prepare songs and plays for community events. In December she played the title role of "the Spirit" in the church youth group's Christmas presentation, "The Spirit of the BYPU." She also participated in the lives of her students outside of the classroom, directing children's games at a birthday celebration for two eight-year-olds. Marie increasingly took photographs of her friends, recording her many social activities. Now that her salary had improved, she could better afford the costs of having the pictures developed into physical copies.

***

After the Great War ended, North Alabama avoided a race riot such as Knoxville experienced, but it faced similar issues. A general dislike of immigrants and fear of communism festered in both places as well as throughout the country. Racial prejudice and inequality remained fundamental problems, although Etowah County held varying points of view on these issues. The Ku Klux Klan (KKK), for example, was controversial. Articles in the *Gadsden Daily Times-News* stressed an unwelcome attitude toward the organization. When one Klan rally drew a large crowd, the paper admonished the attendees and commented how much more good the Boy Scouts could accomplish with that level of support.[225]

The city of Gadsden and the KKK came into direct confrontation when the Klan inducted several hundred locals. The Rotary, Kiwanis, and Civitan clubs joined forces in order to counter this influence.[226] Since Klan members covered their faces in public, a town committee decided that outlawing the wearing of masks in city limits would curtail the organization, or at least keep it from gathering on city streets.[227] Town leaders scheduled an open meeting to discuss the idea, and a national representative of the KKK asked to speak. His presentation would be followed by a local preacher who opposed the Klan. Unfortunately, the committee in charge of instituting the ban on masks identified a problem: doing so would essentially outlaw Halloween costumes in Gadsden.[228] Wanting to avoid an uproar, the town abandoned the plan, but the struggle against Klan influence continued.

The Klan challenged Gadsden society, but an old foe proved even more disruptive—disease.

Ominous tidings hid among the lighthearted news of a Burns Academy society column in December of 1922. Professor Hand had recently suffered a serious bout of pneumonia, a common aftereffect of influenza, and several of the school's students were battling the flu. Etowah County had previously experienced bouts of the disease, including a serious outbreak in 1920. Now the illness had returned. Three years after the nationwide calamity of 1919, the flu still outgunned the era's medical abilities. As the 1922 epidemic spread and families suffered, those in Smokeneck supported each other. Marie and her mother, Ninnie, took dinner to the home of a local family whose mother was too ill to cook. They left a basket of food on the front porch, then backed off and yelled until a family member heard them. When a child emerged from the cabin and retrieved the basket, Marie and Ninnie left. They didn't dare go any closer to the house.

Such safeguards soon proved ineffective. Before Marie's Christmas break ended, communities throughout Etowah County began announcing school closings due to the outbreak. As usual, influenza targeted the young and healthy. Marie's best friend died of the disease, and in January, one of her younger sisters, Faye, became seriously ill.[229]

During the epidemic, normal life ended, and sobering announcements became common. Some revealed the deaths of small children and infants, now referred to as "little angels." Thirteen-year-old Faye almost died, and Ninnie, susceptible from caring for her daughter, also fell ill. She shocked her children by lying listlessly in bed. Marie and Grace tried to fulfill their mother's duties by tending the sick, watching over their younger sisters, and preparing meals. As if influenza didn't provide enough challenges, Grace contracted the measles. Marie and her siblings sometimes kiddingly called their father a "prophet of doom" because of his anxious outlook on life, but after disease ravaged the countryside and their family, he seemed to have a point. Etowah County's high death rate continued for weeks.

By late March 1923, Faye had recovered enough to participate in a Sunday night singing event, and Ninnie's health improved to the point that she encouraged her daughters to enjoy themselves. The resulting social events were immediately publicized. Marie and her cousin Frank went shopping in Gadsden, and Grace spent the night with friends.

* * *

Issues of race and illness constituted the region's most serious problems, but they weren't the only challenges. The women of the Progressive era had fought obstinately for change, confronting the use of child labor, the general population's alcohol consumption, and women's inability to vote, but even they didn't envision the vast social changes of the 1920s. Standards of behavior and of clothing swiftly relaxed as movies and advertisements conveyed the newest trends enjoyed by high-spirited, fun-loving youth.

When young people across America adopted these new standards, it challenged their communities. The era's changes wouldn't be halted, though, not even by its influential churches and traditional culture. Some Etowah County elders became greatly concerned at this weakening of standards. Controversy erupted in the neighborhood of Mentone when young men and women cavorted together in the local swimming hole while wearing bathing suits and other informal clothing. Women's swimming garments of the day covered their bodies from neck to knees, but the attire still appalled some locals. Angst-filled residents wrote letters to the newspaper, claiming these "half-naked" swimmers would corrupt the neighborhood children.[230] More controversy arose over the behavior of Gadsden's young people who gathered at Moragne Park, loitering without supervision into the evening. This practice upset the older adults, who grew up in a stricter era of chaperones and parental control. Determined to rectify the situation, city leaders strung lights throughout the park, but the town's youth rebelled. The new light bulbs broke with mysterious regularity, allowing courting couples to regain the cover of darkness.[231]

This loosening of social standards even reached Smokeneck. In Marie's second year of teaching at Burns Academy, she and other school employees motored to Gadsden on a Saturday night to watch the school's basketball team play the steel plant's team. The freedom inherent in her unchaperoned, cross-county jaunt—in an automobile, no less—would have been unheard of just a few years earlier.

In the spring of 1923, after the influenza epidemic faded, the Littles received welcome guests. Patsy and Jim visited from Washington, DC, so their families could meet Patricia, their young daughter, and so Patsy could assure herself of her family's health. The couple traveled from the nation's capital in a Model T, a purchase that signified their success.[232] Jim and Patsy marveled at the freedom an automobile gave them; their daughter learned to dread the hot, bumpy rides from DC to Alabama. To commemorate this particular visit, Patsy took a picture of her family members standing by the car. It features eighteen-year-old Marie, Gladys, who was one of her younger sisters, and three young nieces. Marie smiles shyly and cradles little Patricia so the toddler doesn't fall off the car's running board.

Astonishingly, Marie's hair is bobbed, or cut short. American women traditionally grew long locks, which servants of the wealthy styled into coiffures and average women pinned or braided themselves. Then silent film stars began cutting their hair, disrupting the status quo. Because long hair was considered sweetly feminine and short hair sporty but defiant, a girl's hair style became social commentary. The bob quickly gained popularity among the young. At first, hair salons for women didn't exist outside of major cities,[233] so attaining the style required ingenuity. Some women asked male barbers for a cut, but usually sisters or friends wielded the scissors. Lucky was the woman whose sister had a talent with shears. Since society often frowned upon short hair, many girls regretted their daring, especially after a botched cut or upon discovering the style didn't flatter them.

Adventurous young women accompanied this revolution with vastly reimagined clothing. Just a few years before, dress hemlines had been floor length, and corsets dictated a woman's shape. In a photograph of Patsy, Grace, and Marie taken six or seven years earlier, Patsy wore a Gibson Girl outfit, with a carefully coiffed up-do and a high-waisted, tiered dress that cascaded toward the ground. Since then, hemlines had shortened and waistlines disappeared, so frocks hung from the shoulders, skimmed over hips, and ended just below the knees. Tall, slender girls best wore this new fashion because the dress's thin material hung attractively on them while also revealing the lack of a corset.

In the picture taken by the automobile, Marie's dress falls to just above her calves. It features an immense white collar and the popular dropped waistline but is made of heavy, dark fabric. Since she isn't much over five feet tall, the color and extra material at the waist overwhelm her frame, making her look dowdy. Like many women, though, she wore the fashionable style whether it flattered her or not.

The short hems and bobbed hair of the 1920s announced women's rejection of the old order. They left farms wearing long, plaited hair and ill-fitting shoes; after a few paychecks from town jobs, they sported haircuts, updated clothes, and cosmetics.[234] But their aspirations went beyond fashion. They wanted tangible advancement. Armed with an education provided to them by the Progressive era, they sought employment as office workers and salesclerks. Dubbed the "new women," they enjoyed more opportunities than their gender ever had before.

Many in society considered them a passing fancy.

Standing by the Model T, Marie looks bashful, more sweet than sophisticated. She appears very much a girl, albeit a girl with a carefully displayed wristwatch and newly bobbed hair.

* * *

One reason for Marie's updated look might have been an exciting addition to her life: a boyfriend. In late April, she participated in an evening of community entertainment that featured songs, recitals, and a play. She had a lead role in that production as the daughter of a rich mine owner who had a secret fiancé, played by local boy Clifford Johnson. If Marie and Clifford weren't courting when rehearsals began, they soon were. Pictures show them standing close enough that their bodies touch. A head taller than her, his frame extends solidly above hers. She looks a bit pudgy in her waist-less dress, but her short hairstyle suits her, and she smiles with delight. They make an attractive couple.

Clifford had long been a favorite of the Little girls. Grace mentioned him in one of her first newspaper columns four years earlier. His family owned and farmed land in Smokeneck, and his younger brothers attended Burns Academy. Clifford enjoyed more opportunities in life than Marie. Unlike her, and even more unusual for boys, he attended high school after graduating from the seventh grade. Since both were well known in the community and Marie was a teacher, their courtship likely remained a traditional one, enduring not just formal supervision but also impromptu chaperoning whenever they were together.

* * *

In the fall of 1923, Marie began her second year of teaching at Burns Academy. However, the community of Smokeneck had been renamed "Southside" and the academy was called "Southside School." The Etowah County School System had taken over the county's rural schools, enlarging some facilities and closing several one-room schoolhouses. Southside School employed three teachers and occupied a new building. One hundred forty students attended, with Marie teaching the newly added high school grades.[235] She surely thrilled to her new position, but it revealed a weakness in the local educational system since she had never been to high school herself. An extended school year also proved elusive. Fall classes didn't begin until November 1.

With its new identity, Southside School teemed with ambition. At the Etowah County fair, it won first place for best exhibit, taking a $150 prize. A Thanksgiving program benefitted the school's library. Attendees brought a book to donate, then were entertained with songs, short plays, a debate about men's minds verses women's minds, and Marie reading a short essay called "The Busy Body." After this successful fundraiser, she plunged into another project: cohosting a Christmas party for the school basketball team. At least forty revelers attended, including several of Marie's sisters and her beau, Clifford. They played games, entered contests, and ate free candy.

Now age nineteen, Marie thrived as an independent young adult with a host of friends. She taught Sunday school at Cedar Bend Baptist and attended its frequent church socials. She even participated in the local Methodist church's Easter egg hunt. When the Rebekahs, a service-oriented organization devoted to friendship and truth, convened at Cedar Bend Baptist, Marie gave the welcome address. She greeted participants, the local paper noted, "in her charming way."[236]

Marie's enthusiasm for informing the community of her social activities, however, had drawn negative attention. Some readers viewed her articles as self-promotions that overstepped the acceptable limits of modesty. This condemnation included her emphasis on the Little family. In April, she wrote a newspaper column that, although it was brief, mentioned half a dozen Little relatives by name and used the word as an adjective several other times. A nearby article from the Sand Rock community seemed crafted to draw attention to her habit. It mentioned "little" seven times, always in reference to young children. Marie's columns continued, however. She often dined with female friends and returned to her parents' house for a dinner party when out-of-state relatives visited. Ninnie had prepared a four-course meal to welcome the Bean family of Knoxville, Tennessee. Marie soon hosted an elaborate dinner party herself, which featured full place settings for thirteen guests, including Clifford. She showed off her homemaking skills in case someone should notice them. As she had learned from her mother, Marie hovered nearby while the visitors ate, fetching items from the kitchen, replenishing the serving bowls, and refilling water or tea glasses. Not incidentally, state officials had recently decided that Alabama's teachers could marry. In March, Marie's beau again dined at the Little household, this time at a party for eight hosted by Ninnie.

Soon afterward, in the early summer of 1924, Marie and Clifford's relationship ended. They had dated about a year. He bowed to his family's opinion that her social status lay too far below his to allow for marriage.[237] Quite simply, they convinced him that he could do better. Marie abruptly quit publicizing her social activities, a sure sign of her distress. Someone else wrote an April newspaper article that reported events from Southside. Devoid of interesting tidbits, it recommended that households begin their spring cleaning, complained about an unsafe bridge over Black Creek, and noted that work would soon begin on Mt. Zion Church.

As for Marie, she did what any self-respecting New Woman would do after a broken relationship.

She left the state.

CHAPTER 11
Credit Man

AFTER HIS HARROWING EXPERIENCE DURING Knoxville's race riot, Earl moved out of his room at the YMCA and in with his favorite sister, Mae, and her husband, Clarence Smith. The couple lived in one of Knoxville's eastern suburbs near Magnolia Avenue, away from the congested and dirty central city. Earl still worked on Gay Street at Woodruff's Hardware, however. The owner, W. W. Woodruff Jr., was a devoted Christian, and Earl fit with the company culture, having attended church in Sevier County. He continued to do so in Knoxville and joined the ABCs, or Associates Bible Class, which met in the Strand Theatre. Mae's husband, Clarence, and Earl attended these services for years and, at one point, earned pins for participating twenty-six Sundays in a row.[238] Earl also served as usher for a special event based on the sermon "Can a Man be a Christian in Business?"

To highlight his position as a town man, and perhaps his nineteen-year-old good looks, Earl had his picture taken. Like most Americans of his era, he believed that clothing revealed an individual's prestige, or at least his aspirations. For the photograph, Earl wore a newly purchased dark suit, along with a dark patterned tie and white shirt with a high, stiff collar. He paid for a shave and haircut, opting for a hairstyle called the undercut where the barber shaved the sides of his head but left his hair long on top. That hair was slicked back over his head and kept in place with Brilliantine. The sticky gleam of this product might have spurred the term "city-slicker," a designation that would not have offended Earl. The undercut style could be unflattering, though, especially if it exposed protruding ears. On Earl, it showcased his even features and candid, blue-eyed gaze. He looks a bit proud of himself in the photograph.

Economically, Knoxville had recovered from its post-war doldrums and even outgained comparable Southern cities in population, partly though annexation. Many residents thought it would continue rising into prominence because it had so many advantages. In 1923, the city's streetcar system provided nearly twenty million rides between homes outside of the city to jobs within it.[239] Gay Street contained diverse businesses that ranged from stores and offices to Lloyd Branson's artist studio where he showcased East Tennessee landscapes and portraits of the town's wealthy. The city's textile mills, especially Standard Knitting Mill, provided employment, and in many ways the downtown area was thriving. The recently enlarged courthouse stressed Knoxville's importance as the county seat and home of East Tennessee's federal court. A recently finished Gay Street hotel had been named after a local hero, Admiral David Farragut. He was famous as a United States Navy officer during the Civil War, who (somewhat apocryphally) commanded his crew to "damn the torpedoes, full speed ahead" in order to capture Mobile, Alabama. Born in west Knox County, Farragut's family left the region during his childhood, long before he gained fame for his torpedo-dismissive attitude. Since Unionist views still prevailed in the region, East Tennesseans applauded his achievements and claimed him as a native. Hotel Farragut's opulent dining room and coffee shop offered visitors an upscale experience. Plus, every guest room contained a bath and ceiling fan as well as fireproofing.

The University of Tennessee, located several blocks west of downtown, had just opened its flagship building, Ayres Hall. A women's dormitory named Sophia Strong Hall was under construction, and the new athletic stadium held seating for thirty-two hundred. Its irregular playing field prevented fair play, however, so faculty and students evened it themselves. The university's president canceled classes for a day, and the university's men moved dirt to even the pitch while the co-eds provided barbeque.

These volunteers might have drunk Coca-Cola with their meal, a drink so well-loved in town that all soft drinks became "cokes," no matter the brand. Other popular foods included ice cream, which could be found at Kern's Bakery near the Market House and in the former Patrick Sullivan's saloon. Knoxville's quality dining establishments included Good's and the Regas Brothers Cafe. Owned by Greek immigrants, Regas served excellent meals in a modern, art deco setting of mirrored walls. It also had a thriving lunch counter.

These many advancements thrilled Knoxvillians, but instead of beating its competition, the city was actually participating in nationwide prosperity. Nevertheless, an undeniable energy pulsated throughout the 1920s, one that was widely noticed in the city.

The automobile best symbolized this vitality. Soon to become an essential part of the American identity, cars allowed citizens to move across the country's vast spaces in search of entertainment and opportunity. Railroads might have opened up the country as a whole, but automobiles expanded the number of choices available to individuals. A car-buying frenzy erupted in Knoxville during the twenties, causing their numbers to more than quadruple.[240] Earl's generation was the first to fully experience the freedoms that an automobile granted: the expanded options in where to work, live, and play. Many a young man, including Earl, aspired to own one, especially since doing so conveyed prosperity and forward-thinking.

The burgeoning number of automobiles caused fundamental problems for cities. Roads that had worked for a town full of horse-drawn carriages now barely functioned. Gay Street became a sluggish crush of vehicles as automobiles competed with the city's streetcars, carriages, and wagons. Finally, the town installed eleven transportation stands that towered eight feet above the roads. Policemen operated these towers by spotting oncoming congestion and communicating with each other via telephone.[241] To actually direct traffic, they changed the colors of large lights mounted underneath their platforms. Most of the new lights lined Gay Street, but the transportation revolution also affected other parts of town. Near Earl's former lodgings at the YMCA, business owners sorted out the evolving demand as liveries, blacksmiths, and a wagon-repair business commingled with a twenty-two-car garage and an automobile repair shop.[242]

Speeding vehicles soon became a hazard. One motorist drove forty miles an hour down Kingston Pike, resulting in a state warrant being issued against him. Several others sped in the suburbs, going thirty-two miles per hour or faster on Magnolia Avenue. Fines for these crimes ranged between twelve and twenty dollars. The ever-increasing number of automobiles added to the pollution that already streamed from Knoxville's coal-fueled factories and homes. Smog hovered over town and settled onto buildings, turning them an ugly dark gray. Disconcerted by the unsightliness, Knoxvillians blamed the pollution for lingering health issues. On the other hand, they also thought that automobile exhaust improved upon the foul-smelling product created by horses. In this way, cars made a town look cleaner and updated, and they fascinated most Americans.

A less-tangible twenties innovation would also be problematic: easy credit. Previously, loans to individuals had come from pawnshops, banks, or personal agreements between two men. Some East Tennesseans loaned money based on an IOU written on a scrap of paper and kept in a pocket. Then stores began issuing credit for large purchases, and American consumers signed up. Families whose homes had electricity, for example, could benefit from a plethora of labor-saving devices. Appliances new enough to be featured at Knoxville's 1923 Tennessee fair included an electric range, portable heater, refrigerator, water heater, food mixer, toaster, percolator, and grill. Advertisements of these items, another emerging concept, appeared in newspapers and magazines, spurring an economy that encouraged consumption.

Woodruff's Hardware sold any number of items that local families had difficulty saving up to buy, so the company started issuing credit. Invariably stores that did so found themselves with overdue payments, so they created collection departments. In a city small enough that word-of-mouth mattered, such as Knoxville, soliciting this money required finesse because the process could generate ill feelings toward a local business, even when it was justified.

Earl had advanced through the ranks at Woodruff's in a series of promotions. He first went from office boy to assistant cashier, then became an assistant bookkeeper two years later.[243] With his ambition and attention to detail, he soon received yet another promotion, finding a niche as the company's assistant credit manager.[244] His job was debt collection, soliciting payment from customers with delinquent accounts. Earl's nature wasn't to strong-arm anyone, so he adopted a more gentlemanly approach, relying on a trait developed in childhood. His older brother, Lem, stuttered badly and became frustrated if asked to repeat himself. As the younger sibling, Earl had learned to wait quietly while Lem laboriously conveyed ideas. When collecting debts, Earl drew on this patience while listening to the borrowers' hard luck stories. He also doggedly chased payment owed the store, aiming to succeed without alienating customers.

On the job, his rural background often gave him an advantage. Sometimes Woodruff's Hardware issued credit for relatively inexpensive purchases, so its delinquent bill-payers could stem from the city's large population of Appalachian migrants, whom Earl treated with kindness instead of disdain. He didn't mind visiting the city's shantytowns in order to collect payment. While navigating the narrow alleys and tenements, he accepted the residents' mountain accents and could conjure up one himself. Like many middle-class migrants, Earl submerged much of his original dialect, which surfaced when he felt relaxed. Or when it worked to his advantage.

In a few short years, Earl had evolved from farm boy to assistant manager, and he intended to go from streetcar-rider to motorist. But his connection to Sevier County remained strong, even though he didn't want to live there and bristled at being stereotyped as an ignorant hillbilly. A picture taken on the family farm reflects this inner contradiction. He and Lem stand on the edge of a forest with guns in hand, clearly either leaving to hunt or just returning from doing so. Earl's high-maintenance hairstyle clashes with the rustic scene, revealing his attempt to straddle two cultures. A feat tried by migrants throughout time, this delicate balance often resulted in their feeling like an outsider in both communities. In some ways, Earl's happiness in life would depend upon how successfully he managed to come to terms with this core conflict.

* * *

Earl's most exciting experience as a credit man came while pursuing a small debt owed by a Knoxville widow. As he talked with the debtor, Mrs. Dinwiddie, he became fascinated by her story. Her husband had been a Knoxville policeman who was murdered years earlier by Harvey Logan, one of America's most infamous criminals. Also known as Kid Curry, Logan had belonged to Butch Cassidy's "Wild Bunch," a group of western train robbers. After the gang broke up in the early twentieth century, Logan migrated east. Mrs. Dinwiddie's husband and his partner were working a shift in Knoxville's Bowery when they noticed Logan misbehaving in a bar.[245] Unaware of the outlaw's real identity, they tried to arrest him. Logan shot both men, who soon perished from their wounds.

Tried and convicted in Knoxville of a lesser crime, Logan received a twenty-year sentence. While in the Knox County jail awaiting transfer to a federal facility, he captured a guard using a wire noose, then snagged a box of guns.[246] With firearms and a captive, Logan gained his freedom and rode off on the jailer's horse. He then moved back west. A year after this escape, he robbed a train in Colorado. Seriously wounded during this crime, he killed himself rather than be captured.[247]

The outlaw's demise did nothing to improve the finances of Dinwiddie's widow. She and Earl talked about her husband's death and her struggles afterward. Her story, which included unresolved justice and a felon's escape from the Knox County jail, evoked Earl's family experience with Ehude Fellows. Earl sympathized with her, commenting that she didn't owe much to Woodruff's Hardware, only a "little ole five- or six-dollar bill."[248] He freely admitted that he never collected her debt to the store.

The widow Dinwiddie's poverty reveals a lesser-known aspect of America during the 1920s: not everyone prospered. The era's economic boom bypassed most of the country's poor. In Knoxville as elsewhere, inflation proved a major problem, as it continually outpaced a day laborer's wages. In order to counter rising prices and frequent unemployment, the city's lower-income residents needed two breadwinners, so wives also worked.[249] Living in the town's low-rent areas, they could only dream of the automobiles, electricity, and running water enjoyed by Knoxville's wealthy and, increasingly, middle class.

A less serious but oft-discussed disappointment of the early twenties stemmed from Earl's favorite sport. Tawdry details of cheating by professional baseball players became public knowledge. The travesty started when team owners changed how they compensated players during the World Series, paying the athletes a flat fee instead of a percentage of ticket sales. This drastically cut the players' income while boosting that of the wealthy owners.[250] Angry over this ploy, several members of the Chicago White Sox accepted bribes and deliberately lost a 1919 World Series game. Eventually, players confessed to throwing multiple games, causing an enormous scandal. Similar to most Americans, Earl considered playing baseball for a living to be the ultimate career, one wasted on these cheaters.

Around the time that baseball was losing fans because of this disgrace, motion pictures exploded in popularity. They still conveyed dialogue through placards and only contained shades of black and white, but the excitement of early films overshadowed the older-style nickelodeons and familiar vaudeville routines. Going to the motion picture show became an increasingly popular pastime. Most of Knoxville's movie houses, such as the Queen Theatre, featured reputable pictures enjoyed by middle-class patrons. The Riviera added a glamorous feel to town through its seventeen-foot lighted sign and pink Tennessee marble construction.[251]

This outward respectability countered the risqué subject matter found in many early movies. *Sex*, a popular 1920 film, shocked viewers with its happy and immoral female protagonist.[252] The title of *Men Who Have Made Love to Me* raised some eyebrows, as did Betty Blythe's comment on her wardrobe for *Queen of Sheba*: "I wear twenty-eight costumes, and if I put them on all at once, I couldn't keep warm."[253]

In Knoxville, risqué films showed at the Ritz and, shortly before it closed, at the Staub Theatre. The latter was a major entertainment venue that sat across the street from the Bijou Theatre. The Staub ended life with a scandalous lineup that included *The Whirly Girly Show* and a feature with "twenty wondrous girls under twenty."[254] It also brought *Birth of a Nation* to Knoxville, where the movie's blatant racism garnered both approval and condemnation from its local audience.[255] Other films of the era depicted equally unsavory topics: *Human Wreckage* from 1923 addressed morphine addiction, and by that year at least three films had featured scenes of women being branded.[256]

Early opponents of movies had feared they would inspire lust and sinfulness,[257] and these depictions of sex and brutality reinforced their concerns. Scandalous movies generated so much attention that religious organizations and women's groups throughout America protested against them. In Knoxville, for example, the League of Women Voters lobbied for the town to create a censorship board. In response to these concerns, the heads of the motion picture studios eventually agreed to self-censor, appointing an overseer to ensure morality in American film.

Movies would be censored for decades, but this didn't stop an increasing acceptance of sexual topics in American culture. Popular literature took on a racier edge. One of Earl's favorite magazines was *True Story,* which featured short tales about crime. Its covers featured buxom dames and text which implied that lurid details could be found inside. Decidedly low-brow, crime magazines enjoyed a wide readership.

Movies and advertisements, which newspapers and magazines increasingly depended on for cash, inadvertently worked together to begin a new phenomenon: fads. Bobbed hair, miniature golf, peanut butter, and crossword puzzles surged in popularity. Earl got so good at solving the latter that he just gazed at one until he knew its answers, then inked them all in at once.

As exciting new technologies combined with fewer social restrictions, the 1920s seemed to glisten with promise and would eventually be recognized as America's first modern decade. Thus, in spite of problems, they "roared."

* * *

Many Americans found the era's swift pace of change to be disconcerting. Some of them countered this unease in positive ways. *Reader's Digest,* a magazine that highlighted traditional values, gained great popularity. Interest in historical events increased, along with an appreciation for antiques and artifacts. In Knoxville's city center, several buildings had survived from East Tennessee's frontier origins. They included the home of William Blount, the region's first territorial governor who helped Tennessee gain statehood and then served as a US senator. By 1925, his wood-framed home, called Blount Mansion, had become a disintegrating apartment building slated to be demolished and replaced by a parking lot. [258]

A few blocks away, another eighteenth-century structure called the Chisholm Tavern served as a low-income boardinghouse. Because these relics sat in the oldest part of the city, not far from the river, they had been engulfed by its disreputable neighborhoods. The tavern didn't survive, but a group of ladies, one of the era's typical women's clubs, bought Blount Mansion and saved it from demolition. Another historical structure, built in the lavish Greek Revival style, sat a few blocks west of Gay Street. It had served as a school for the deaf and a Civil War hospital. Knoxville eventually bought the building and converted it into its city hall.

Some Americans felt threatened by the decade's swift transformations and searched for scapegoats. The Ku Klux Klan provided one such channel in Knoxville, just as it had in Alabama. In fact, this national group exploited local tensions, rallying against Catholics in the North, Asians in the West, and Black people in the South. Locally, the organization held a huge rally in Chilhowee Park, initiating new members beneath a twenty-foot-tall burning cross. Just as in Gadsden, some Knoxvillians disliked the Klan. Local newspapers didn't strenuously object to the group, but they published viewpoints that opposed it. One article, for example, quoted a Klan member who claimed the organization abhorred lynching and had over 400,000 members in Indiana. Elsewhere, that day's paper claimed the Klan was dying in Texas.

A fresh start in Knoxville's governing structure was a change sought by most everyone. After the 1917 annexations, the city failed to expand basic services to all its new neighborhoods, vexing their residents. Corruption flourished in the city government, which was run by five powerful commissioners. They consolidated power for the town's elite by negating the votes of the White and Black underclass.[259] Because city commissioners wasted so much money and failed to do their jobs so utterly, the board of commerce decided to sue them.[260] Obvious problems abounded. Knoxville's water plant contained illegal levels of bacteria, and the hospital superintendent controlled the medical facility to the point that he strong-armed the workers' votes, providing a block of ballots for the police commissioner.[261]

Knoxville's Board of Commerce was joined by its newspapers in supporting a change in city government. So did Lee Monday, a member of the city council from South Knoxville. He represented the town's White, lower-income citizens and berated those who ran the city, insisting that they squandered tax money. City leaders disliked him, partially because he gave a voice to the problematic Appalachian in-migrants. Outrage over corruption and the inability to stop it grew until citizens demanded and voted for change. A city manager and a city council would run Knoxville's new government. Improvements included establishing a board of education.

The turbulent process required to dislodge these corrupt officials foreshadowed decades of contention among Knoxville's leaders. The city's political scene became a "rough and tumble" game, one that would eventually ensnarl Earl.[262]

CHAPTER 12
DC Adventures

MARIE TOUCHED THE WARM MARBLE AND looked upward where the famous monolith soared toward the heavens. Her neck cramped from the uncomfortable angle, so she gazed across the expansive lawn, then strolled toward work. Her flight from a broken relationship had turned into a satisfying adventure. The Gadsden newspaper announced her departure in its town society column, declaring she would be in the District of Columbia for the summer while taking an English course at Washington University.

While in DC, it's unclear whether or not that college course panned out, but Marie lived in an apartment on 18th Street, found work, and rode the streetcar wherever she wanted to go. In the summer heat, she dressed like a city girl, wearing pants that ended at her knees. Dark hose covered her lower legs, preserving her modesty while being stylish and comfortable. Finding a job had been surprisingly easy. Her self-taught typing abilities gave her employable skills, and her sister Patsy had known of available positions. By this time, women such as Marie comprised about a fifth of the country's workforce, but clerical jobs represented a new opportunity for them.[263] The coveted work had more prestige and a better possibility of advancement than women's traditional positions as servants, mill workers, and teachers.

Marie found employment in a temporary government office specifically established to help Great War veterans. An inability to find work had magnified the men's resentment over poor pay during their service and shoddy treatment afterward. These veterans lobbied hard for more compensation and gained some success with the help of the American Legion. In 1921, President Harding created a Veterans' Bureau to support and care for the two hundred thousand men wounded in the conflict.

The new bureau's leadership proved to be staggeringly corrupt. Its head, Charles R. Forbes, sold warehouses full of taxpayer-bought supplies, pocketing much of the proceeds.[264] He hosted extravagant events and dinners for the famous, including luminaries of stage and film.[265] The bureau used surreally complicated procedures to stymie the veterans who asked for help and ignored hundreds of thousands of their letters, all while diligently stealing public funds.[266] Within two years, a scandal erupted, and Congress investigated.

When President Harding died, veterans' groups kept pressure on the government, including the country's new leader, Calvin Coolidge. Mainly, they wanted more pay for their service. Congress finally passed a bill granting them extra compensation, but Coolidge promptly vetoed it, saying that "patriotism ... bought and paid for is not patriotism."[267] In the spring of 1924, more than five years after the war ended, Congress passed a second bill and overrode a second presidential veto. This created the Adjustment Compensation Act, or Bonus Bill, which paid veterans in the form of bonds that would mature in 1945. The men would receive varying amounts, with overseas service more highly rewarded. Thus, before each bonus could be figured, a soldier's time in the armed services and the locations where he served had to be verified. The federal government hired thousands of clerical workers to complete this paperwork.

Marie believed in this extra compensation, partly because she felt personally connected to it through her brother Jim, who served in the Great War. She began working on the project in June of 1924, earning a yearly salary of $1,140.[268] The daily routine of government service varied widely from her teaching experiences. Bonus Bill clerks worked in large rooms where dozens of mostly female employees chatted softly throughout the day. Marie thrived amid this busy camaraderie. Teased for her Southern accent and Alabama's political idiosyncrasies, she laughingly replied with her own verbal zingers. She improved her clerical skills during her time at the bureau, starting as a grade one typist and clerk, then advancing to grade two within a few months. This raised her salary to $1,320 a year.[269] When the official portrait of the Adjusted Compensation Bureau workers was taken, Marie stood proudly among their ranks. She displayed a copy of the photograph in her home, although she had to identify her likeness among the hundreds of figures.

The District of Columbia teemed with activity during the mid-1920s as it evolved from a midsized Southern town into a modern national capital. Marie likely first rode an escalator while living there and perhaps saw her first airplane. Similar to Knoxville and virtually every other city in the country, Washington struggled to adjust as automobiles became the primary form of transportation. New and better roads were built, including a bridge that connected the Lincoln Memorial area to Arlington Cemetery. Other improvements included traffic lights for 16th Street, a revamped sewer system, and regular trash collection.[270] Even frugal President Coolidge agreed that the city needed updating. While Marie lived in DC, new Internal Revenue Service and Commerce Department buildings were in construction.[271] In May of 1926, Congress went further, providing for fifteen new buildings in the district. The nation's capital needed these facilities, but it would struggle to deal with the resulting construction chaos while also providing housing for legions of manual and clerical workers.

Many Washington, DC, sites that Marie enjoyed would be familiar today. The White House and Washington Monuments were already iconic tourist attractions. The Lincoln Memorial had been dedicated two years before, and two reflecting pools graced the National Mall. The mayor of Tokyo had already given a number of cherry trees to the city, but the first Cherry Blossom Festival wouldn't take place for a few more years.

The Coolidge family added pizzazz to Washington, mostly because First Lady Grace Coolidge had forward-thinking ideas. She favored fashionably short skirts and wore her hair in the trendy, marcelled style with its short waves. Her official White House portrait included one of her pet dogs. Americans connected with this first family, but tragedy made the Coolidges even more approachable. During the summer that Marie lived in Washington, their sixteen-year-old son, Calvin Jr., died from an infection that resulted from a common blister. The nation mourned alongside his parents. His death put the first family on the same level with countless other Americans, such as the Littles, who had lost loved ones to disease and illness.

Marie worked for the Adjusted Compensation Bureau into the fall, including during its busiest month, October 1924.[272] During this high point of applications, thousands of veteran claims were handled each day. As much as Marie enjoyed her job, however, working on the Bonus Bill didn't provide her with the long-term employment that her teaching job did. The clerks functioned so efficiently that they completed their entire assignment in just over a year. By late October, Marie resigned her position. Grace had come for a visit, and the sisters left Washington together.

They returned to Alabama for an important celebration—Grace's wedding to her longtime sweetheart, Edward McDill.[273] Ed worked as an assistant manager for a Gadsden wholesaling company and had solid prospects. A small group of family and friends, including Marie, attended the nuptials. The bride wore a three-piece traveling outfit trimmed with gray fox. As for Marie, during her adventure in the nation's capital, she had worked to put her broken relationship behind her. Now she had another life-changing event to confront. Grace held an enormous place in Marie's life as a sister, companion, and sometime adversary. With Grace's marriage, Marie was a bit more on her own.

She resumed her teaching position at Southside School, near her parents.[274] After the freedom of living in Washington, returning to Alabama required adjustment. The school system still dictated where its educators lived. This time, Marie roomed in Gadsden with six other teachers: Cleo Durham, Eva Kennedy, W. E. Hughes, C. C. Sellers, and Lucile Sisson.[275] Since W. E. and C. C. were probably men, a landlady likely oversaw the facility—and the young people. As a growing institution, Southside now employed six teachers. They each had an appointed classroom, but their pupils might range across seven grade levels.[276] Thus, the school used much the same system as the one-room school where Marie had taught five years earlier. Alabama still expected miracles from its educators.

Even though she had an escapade in the nation's capital with which to impress Etowah Countians, twenty-year-old Marie stopped submitting columns to the Gadsden paper. After years of regaling North Alabama with accounts of her girlish sleepovers and dinners with friends, the self-promotions ended. If she dated during this year, she didn't advertise it. Her broken relationship and months in Washington, DC, had matured her. They inspired her as well. Determined to experience the nation's capital more fully, she made plans unheard of in her family.

Marie resolved to take a vacation.

In the summer of 1925, she returned to Washington, DC, as a tourist. Mysteriously, because she refused to explain her motive, Grace also felt the need to leave Gadsden. She had been married less than a year. After a long train ride, the sisters arrived in DC's Union Station, which Marie labelled one of the most beautiful railway stops in America. They stayed with their sister Patsy and her husband, Jim, just outside of the nation's capital in northern Virginia. The couple had thrived after moving north. Jim had a career in the postal service, and Patsy worked as an administrative assistant, then called a "secretary." She would further her education and eventually rise through the ranks of government employees to become the private secretary of Wayne Chatfield Taylor when he served as the president of the Export-Import Bank and as Franklin D. Roosevelt's Undersecretary of Commerce.[277]

During their visit, Marie and Grace cared for their five-year-old niece, Patricia. In their free time, they toured the district, enthusiastically snapping photographs. Pictures of the Capitol Rotunda and Union Station made their way into Marie's memory book. She and Grace posed for the camera in front of the Washington Monument and while perched on the Capitol Building's back fountain. At the White House, they stood unattended while being photographed just a few feet from the steps of the north entrance.

In spite of their meager finances, the sisters attempted to be fashionable while in the city. They sewed their own dresses, a skill learned in childhood from their mother. Marie, for one, never became an expert seamstress, and the pleats on her outfits tended to protrude awkwardly instead of lying flat. Both women owned cloche hats that fit snugly over their heads and had low brims that almost reached their eyes. Stylish outfits of the twenties always included hats, with the cloche variety especially popular. In the sweltering DC heat, however, the sisters invariably carried their headgear instead of wearing it. In order to look like they had larger wardrobes than they actually did, they borrowed each other's dresses and took turns accessorizing with a long, lightweight scarf. Grace, however, owned a string of pearls that only she wore.

Some days the sisters ventured outside the city. They stood amid the tobacco fields of a friend's farm in rural Maryland and visited Chesapeake Beach with its popular roller coaster. A tour of Mount Vernon, George Washington's home in Virginia, proved inspiring. Marie and Grace lounged on a bench in front of the stately house and strolled through the backyard flower garden. Whenever possible, Patsy and her daughter, Patricia, joined these excursions. On sweltering summer days, the sisters went swimming and, amazingly, took pictures of themselves in bathing costumes. Patsy and five-year-old Patricia looked adorable in their matching black swimsuits and hats. Grace, Marie, and a friend also sported bathing attire, along with vividly decorated swimming caps. Grace seemed uncomfortable to be caught wearing the era's skimpiest outfit, but a slimmed-down Marie grinned widely.

Washington, DC, was more than just a center of government in the midtwenties. Tourists and natives alike enjoyed its lively selection of arts—plays, motion pictures, and chamber music. During the summer of 1925, however, the city nurtured a true American phenomenon that dominated the local popular culture and soon that of the country: jazz music.

Jazz conveyed an energy that illuded most art forms, and it attracted fans of both races. Duke Ellington, who began his career playing gigs across DC, deserved much of the credit for the music's incredible popularity there. One of jazz's most accomplished musicians, Ellington was born in Uptown, the Black section of segregated Washington. There, he attended excellent schools where teachers encouraged his musical abilities. In fact, the upper- and middle-income inhabitants of Uptown lived in a fashion denied to most Black Americans. The neighborhood had Black-owned businesses as well as artistic and literary groups, and it housed Howard University, America's premier historically Black university.[278] Much of Uptown oozed sophistication, as reflected in Duke Ellington's famous elegance.

DC's appreciation for jazz evolved into a love of dancing, the city's most popular midtwenties pastime.[279] The advent of electricity made underground clubs more appealing, although hotels often held dance parties on their rooftops, under the stars. Meanwhile, an influential musical featuring Black actors opened in town. *Running Wild* showcased a distinctive song and dance that became feverously popular: the Charleston. Evolving out of an African tradition, it featured fast, flamboyant movements. Because doing the Charleston involved swinging arms and pumping legs, women dancers had to discard any inhibiting clothing for loose-fitting, sleeveless dresses with short skirts. The dance screamed "scandal." Variations of the Charleston include the Shimmy-Shake (or just "Shimmy") named after the dancer's shaking breasts, and the Black Bottom, which references her protruding behind.[280] Elder Americans who remembered the Victorian era frowned mightily at the Charleston. Naturally, the craze swept across the nation and ultimately reigned as the quintessential Jazz Age fad. When it reached Knoxville, alarmed administrators at the University of Tennessee tried to prevent students from participating by predicting that its dancers would hurt themselves and suffer from intestinal problems.[281]

Marie danced the Charleston, most likely learning it in DC. Even though her moral compass prohibited her from trying alcohol and having premarital sex, she bloomed as a "flapper," one of those carefree women who celebrated their femininity and freedom. Having overcome significant drawbacks, including birth into poverty and a childhood marked by restricted opportunities, she flourished as a modern woman who voted, provided for herself, and danced.

Decades later she would teach the Charleston to a granddaughter, its movements firmly etched in her brain.

CHAPTER 13
Clean Thinking

KNOXVILLE'S SWITCH TO A NEW SYSTEM of government in the mid-1920s didn't fix all of its problems ... or end its ambition. Infused with optimism and a belief in positive change, both the city and Earl undertook enormous endeavors. Earl aspired to a profession. City leaders, aided by the local press and community support, advocated for a national park in the Southeast, a decision with massive, long-running consequences.

America's leisure activities had evolved alongside its automobile ownership. In the past, enormous vacation and health resorts had flourished in rural areas. East Tennessee contained several that attracted wealthy visitors to the region's mountain air and lush beauty. In Grainger County, just north of Knox County, the Tate Springs Hotel welcomed the Rockefellers, Fords, and Firestones. These families arrived in private railroad cars, then took plush carriages to the resort where golfing, swimming, fox hunting, picnicking, and billiards awaited them. Automobiles, however, enabled Americans to personally visit the country's far-flung scenic wonders. After the establishment of Yosemite and Yellowstone National Parks, this "sightseeing" became all the rage, gradually putting hotels such as Tate Springs out of business but increasing the popularity of America's remote landscapes.

Supporters who called for a national park in the Southeast ranged from the economic elite to ordinary East Tennesseans. Some wealthy Knoxvillians vacationed in the nearby mountains in an old logging camp that had been transformed into a popular retreat. Many of them wished to preserve the region's remaining natural glories.

Rural residents such as Earl also felt an affinity with mountains. He spent his youth in nature amid the green foliage, mountain streams, and arched foothills. A lover of trees, he not only knew the difference between an elm and a walnut but could tell a white oak from a red oak from a black oak. He would lament the plight of his favorite species of tree, the massive chestnut that supplied wood to farmers and nuts to the forest's wildlife. Tragically, a blight had entered the US from overseas, starting a die-off of chestnut trees that would alter the ecosystems of most eastern US forests.

Logging also destroyed East Tennessee's forests. At one time, wooded areas covered the region's mountains and foothills, including in Earl's home county of Sevier. Early settlers such as the Laymans cut trees on their land, creating fields and using the timber to build their homes and barns. This practice had long since gone commercial. Lumber companies owned vast swaths of Sevier County land and dominated its economy. Clear-cutting was the preferred logging method, although it destroyed entire forests, caused erosion and ruined mountain streams. The technique was so widespread that over 65 percent of lands considered for the national park had already been clear-cut.[282] The southeastern forests were truly being assaulted.

Even with support from several levels of society, the creation of a regional national park faced serious challenges, making it a long-term goal. Just deciding where to locate it—North Carolina or Tennessee—proved contentious. Advocates quibbled over the site for months, then compromised, agreeing that the park would include property from both states. The proposed area included sections of East Tennessee's Sevier, Blount, and Cocke Counties. The first two border Knox County, with Blount containing Elkmont, the former logging camp.

Not everyone wanted a protected national park. Some advocates agreed with the timber companies who considered the forests to be a replaceable commodity. They lobbied for a national forest that could be logged. For some time, this difference of opinion couldn't be resolved. Horace Kephart, an early conservationist, passionately advocated for a national park that would save the region's remaining fifty to sixty thousand acres of old-growth trees. He asked, "Why should future generations be robbed of all chance to see with their own eyes what a real forest, a real wildwood, a real unimproved work of God is like?"[283] Kephart's words helped convince the public to value old-growth forests, majestic wonders that only a national park would protect.

Naturally, funding presented a major obstacle. Forming the Yosemite and Yellowstone Parks had been cost effective because the US government already possessed the land. Native Americans who lived in Yellowstone were unceremoniously kicked out. In the Southern Appalachian region, most acreage would have to be donated or, more likely, purchased from companies and individuals. Multiple levels of government decided not to help. The US Congress failed to contribute any funds, although it approved the park in 1925. Likewise, Tennessee Governor Austin Peay supported the endeavor, but state legislators declined to supply any money.

When a major lumber company offered to sell some of its Blount County holdings in 1925, park advocates had to act. No other branch of government stepped forward, so Knoxville's mayor, Ben Morton, decided that his city would. Thus Knoxville, not the state or the federal government, funded a third of the initial purchase of seventy-six thousand acres for the Great Smoky Mountains National Park.[284] City residents eventually supplied over half a million dollars to the cause.[285] Most famously, East Tennessee schoolchildren contributed by sending in their pennies.

Slowly a park started to emerge, even though the lumber companies often asked exorbitant prices for their holdings. Individuals resisted selling too, some of them mountain farmers devoted to their land. With so many unresolved issues, the quest for a regional national park would extend into the next decade.

* * *

As the city of Knoxville tried to influence the future of the southeastern United States, Earl also focused his ambition. The concept of social mobility dominated the twentieth century; and the aspirations of many an optimistic American centered on it. During his six years in Knoxville, Earl had matured from country-boy-in-town to a long-term employee of one of the city's best-known businesses. He appreciated the opportunities that Woodruff's Hardware had given him as he rose from office boy to assistant credit manager. But he didn't find squeezing cash from the obstinate or poor, no matter how benignly, to be fulfilling. His aspirations still centered on Knoxville, however. Although he felt closely tied to Sevier County, the family farm had become his brother's domain.

In spite of a secondary education limited to a few months at Farragut High and some classes at the YMCA, Earl enjoyed learning. During his spare time, he read, did crossword puzzles, played checkers, and memorized poems, such as Poe's "The Raven." But he had few options for formal education. Even if the University of Tennessee had accepted him without a high school diploma, he couldn't afford to pay its tuition. Earl also lacked the preferred background. Universities catered to the upper class, not to students paying their own bills. The University of Tennessee was typical in only holding classes during the day when working men couldn't attend.

Fortunately, the university had recently divested itself of several faculty members, alienating a particularly brilliant attorney and native Tennessean who had a propensity to help those in need.

That attorney, John R. Neal, possessed a natural, multifaceted intellect. He also had impressive educational credentials, starting with an undergraduate degree from the University of Tennessee and two higher degrees from Vanderbilt, including one in the law. Neal then earned a doctorate in philosophy from Columbia University. A student of public discourse who specialized in constitutional law, he often visited Washington to watch Congress or the Supreme Court in session and to attend presidential inaugurations. He enjoyed traveling and—in an era when most Americans didn't leave the country—had visited Sri Lanka, India, and Singapore.[286]

In 1909, when the University of Tennessee School of Law hired him as an instructor, Neal returned to his native state after eighteen years of teaching law in Colorado. He then started a decades-long habit of running for political office. At first, he had success, serving one term as a state representative and one as a state senator. Neal fervently believed in service to others, and during his time in the Tennessee legislature, he worked to improve education and aid the underprivileged. In the House of Representatives, he supported a successful bill to establish four normal schools, one of them for Black students, and to establish high schools in Tennessee counties.[287] After learning that authorities planned to publicly hang fifteen men in the western part of the state, he introduced a successful bill requiring all state-sanctioned executions to be conducted inside prisons.[288] This ended hanging-as-entertainment in Tennessee. As an attorney, Neal often represented members of the underclass, such as mill employees, frequently doing so without pay.

In 1923, about the time that Earl tired of being a credit manager, the University of Tennessee (UT) abruptly declined to rehire Neal and several other professors. The administration filed fourteen specific charges against Neal that included missing too many classes and inadequate testing and grading.[289] They also objected to the attorney's "slovenly appearance, rants on current events, and love of liberal causes," calling him more of an entertainer than a professor.[290]

"Liberal causes" likely referred to evolution, which Neal believed in. Charles Darwin's theory challenged the belief systems of many Tennesseans, and the state had recently enacted a law making it illegal to teach. UT's administration encouraged this conservative viewpoint and actively wanted to comply with the law.[291] The instructors purged by the university had adopted textbooks that covered evolution.[292]

This decision to fire the professors, especially Neal, caused an immediate brouhaha in Knoxville. Almost all of UT's law students signed a petition against his firing, and many alumni quickly came to his defense.[293] A former student who was the United States District Attorney defended Neal, saying that Neal tried to "develop the minds of his students."[294] When the *Knoxville News Sentinel* took up Neal's cause and that of the other ousted professors, it printed attention-getting headlines to accompany its front-page articles on the subject. One editorial that attacked UT's administrators began with the caption, "Someone Should Stop Them."[295] Even the University of Denver Law School joined the cause by inviting Neal to rejoin its faculty. At his well-attended hearing in Knoxville, Neal admitted to the charge of smoking in Ayres Hall, which surely amused his audience. After all, everyone smoked indoors. More seriously, he asserted that the other charges were "glaringly false" and that he put his "very life blood into his work."[296] Nevertheless, the university held firm in its decision, refusing to rehire him.

Neal responded to UT's action with resourcefulness and vision. Having inherited wealth, unemployment didn't threaten his lifestyle, but he came from a family that regularly championed causes. His brother had served as an admiral during the Great War, and his sister had advocated for temperance. Soon after UT's decision, Neal started tutoring law students in Knoxville. To become an attorney in the 1920s, it wasn't necessary to have a college degree. One only had to pass the state's bar exam, a technicality that negated the university's usual stranglehold on higher education. Neal took advantage of this loophole and started helping students prepare to take the lengthy test. Some of his former University of Tennessee law students left the university to study with him, fueling his success.[297] Soon he had dozens of enrollees in what he referred to as the John R. Neal School of Law.

Several of Earl's life experiences had involved legal matters, from dealing with debtors at Woodruff's Hardware to his family's saga with Ehude Fellows. He had also gotten to know the young lawyer who handled Woodruff's legal work, Ben Winick.[298] Through Winick, Earl glimpsed the daily life of a Knoxville attorney. Ben had graduated from UT's law school,[299] attending while Neal taught there, and almost certainly gave Earl a complimentary report on the professor. Earl apparently found legal matters to be interesting and was probably attracted to the profession's prestige. At age twenty-four, he knew that Neal offered a rare opportunity to a young man without a high school education. Approximately a year after the professor left UT, Earl began studying with him.

Passing the bar exam wasn't easy, especially when preparing for it through unconventional means, but Earl had the necessary reading and analytical skills. His success also depended on a strong work ethic. Since he worked for Woodruff's Hardware during the day and studied with Neal at night, he essentially had two full-time jobs.

Neal's entrepreneurial tendencies, intellectual curiosity, and concern for his fellow man combined to create a striking personality. He also possessed some puzzling traits that Knoxvillians gossiped about, such as his lackadaisical attitude toward money. He had so frequently failed to pick up or cash his paychecks while working at UT that it disrupted the university's bookkeeping system. Neal's odd habits with money didn't just stem from absentmindedness. He would sometimes destroy a tuition check that had been written to his law school, commenting, "That boy can't afford to pay."[300]

This generosity mattered greatly to that particular student but also caused animosity because it resulted in students paying different tuition amounts for the same services.[301]

As Earl studied with Neal, he encountered more of the lawyer's eccentricities. A bachelor, Neal neglected to send his clothing to be pressed or cleaned as often as society dictated. He wore garments until they grew shabby and only acquired a new suit when he visited Washington, DC. Even then, he didn't necessarily desire the clothing. Upon his arrival, his brother immediately took him shopping.[302]

A general lack of personal hygiene compounded the problem of Neal's unwashed clothing. By all accounts, he often went unshaven, wore his hair long, and didn't regularly bathe. In having prestige and inherited money but not grooming appropriately, Neal confounded his culture. Wealthy men just didn't go unshaven or wear dirty, wrinkled clothes in the 1920s. Many households lacked the running water that made personal hygiene easier, so daily bathing delineated those of solid income who could easily wash from the poor who didn't have indoor plumbing. Neal's grooming habits worsened over the years. Later in his life, management at the Watauga Hotel in Knoxville asked him to vacate his lodgings there. When he did so, they found the bathtub to be unusable because it held stacks of books.[303] As one local attorney put it, calling Neal "eccentric" showed kindness.

Because of his appearance, strangers often overlooked the professor until he spoke. Articulate and courteous, his background as a wealthy, educated Southern gentleman resonated through his speech. So did his intellect. Similar to many lawyers, Neal enjoyed conversation, and articulately explained his position to others.

While he studied with Neal, Earl also worked for E. G. Stooksbury, a respected Knoxville attorney.[304] Stooksbury had graduated from UT's law school and taught criminal law there,[305] so he also knew John Neal. Perhaps most importantly, Ben Winick, Woodruff's attorney, was a member of Stooksbury's small firm. A city of Knoxville's size depended on such relationships. Neal and Winick likely vouched for Earl's character and ability, helping him to get the position with Stooksbury. When used ethically, this informal system of vouching for others allowed citizens to inquire about a man's morals and work habits from those who knew him, providing references at a time before formal resumes. If abused, it could become a "good ole boy's network" that denied opportunity for outsiders, including Black citizens. Earl's work for Stooksbury was called "reading the law," and it allowed him to experience the practical aspects of being an attorney. He functioned much like a clerk would in later years, researching cases, searching for legal precedents, and running errands, most of them mundane, such as filing papers at the courthouse.

The summer of 1925 proved pivotal for Earl and his mentor. After studying with Neal for a year, Earl took the Tennessee bar exam. Then he began waiting on the results. Neal, however, contributed to one of the twentieth century's greatest public debates. The event started near his ancestral home in East Tennessee's Rhea County and involved one of Neal's passionate beliefs—evolution.

The leadership of Dayton, Tennessee wanted to bring attention to their town by challenging the Butler Act, the state law against teaching evolution.[306] Several lawyers from the area, one of them almost certainly Neal, had attended that decisive meeting.[307] In any case, Neal volunteered to defend John Scopes for teaching evolution in a Tennessee high school. Soon, a nationally prominent attorney, Clarence Darrow, also signed on to defend Scopes in the famous confrontation over evolution, *The State of Tennessee v. John Thomas Scopes.*

Neal had a different conception of the lawsuit's goal than Darrow. As an expert in constitutional law and a supporter of education, Neal wanted the trial to center on the freedom to teach.[308] His experience with the University of Tennessee undoubtedly influenced this preference since a victory would counter the state's ability to fire educators because they supported evolution. Darrow wanted a broad confrontation between science and religion. The more famous attorney prevailed, and the "Scopes monkey trial" became a national obsession, especially when William Jennings Bryan, famous evolution denier and former presidential candidate, volunteered to lead the prosecution. Journalists flocked to Dayton, Tennessee, from around the country, as did onlookers and salesmen, religious leaders and flimflam men. Bryan and Darrow received intense publicity for their roles in the trial. In fact, their names became synonymous with it. But John Scopes, the man who was actually being tried, praised John Neal's contribution to his defense. He complimented

Neal's sense of compassion and his "keen and analytical mind." Scopes also called Neal's participation "fortunate."[309] When the national press focused on Neal's dishevelment, Scopes alluded to his counselor's genius when he called him "a clean thinker, a much rarer person than most spotless, clean-shaven and shorn clotheshorses."[310]

The trial's verdict went against Scopes, upholding Tennessee's law against teaching evolution. John Neal would spend years working to overturn that legislation.[311] The professor apparently parted on good terms with Clarence Darrow. Neal soon announced that the famous litigator would give his law school's commencement address, speaking on "The Philosophy of My Life."[312] The general public was invited to the event, which was scheduled to occur a few weeks after the Scopes trial ended. Darrow's visit placed Neal's law school in opposition to UT's, which didn't dare defy the state legislators' stance on evolution.[313] It isn't clear whether Darrow actually spoke, but at this commencement, twenty-eight students received degrees from John R. Neal's school. One of them was Earl who received a Bachelor of Law degree.[314] His achievement wouldn't mean much, however, if he didn't pass the Tennessee bar exam. Only that feat would allow him to open a law practice in the state.

In 1925, a mere two years after being let go by UT, John Neal formally opened a law school campus in downtown Knoxville. Located on Market Street, the school occupied the second floor of the Todd and Armistead Drugstore and became an undeniable success. Neal taught many of the courses himself, and several well-known Knoxville attorneys pitched in.[315] Some of his students came from prominent families, such as George Dempster who became an entrepreneur, inventor, and Knoxville mayor. Neal's law school often graduated more students than UT's did.[316] It held night classes and accepted part-time students, providing opportunities to ambitious young men who were snubbed by the university.[317] Because his school was popular, Neal accepted these nontraditional students because he wanted to, not because he had to. He offered higher education to average citizens decades before the state decided to do so. Tennessee didn't begin providing easily accessible, post-secondary education until it opened three community colleges in the late 1960s.

In an era that valued conformity and expected social status to be revealed through one's appearance, Knoxvillians sometimes mocked Neal. Many didn't appreciate his public service or realize the scope of his contributions to the state. For all Neal's oddities, though, John Scopes wasn't alone in defending him. Earl spoke well of his mentor and treated him courteously, even as the attorney became more eccentric with age.[318]

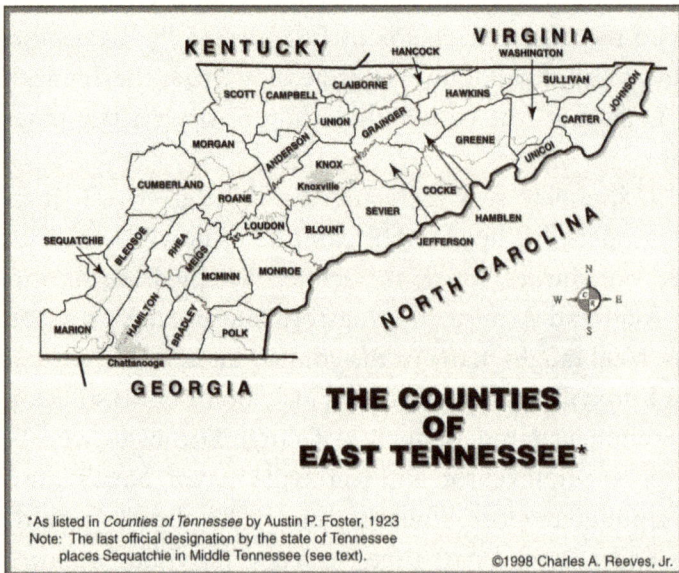

THE COUNTIES
OF
EAST TENNESSEE*

*As listed in *Counties of Tennessee* by Austin P. Foster, 1923
Note: The last official designation by the state of Tennessee
places Sequatchie in Middle Tennessee (see text).

©1998 Charles A. Reeves, Jr.

The Layman family in Sevier County, circa
1893. From left: Mitchell Layman, Florence
Layman, Sallie Shultz Layman, Ola Layman.

Earl Layman and Clarence Smith circa 1919. The
house behind them is probably where Clarence and
Mae lived in Knoxville.

Earl Nichols, son of Pete Nichols and Earl Layman's
first cousin circa 1919.

From left: Marie Little and Hazel Myrick in
Southside, Alabama circa 1919 Possibly one
of the first pictures taken with Marie's camera,
her dress is clearly homemade.

Marie Little and Clifford
Johnson, Alabama circa 1924.
Marie's penchant for writing on
photographs proved helpful when
identifying her companions.

From left: Grace Little and Marie Little. Labelled as being taken
on Labor Day, this photograph was probably shot at Alabama's
Noccalula Falls. Circa 1923-25.

From left: Grace Little McDill and Marie
Little at the Washington Monument, 1925.

From left: Marie Little and Grace Little McDill on the
White House lawn, 1925.

From left: Patsy Little Robertson and Patricia Robertson, 1925. Northern Virginia vicinity.

W. Earl Layman in one of several photos taken in his office soon after starting his law practice. Circa 1926

From left: Grace Little McDill, unknown, Marie Little circa 1926.

From left: Richard Layman and Bobby Earl Layman. Taken circa 1940 at the United States Capital Building fountain, Washington, DC.

W. Earl Layman's wedding photo, 1929

Marie Little Layman's wedding photo, 1929.

From left: Marie Little, W. Earl Layman, Charlie King, Carmen (no last name). Taken on the trip to Sevier County before Earl and Marie's marriage, Marie looks particularly anxious in this picture, 1928.

CHAPTER 14
All Over the World

AFTER THEIR SUMMER IN WASHINGTON, DC, Grace and Marie returned to Alabama, the former to a newly appreciative husband. He met her at the train station, telling her that she was never to leave him again.

Marie returned to less acclaim, but she did have a new goal. She found a job working as a bookkeeper and stenographer for Moss Furniture in Gadsden,[319] then resigned her teaching position in Southside. Her new job duties included recording the store's daily sales and purchases as well as taking dictation, then typing the results. As a clerical worker, Marie enjoyed more freedom than she had as an educator. With the school system no longer dictating her housing options, she found lodging in Glencoe, a neighborhood close to downtown Gadsden. She made a higher salary than before, although it was still about half that of her male coworkers.[320] In order to stretch their income, working women such as herself often shared rooms in a boardinghouse, an arrangement that suited the sociable Marie.

As America's middle class grew, stores such as Moss Furniture offered a host of popular and functional items that went beyond beds and bureaus. Since most homes lacked closets, chifforobes or wardrobes offered space to hang clothing. With kitchen counters not yet standard, Hoosier cabinets provided work and storage space for cooks. They contained shelving, drawers for silverware, a flour bin, and a small counter for making biscuits. Every cook aspired to own one.

Gradually, Marie's focus drew away from her previous rural life to center on her new occupation and youthful companions in town. She joined the Gadsden Business and Professional Women's Club. It promoted local businesses, lobbied for better working conditions and higher pay for women, and provided scholarships for worthy girls. Single women dominated the group, but a half-dozen members were married and still working, anticipating a future social change. In November of 1926, Marie and sixteen other members of the Gadsden club drove to nearby Anniston, Alabama, for an exchange program.[321] Through such gatherings, these women supported each other and expanded their business connections. Someone in the group, quite possibly Marie, also understood the power of publicity. The Gadsden newspaper ran a short article touting the women's joint meeting.

As America's economy grew throughout the 1920s, these white-collar working women benefitted from an increased standard of living.[322] Despite their low pay, many of them began to accumulate the unthinkable—disposable income. This buying power drew national attention, and advertisers targeted them, which increased their influence.[323] Magazines such as *Life* and *Vanity Fair* celebrated their achievements in articles and photographs while actresses such as Clara Bow and Louise Brooks portrayed them in motion pictures.

In the growing consumer society, entire industries centered around providing goods for women. Marie, for example, detested sewing and eagerly spent her cash on ready-made clothing, which companies such as Sears and Roebuck sold through catalogues. Women raced to purchase these offerings, especially since flapper-era dresses, with their thin material, defied easy construction. Store and catalogue clothing tended to have more updated styling than handmade outfits, so their popularity brought women's fashions to the masses.

Other products bought by women challenged society's traditional standards. Previously, only prostitutes had worn cosmetics. In fact, "face paint" signified their profession. Marie's generation changed this long-running stigma. Lipstick had exploded in popularity by the mid-twenties while almost every woman used powder foundation.[324] Marie wore both, but she especially fancied another cosmetic invention of the 1920s: nail polish, specifically mauve-colored polish. Spurred by these changes, society gradually accepted that unmarried women enjoyed an adventurous life instead of being sad, sexless old maids.

Marie had a photograph taken that showcased her vitality. She wore her hair shorter than before, emphasizing her fine features. A flattering marcel wave took advantage of her natural curls. Her blouse almost certainly came from a store or catalogue because her bare arms showed thorough the cut-out sleeves, a feature that would cause complications for any casual seamstress. A long necklace hung almost to Marie's waist and completed the Jazz Age styling. The photograph reveals a fashionable woman with a confident gaze and open smile.

While working at Moss Furniture and living in Gadsden, Marie gravitated toward one of the twenties' best innovations—having fun.[325] Motion pictures, radio programming, and sports provided much of this amusement. Because young people were marrying later, they enjoyed these activities with friends. Marie had a wide circle of companions, several of whom liked to travel. One group took a day trip to Lookout Mountain in Chattanooga, Tennessee. With its view of seven states, the tourist attraction made a perfect, day-long excursion from Gadsden—if traveling by automobile. In photographs, Marie and a gentleman named Hector McDonald perched together on Umbrella Rock, a precarious natural formation.

With Americans' scope of travel still expanding, the wealthy now enjoyed long-distance vacations. Exotic destinations included the North Beach of Miami, Florida, with its colorful art deco hotels.

Cruise lines advertised Caribbean adventures that included fine
dining, an ocean view from the cabins, and trips ashore. The middle
class also traveled. In Knoxville, railroads like the Louisville and
Nashville (L&N) transported passengers to Yellowstone National
Park for eighty-nine dollars or to Niagara Falls for forty-two.[326]
Closer to Marie, the L&N had opened railroad lines to Birmingham,
Alabama, in order to acquire coal for its engines. The closest midsized
city to Gadsden, Birmingham became heavily industrialized, with
soot permeating its air and coating its buildings. Another result of
the railroad's attentions, however, was the passenger trains that ran
from Gadsden to Birmingham and beyond, making Mobile, Atlanta,
Savannah, and other Southern cites accessible to Marie.

By the fall of 1927, she had enough money to indulge in another
vacation. Once the summer heat subsided, she and several friends
traveled to the Gulf Coast, a trip that would have been unthinkable
for unmarried women just a few years earlier.

They first stopped at Gulfport, Mississippi, for a stay at the
Great Southern Hotel. The 250-room resort had opened in 1903,
wowing guests with hot-and-cold running water, a telephone in
every room, and a shared bath for every two rooms. Rose gardens
and palm trees surrounded the three-story building, and its balconies
provided stunning views of the Gulf of Mexico. Marie, who had
uncharacteristically left home without a camera, bought a souvenir
album containing several small photographs of the resort's wonders.
At the Great Southern Hotel, guests played golf or tennis, then shot
billiards in the evening. They also lazed on the beach and frolicked
in the warm, blue surf.

Soon, the group ventured onward to New Orleans, a city whose
blend of French, English, Spanish, and African cultures had long
created a distinctive atmosphere. Recent Greek and Italian immigrants
contributed even more flair. Sitting at the mouth of the Mississippi
River where it flowed into the Gulf of Mexico, New Orleans was
the Deep South's financial powerhouse and America's second major
port after New York City.[327] In 1927, ships from one company sailed

between the two cities twice a week, all year long. Over four hundred thousand inhabitants called New Orleans home.[328]

The river and the city had a symbiotic relationship that resulted in jobs, seafood, and a distinct ambience. That spring, however, before Marie and her friends visited, the Mississippi had delivered the worst flood in United States history. Months of heavy rains had caused the river to overflow its banks in the northern plain states. Modern farming techniques contributed to the disaster because farmers had plowed over natural, water-absorbing vegetation in order to sow their crops.[329] Unprecedented amounts of water channeled into the Mississippi and gradually flowed downriver in a slow-moving disaster. Due to newspapers and the ever-increasing phenomenon of radio coverage, the South and even the country learned of the ongoing destruction. Levees started breaking as the waters crested farther and farther downriver. New Orleans, which was not much over sea level, would invariably flood when the deluge arrived. Authorities saved their town, but at a cost. They destroyed a levee thirteen miles south of the city and allowed that area to flood. Fewer people lived there than in the city, but the river still decimated homes and neighborhoods.

By the time the disaster ended, the flooding had affected seven states, killed hundreds of Americans, and left over six hundred thousand homeless.[330] As the nation watched, the Mississippi River had shown its legendary power.

Similar to the timelessness found in the District of Columbia, much of New Orleans enjoyed by Marie and her friends would be familiar today. Tourists gawked at the city's distinctive architecture with its ornate ironwork. They admired its gracious homes, although genteel living in New Orleans often occurred in hidden courtyards, not the front porches common throughout the South. Decades before an acclaimed food culture arrived in most of the country, restaurants provided exquisite dining experiences using locally caught seafood. In cooler weather, Marie and her friends could have sipped on a hot beverage, for New Orleans adopted coffee breaks long before they became a nationwide obsession.[331] The women might have splashed in bathing pools, toured tropical gardens, and referred to New Orleans' most celebrated neighborhood as the *Vieux Carre*. Now usually called the French Quarter, the Cathedral-Basilica of Saint Louis dominated the area, along with a statue of Andrew Jackson. This Tennessean famously protected New Orleans from the British in 1815, using soldiers who ranged from Native Americans to seagoing privateers, settlers to enslaved Black people. In Marie's day, the French Quarter possessed a Bohemian flair because of the artists who lived there in surprisingly cheap accommodations. The celebrated writer Sherwood Anderson had been a resident not long before. His houseguest, the young, unknown William Faulkner, stayed so long that the Andersons forced him to seek his own lodgings. The musician known as Fats Domino, who would influence blues music and help create rock and roll, was about to be born into a local Creole family.

Near the end of their vacation, Marie's friends decided to watch a motion picture. She parted ways with them, then strolled through the city in the direction of America's greatest waterway. Her father had worked on Alabama's river locks; a flood had obliterated his family farm. Marie knew about the power of water and understood the Mississippi's famed place in American history. She wanted to see it, an urge that wasn't unusual. New Orleans residents frequently visited the river, sauntering to its banks in the relative cool of evening. There, families watched the dockworkers, contemplated the rolling vista, and soaked in the colorful atmosphere. Since the river dominated the city's economy and culture, locals considered these moments to be a loving tribute.[332]

In the midtwenties, New Orleans' harbor had not been modernized, so loading docks lined the city's riverbanks in an elongated port.[333] Hefty, heat-infused odors rose from the muck, fish, produce, and human sweat that dominated the wharves. The quick cadence of New Orleans English competed with the French and Italian languages and African American dialects as hundreds of longshoremen unloaded bales of cotton, sacks of rice, and barrels of supposedly legal liquids. White and Black laborers worked side by side here, making a respectable amount of money and enjoying regular employment.[334] The intense activity continued onto the river. The paddle wheelers gathering around the cotton docks might have included the famous Delta Queen, which was built the year Marie visited the city. Massive ocean liners also docked in New Orleans, as did john boats and ramshackle banana boats.

Thankfully, Marie enjoyed her solitary adventure to the river. That motion picture her friends saw in the fall of 1927 was *The Jazz Singer*, the first movie to include spoken dialogue. It became an instant phenomenon, making more money than any other film that year. A cultural marker, it heralded the coming of "the talkies," a new era of entertainment. When the travelers returned to Gadsden, Marie's friends could rightfully brag about seeing it.

But Marie had a story too as she described what she saw from the New Orleans riverbank. The massive Mississippi had rippled and roared, clearly capable of wiping out huge amounts of real estate. Graceful, ocean-going schooners impressed her with their tall masts and colorful flags that denoted their countries of origin. She marveled that "those ships came in from all over the world" and felt connected to places far beyond her Alabama roots. No longer a freckled farm girl with unruly hair, in New Orleans Marie sensed an enormous world thriving just beyond her, and she found that knowledge invigorating.

Soon after this trip, having worked three years at Moss Furniture, Marie decided to update her office skills. Since Gadsden didn't have a business school, she would have to temporarily relocate. She carefully considered her options. Once more, Marie would be on the move.

CHAPTER 15

Lawyering

As Marie grew restless in Gadsden, Earl endured an agonizing wait for news that could change his life. Finally, he learned that he had passed the Tennessee bar exam.[335] He immediately started a law practice, a step made possible when attorneys E. G. Stooksbury and Ben Winick invited him to occupy the empty room in their suite of offices.[336] Earl's decision to study with John Neal had propelled him toward an opportunity surpassing any he had dared hope for, a victory that had been unimaginable when he left home. Grateful for the ways in which Neal allowed him to better his life, years later, Earl would christen one of his children "Richard Neal Layman."

Earl wasn't alone in craving advancement. Spurred by the nation's soaring economy, a preoccupation with status flourished during the 1920s. One way for a business to show prestige was through its location. Downtown Knoxville reigned as East Tennessee's business center, and Stooksbury and Winick's law firm sat in the midst of it in the Holston National Bank. The Holston building had been built decades before at the corner of Gay Street and Clinch Avenue, and its impressive lobby featured Grecian-style columns and lustrous white marble walls. Upstairs, two floors had recently been added, giving the building a coveted title: skyscraper. Throughout America, having offices in these structures increased a business's reputation, especially if they occupied a top floor.[337]

Stooksbury and Winick's twelfth-floor office was one of the highest in Knoxville, but it reflected stability more than pretentiousness. Clients entered through an oak door that had frosted glass for its top half. The office's room number was painted in black directly onto that glass. Inside, a cramped waiting room housed several wooden chairs meant for clients and the desk of an overworked secretary. Employed by all three attorneys, she was often surrounded by stacks of papers. The firm kept two telephones with separate numbers because the city still had two providers, just as it had when Earl arrived in town a decade before. Soon, though, Southern Bell would purchase its competitor and finally consolidate Knoxville's phone systems. From the waiting room, three doors led to even smaller offices, with Earl to the right, Winick to the left and Stooksbury, the most established of the three, straight ahead. Presumably, his office faced the outer walls and had windows overlooking the city.

The white walls of Earl's office held a calendar that he got for free and a framed copy of his license to practice law. He worked at a simple wooden desk and sat in an oak swivel chair. Immensely proud of his accommodations, Earl had photographs made to celebrate one of his first days in the office. In one pose, he leaned back in his office chair, radiating satisfaction as he gazed into the camera. His light gray suit showcased his blue eyes and fair hair. Several pictures featured him talking on the telephone, stressing his work ethic and white-collar professionalism.

Although he had passed the bar exam, that achievement didn't automatically prepare Earl to be a practicing attorney. Working with Stooksbury and Winick allowed him to experience the practical aspects of his profession as he helped them serve the local individuals and small businesses that made up their clients.[338] Stooksbury, however, would soon become judge over the city's juvenile court, leaving the twelfth-floor offices to Ben Winick, Earl, and a series of other lawyers.

Ben and Earl's friendship solidified during these years. Neither came from Knoxville's higher society. Winick's parents were Rabbi and Mrs. Isaac Winick, who had immigrated to the city from eastern Europe. Their home at the corner of Vine Street and Temperance Avenue doubled as the Heska Amuna Synagogue and school. Born in the United States and raised with orthodox Jewish beliefs, Ben was outgoing, ambitious, and devoted to his religion. By the time he and Earl met, he had graduated from the University of Tennessee and served in the Great War.[339]

Ben had recently fallen for a girl from Knoxville's Reform Jewish community at the Temple Beth El. This congregation was less orthodox but more wealthy than that of Heska Amuna, and some tension existed between the two groups. In the interest of courting, Ben worked to smooth relations between them. He wrote a public letter to Temple Beth El members, entreating the congregations to "cast aside all petty prejudices and work in harmony for what we all desire—a bigger and better Jewish community in a bigger and better Knoxville."[340] His efforts succeeded in one area: he and Clara Katz would marry by the end of the decade.

As Ben's background shows, religious diversity existed in Knoxville. Baptists and Methodists predominated, but the city also had Catholic and Jewish congregations, along with other, smaller denominations. Disagreements sometimes flared within these groups. In the previous century, the point of contention had been the Civil War; now it was evolution. Debates that had raged during the Scopes trial continued afterward and weren't restricted to religious groups. One League of Women Voters meeting included a testy exchange over whether the group should encourage the Tennessee governor to veto an anti-evolution bill.

* * *

As Earl struggled in the early days of his career, his family provided some support. One of his first cases came from a relative on his mother's side, Lloyd Shultz, who lived in Burlington, a suburb east of Knoxville. Shultz had declared bankruptcy, and his creditors elected Earl as trustee of the proceedings. Meanwhile in the Fourth Circuit Court, Juvenile and Domestic Relations, Earl helped Ben Winick represent several women in divorce cases. At this time, the dissolution of a marriage almost always stemmed from serious problems. Religious groups and society in general frowned upon divorce, and women, who often instituted the proceedings, usually did so because of abuse or desertion. Maggie Crigger, for example, charged that her husband of seventeen years drank heavily, mistreating her and their two daughters. These cases weren't lucrative and had zero prestige for the lawyers, but they at least got Earl identified as an attorney in the local newspaper.

Earl and Ben's profession did allow them to enter one of the era's biggest moneymaking ventures: the stock market. In the twenties, Wall Street flourished to the point that stocks of select companies bought early in the decade were worth almost four hundred times more by the end of it.[341] With profits like this, investors ignored the instability that accompanied these gains. Speculation ran rampant, and even non-stockholders kept track of the market.

The friends' foray into stocks focused on local companies. As the two attorneys helped entrepreneurs begin small businesses, they received stock as payment. These enterprises represented surprisingly diverse products and included a Good Humor Ice Cream charter with $50,000 in capital. Located near the University of Tennessee campus on West Cumberland Avenue, this shop would sell ice cream, cakes, sandwiches, confections, and dairy products. In the summer of 1927, Ben, Earl, and two other men applied for a variety store charter. Later, Earl joined several businessmen in chartering the Stone Tile and Supply Company, which produced building products such as brick.

* * *

Earl's new profession allowed him more leisure time than he had while collecting debts for Woodruff's Hardware. He focused much of it on a national obsession: sports. During the 1920s, sports figures first began attracting fans similar to those who followed movie stars. Both Earl and Ben Winick loved baseball, and the twenties overflowed with titans such as Babe Ruth who had rescued the sport after the 1919 cheating scandal. Ruth, also called "the Sultan of Swat," "the Bambino," and other catchy nicknames, would soon participate in Murderers Row, a group of New York Yankee players named for their treatment of opponents. Ruth energized baseball, turning it from a game of few hits into one with spectacular home runs.[342]

But even the Babe had competition as the era's top-tier athlete. Other baseball players such as Ty Cobb competed for that title, as did world heavyweight boxer Jack Dempsey whose aggressive style helped him to annihilate opponents. Red Grange had just signed to play professional football with the New York Giants, while Knute Rockne's superior coaching at Notre Dame showcased college football. Rockne's 1924 team featured a quarterback and running backs so powerful that Tennessee-born sportswriter Grantland Rice named them the Four Horsemen, as in the apocalypse. Quality writers such as Rice helped spur interest in sports and coined many of the era's memorable phrases. New technologies also increased the number of fans by quickly relaying game information, making the experience more immediate. Earl and Ben Winick likely experienced the 1925 World Series as part of a crowd who read game updates from a Gay Street marquee.

The twenties also spurred regional sports stars. In Knoxville, Robert Neyland had been hired to coach the University of Tennessee's football team after one year as an assistant. Fan expectations for the upcoming season ran high. Earl and Ben entered a local contest, trying to win tickets for UT's clash against the University of Virginia. Whoever correctly picked the most winners of twenty-one upcoming college football games would be awarded two tickets. The friends didn't win, but they made the contest's honorable mention category by choosing sixteen of twenty-one victors.

Expertise, daring, and personal endurance made other Americans famous. By this time, several pilots had flown across the Atlantic, with the achievement announced afterward. Charles Lindbergh, however, crossed the Atlantic from New York to Paris while flying solo and without stopping. He went forty-eight hours without sleep, including thirty-three hours in flight. Radio accounts tracked his progress, which added to the public's excitement. When he landed, "Lucky Lindy" became an instant celebrity, envisioned by Americans as the spirit of their energetic and innovative era.

Something about the tenacity needed by Lindberg and others like him inspired adrenaline and endurance-related fads across the country. Small aircraft owners went barnstorming, thrilling crowds with simulated, midair battles. They also walked on the plane's wings—while in the air. Average Americans found ways to join the trend. Sitting on flagpoles, or at least on small platforms atop flagpoles, became a popular feat. Dance marathons allowed citizens to test themselves by dancing for forty-five minutes and then resting for fifteen. This doesn't sound too terrible except that the contests could last for days.

For all that he loved watching sports, Earl's leisure activities tended to require brain power. He joined the Knoxville Checker Club and became the group's secretary in charge of scheduling events. In a newspaper article announcing a tournament with players from nearby Johnson City, Earl exchanged barbs with the other club's representative. Johnson City was a much smaller town, but it fielded a confident team that had requested games with the Knoxvillians. Earl addressed the rival club, saying, "We of Knoxville ... are surprised that your ambition has led you to such a rash challenge since our prowess is universally known, and we have always left in our wake broken-hearted checker players with blasted ambitions. Your temerity is certainly to be admired." Johnson City secretary M. Bauer replied, boasting that "heartbreakers and ambition blasters are our self-prescribed diet." Showing more sly humor, he added that if the Knoxville "boys measure up to requirements, we will put you on our mailing list along with other suburbs of Johnson City."[343]

Knoxville's checker team included several acclaimed players, such as F. M. Felker, "checker fiend by profession," and twins Dan and Ezel Moffett.[344] Another team member, W. C. Fraser, served as the city inspector of weights and measures, ensuring that Knoxville's grocers measured dry goods on honestly weighted scales. Charles McAfee, described as one who "wins with modesty and loses with grace," probably did so.[345] A Knox High School sophomore, he would become editor of the school paper, president of the junior class, and an honor fraternity member at UT. These players took the game seriously, and every team member had a favorite opening move. Fraser preferred the switcher method, and H. H. Turnbull liked the laird and lady move, while Earl excelled at the Bristol cross.

The coming tournament was described as a "momentous battle of wits between local master minds … and deadly thinkers … from another town."[346] Earl invited the public to view the match, with "ringside seats" going to early arrivals. He claimed that the winning team would receive engraved corn cob pipes. This promise was probably more tomfoolery, although experts at checkers could earn nice prizes. Earl played on an inlaid wooden board that he won in a tournament.

Unfortunately, the Johnson City team became ill and couldn't make the trip to Knoxville. Earl withheld any verbal jabs at their withdrawal—at least publicly.

Now twenty-seven, Earl enjoyed an active social life. His friends included the checkers players and a young dentist named Charlie Jenkins, but Ben Winick was his closest companion. In what would become a long-standing practice, in late afternoon when the work day eased, the two leaned back in their office chairs and tossed light banter across the waiting room.[347] A haze of smoke trailed from their hand-rolled cigarettes and curled along the ceiling as they enjoyed one of the most popular fads of the 1920s.

How much mischief the checkers-playing attorney got into during these years is a matter of conjecture. Unlike some in his era, Earl felt no religious barriers to drinking alcohol. Instead, he joined the many Americans and plethora of Knoxvillians who disregarded

Prohibition. Where this imbibing took place had changed drastically over the previous decade. The temperance fighters had successfully eliminated many disreputable saloons, but Americans who drank during Prohibition didn't want to buy directly from moonshiners. A safer method was the traditional one: letting a middleman make the purchase and then buying small quantities from him.

Thus, the speakeasy came into being. Knoxville definitely housed several of these concealed bars. In the future, contractors renovating downtown buildings would uncover the hidden rooms and passageways that indicated their locations. Speakeasies ranged from gritty to sophisticated, according to the pocketbooks of their clientele.[348] In East Tennessee, more than one set up shop in a cave. Usually, however, they thrived in cities, tucked behind a small business or into an apartment building. Customers entered through a nondescript alley or basement, then knocked at a door that featured a hidden window or spy hole. The revelers would be inspected and asked for a password before gaining access to the club. This intrigue, which added to the customers' fun, helped to glamorize illegal drinking.

In the pre-Prohibition era, most women never entered a saloon lest they be considered a prostitute. Many speakeasies, on the other hand, deliberately courted them as customers.[349] When liquor was made illegal, some dining establishments moved to hidden locations so they could continue serving alcohol, but they retained their upscale atmosphere. It turned out that women considered sitting at a table adorned with a cloth to be more appealing than bellying up to a saloon bar. If an establishment added a "powder room" to its facilities, women found it even more attractive.[350] Speakeasies also projected an atmosphere of youthful camaraderie, making these new customers feel safe in a way they never would have in a saloon. These changes helped spur the unthinkable: drinking by women began to lose its social sigma.

The idea that consuming alcohol could lead to lighthearted fun entered the culture in other ways. Some citizens served liquor at home, creating a new concept called "the party."[351] At these events, hostesses encouraged the festivities by playing music on the radio or phonograph. They notified guests that the gathering would include alcohol, generating excitement and identifying the possible risk. *Vanity Fair* magazine suggested that invitations include the subtle line "bring your own corkscrew" to convey the get-together's intent.[352] Motion pictures also spurred these changes, including some starring the popular Greta Garbo. Her favorite director, Knoxville native Clarence Brown, asserted that "cocktail parties and speakeasies were definitely a part of" American society, so they should be shown in films.[353] Movies couldn't legally depict characters drinking, so they conveyed the idea through half-empty decanters and raised elbows, clues easily deciphered by adult viewers.[354]

* * *

Late in the decade, Earl invested tangibly in Jazz Age commercialism. He indulged in a coveted purchase and bought a gray sedan.[355] By now Knoxville swarmed with automobiles, resulting in continual car-versus-streetcar chaos, even with the new signal lights.[356] Traffic especially clogged Gay Street because it was the only major thoroughfare that led to a bridge over the Tennessee River. This congestion would continue until a second bridge finally opened a few blocks to the west on Henley Street. Traffic jams rarely deterred those who coveted an automobile, however, because of the prestige that came from owning one. With his purchase, Earl could commiserate with friends about navigating packed roads, searching for downtown parking, and finding a knowledgeable mechanic.

Finally, he had prepared for the future he craved.

PART II: *Knoxville*

CHAPTER 16
Infatuation

EVEN BEFORE SHE MET EARL, Knoxville captivated Marie. As a town with strong Southern and Appalachian influences, much of its culture felt familiar to her. She considered its size to be perfect, larger than Gadsden but smaller and more convenient than Washington, DC. The city's liveliness invigorated her, and any decline from the previous century wasn't apparent to a newcomer. Energetic young adults flocked to town to attend the University of Tennessee, one of the two law schools, the business school that drew Marie, or a well-established college for Black students, Knoxville College. Celebrities such as Amelia Earhart and Duke Ellington came to town, often staying at an elegant hotel which had replaced several Victorian homes near the courthouse. The Andrew Johnson would be a Knoxville hotspot for decades.

One reason Marie viewed the city as having pizzazz is because she landed in the midst of one of its most exciting ventures.

This vitality came from song as the region's musical strengths clamored into notice. While downtown pedestrians could hear strands of blues and jazz emanating from street musicians,[357] "old time" music brought by Appalachian migrants provided the town's most distinctive tones. Fiddling contests and square dances had entertained Knoxvillians since the late 1800s. Chilhowee Park, the Market House, and the Custom House Post Office hosted these popular events. But a new technology was beginning to influence the music business—from Knoxville. One of the first radio stations in the United States broadcast from the St. James Hotel on Wall Avenue, just north of the Market House.[358] Run by Stuart Adcock, it would help develop country music and eventually use the call numbers of WNOX.

East Tennessee musicians had another promoter, James Sterchi, a Knoxville furniture store magnate. Having established the company with his brother, Sterchi now presided over twenty-six stores from its Gay Street headquarters. The business had always sold musical items, offering pianos and organs alongside clocks and cutlery in 1906. In the late twenties, Sterchi's Knoxville showroom still featured a wide range of merchandise. This included musical instruments, the furniture-sized devices called phonographs that played records, and the records themselves. Early on, classical music dominated these discs, but gradually ragtime and other musical styles were also featured. By the late thirties, Black artists would create over six thousand records containing religious and blues songs.[359] In later years, the playlists of radio stations often excluded Black music, but it could still be heard through a phonograph.

Black musicians weren't the only ones to benefit from this technology. In the early twenties, the first recordings were made of so-called "hillbilly" or "old time" artists. Their music featured the fiddle, banjo, and guitar, and had a distinctive sound cultivated in the hills of Southern Appalachia.[360] Songs included the stark, traditional ballads that often told of thwarted love which led to brutal murder. They had been passed through the generations by Appalachian people such as Earl's mother, Sallie, who sang them and gospel tunes as she worked.

James Sterchi, who sold records made by a company named Vocalion, saw an opportunity. In 1926, he sent East Tennessee musicians to New York where they recorded their "hillbilly" songs for Vocalion.[361] In an event hailed as the beginning of country music, the next year a major music label recorded similar artists in Bristol, Tennessee.[362] The music that came out of Bristol proved so successful that in 1929 Vocalion decided to record in Knoxville, seeking regional, hillbilly tunes. When the necessary equipment arrived in town via the railroad, it generated huge interest, and musical acts streamed into the city. Vocalion's recordings showed surprising diversity with almost a fifth of the acts featuring Black artists.[363] Sterchi's involvement in regional music expanded when he bought WNOX, Alcock's radio station. The efforts of these men and others ensured Knoxville's contribution to early country music. In fact, until the late 1930s, the city matched Nashville in nurturing the emerging talent that would create this distinctly American genre.[364]

In the midst of all this excitement, Marie applied for a job at Sterchi's Furniture. She needed money to pay her expenses and likely assumed that her experience working at Moss Furniture in Gadsden would help her get a job. She probably knew little about James Sterchi's passion for regional music, but his store sizzled with activity as customers came in to buy thousands of records a month.[365] Marie soon began working at one of the most popular spots in town.

Through her network of relatives, she also found affordable housing, rooming with one of her many cousins, Pete Bean, and his wife, Irma. The couple lived in Fountain City, a small town just north of Knoxville where Pete and his brother had bought the first two homes built on Paige Street. This location allowed Marie easy access to downtown Knoxville by briefly walking downhill to Broadway, then taking a streetcar.

Marie planned to live in Tennessee throughout the fall while she expanded her clerical skills at Draughons Business School. Its founder, John Draughons, got his start as an educator at age sixteen while traveling around East Tennessee with a cart full of books.[366] He established his first brick-and-mortar school in Nashville and eventually owned thirty-eight campuses across the South and Midwest. Marie insisted that Draughons was the best business school in the South. The Knoxville branch sat at the corner of Clinch Avenue and Market Street, right in the middle of town. A small store on the building's ground level sold magazines, Coca-Colas, and newspapers.

Eager to prepare for an exciting future, students of both genders flocked to Draughons. In fact, Americans' willingness to update their work skills helped fuel the country's prosperity throughout the twenties. The institutions they attended weren't formal colleges, but they helped fill the niche neglected by the universities' focus on the upper class. Draughons's recruitment material emphasized that a business education would help keep young men from getting stuck in dull, mid-level jobs. It also contained a well-crafted appeal to young women, or perhaps their parents. The school claimed its classes would help women to marry wisely because with job skills they could provide for themselves and therefore be picky when choosing a husband. In this way, Draughons juggled society's conflicting values, encouraging women to better themselves without challenging the traditional viewpoint that their main goal was marriage.

These institutions drew ambitious young people out of the country and into cities, aiding one of the era's major trends. In order to attract rural students, Draughons went to great lengths to ensure their safety. Many parents still considered cities to be dangerous to women and seductive to men. Therefore, a representative from Draughons could meet first-time students at the train or bus station, then escort them to their lodgings. The school provided housing suggestions, so students could find rooms by working for vetted families instead of living in a boardinghouse.

Draughons catered to working students. Marie could enroll for a few months, beginning her studies at any time and taking only the courses she needed. The school offered bookkeeping, shorthand, typewriting, and general business classes.[367] Students received individual attention and learned practical skills, becoming familiar with updated equipment such as Thomas Edison's Ediphone, a dictating machine, and the Burroughs Automatic Bookkeeping

Machine. Since Marie needed real proficiencies in order to advance as an office worker, this practical approach appealed to her.

* * *

It's unknown when Earl and Marie first glimpsed each other. They could easily have passed on a Knoxville sidewalk or sat near one another on a streetcar or in a restaurant. Gay Street's S&W Cafe, which they both frequented throughout life, opened the year before her arrival. As the quiet introvert, Earl probably noticed her first. She would have sparkled brightly as a newcomer with a soft Southern drawl and lively personality. In his favor, Earl was a handsome man, and he dressed well. His profession marked him as a solid breadwinner, an important asset in a culture that expected a man to provide for his family. Earl even owned an automobile. Within weeks of Marie's moving to Knoxville, a mutual friend named Charlie Jenkins did the honors of formally introducing them.

Like many other social structures, courting changed during the twenties. Previously, Earl would have called on Marie at her home or some other supervised location. This most likely describes her earlier relationship with Clifford Johnson when she taught school in Southside. Then, her job had dictated that she live in approved housing and submit to constant oversight. Both sets of parents, who lived nearby, would have kept track of the couple's activities. Traditionally, a girl's parents vetted her suitors, but his did also, as proven by Clifford's family essentially vetoing Marie as a wife. However, when young adults left their home communities to live in the cities, parental control over these matters dwindled. Marie, for example, didn't have a parent in Knoxville, just a cousin who was a few years older than her.

Gradually, society came to expect life partners to find each other instead of being guided in this decision by their parents. As young people enjoyed less supervision, they met spontaneously during casual activities such as dancing, skating, or for some, drinking. During the next major step of courtship, the couple spent time together on a date. The male initiated these events and paid for the activities, giving him increased power over the process.[368] Women rarely asked a man out because it was considered forward or unladylike. Another significant change came in how popularity was measured. Prestige in a social set now came from casually dating one person, breaking up, and then going out with someone else.[369] Premarital sex, however, continued to be rare for unengaged couples.[370] Societal pressure against this act was strong, and many women, such as Marie, considered it a moral failing. A double standard condemned women more than men for any such activity, so prostitutes generally provided sex to men outside of marriage. Brothels, including those in Knoxville, had long made this possible.

So, dating couples in the 1920s rarely had sex, but they sure enjoyed close contact. At one time, women's clothing, in particular corsets, had functioned almost like armor, so when these undergarments became unfashionable, it allowed for increased intimacy. Couples touched each other and kissed, which they called "petting" and which became accepted among the young.[371] Motion pictures, which set societal standards as well as reflected them, showed this activity happening earlier in the courting process, and youngsters admitted to learning about kissing by watching it in the movies.[372] Automobiles probably made the biggest difference in behavior, though, because they allowed young adults to drive away from watchful parents and neighbors. Soon, "parking" would take on a whole new meaning. As Earl and Marie's relationship progressed throughout the fall of 1928, they followed these new norms, discovering a great physical attraction to each other.

The couple also spent time together in public, enjoying the city. On warmer days, they might have visited Patrick Sullivan's saloon, now occupied by an ice cream store. Marie would have approved of the former drinking establishment being overrun with fun-loving children and chatting couples. She also would have shared this opinion with Earl.

On October 1, a fabulous movie palace opened on Gay Street, the Tennessee Theatre. Movie houses in Knoxville had come and gone, but none compared to the extravagant Tennessee. Furnished in a lush style called "Spanish-Moorish," the building had gloriously colorful, intricately ornate features, including enormous crystal chandeliers that capped the lobby. Patterns of red and gold sizzled throughout the carpets, wallpaper, and ceilings. The lobby floor sloped up toward the theater's main level, and a double-sided staircase led to the balcony. Inside, the auditorium had velvet seats, faux Romeo and Juliet balconies, and a red Wurlitzer organ that rose out of the orchestra pit while being played. If all this failed to impress, the theater's ceiling featured a gorgeously decorated and recessed oval design. Outlandish styling so dominated the décor that when the black-and-white marble floors of the power rooms revealed the building's art deco roots, they looked elegantly streamlined, a modern touch amid overwhelming ornateness.

Earl and Marie probably didn't attend the theater's opening, but most of Knoxville society did. Automobiles backed up on Gay Street so that ladies in fur wraps and gentlemen in evening suits could emerge glamorously in front of the venue. The evening glowed with sophistication.

At first, the Tennessee Theatre offered elements of older-style entertainment as well as motion pictures. Its premier included a short vaudeville show and a film, *The Fleet's In* with Clara Bow. Later stage shows included film cowboy Tom Mix doing tricks with his horse and Fanny Brice performing with the Ziegfeld Follies.[373] But venues such as this one wanted to encourage viewers' imaginations and complement the revolution in motion pictures caused by new technologies. Movies had advanced quickly since Marie's friends saw *The Jazz Singer* in New Orleans, and "the talkies" dominated the era's entertainment. Not long after it opened, motion pictures started ruling the Tennessee's playbill. Clarence Brown, who had graduated from the University of Tennessee eighteen years before, directed one of the theater's first showings, a Greta Garbo vehicle titled *A Woman of Affairs*. Similar dramas thrived during the theater's early years, but if Knoxvillians tired of watching Joan Crawford or Marlene Dietrich suffer, they could laugh with the Marx Brothers and Charlie Chaplin.[374]

The Tennessee cost over $1 million to build and thrived as the city's and even the state's premiere movie palace. Reasonable ticket prices allowed Knoxvillians of all incomes to enjoy its exotic atmosphere. Children's tickets cost ten cents during the day and fifteen at night; adults paid forty and sixty cents.[375] The Tennessee Theatre was so popular that Earl and Marie would have visited soon after its opening or risk being considered hopelessly unfashionable.

Another local extravaganza also entranced the couple during the fall of 1928. Support for college football had expanded over the years as local fans turned University of Tennessee games into community events. Women evolved into sports fans as they became athletes themselves through swimming, tennis, croquet, and badminton. Having been raised in Alabama, Marie knew a bit about college football. When the University of Alabama won the Rose Bowl in 1926, a feat comparable to a national championship, it made the front page of the Gadsden paper.

During UT's previous season, coach Robert Neyland had led the team—the Volunteers or Vols—to a record of no losses and one tie. This success propelled an unprecedented crowd of nearly eight thousand to watch the opening game of UT's 1928 season. Marie and Earl might have been among that crowd since they avidly tracked the team's progress and enjoyed watching U.T.'s games.

Neyland's squad warmed up the season with easy victories over its first two opponents. Then it eked out a 13–12 win over Ole Miss. The next game proved especially exciting for Earl and Marie because the University of Tennessee took on the University of Alabama. Much of UT's success came from its quarterback, Bobby Dodd, who challenged the prevailing concept of his position. In the twenties, quarterbacks usually took the snap, tossed the ball to a runner, then blocked an opposing player. Near the end of the game in Tuscaloosa, however, Dodd threw for a touchdown. Next, he punted the ball, pinning the home team within the one-yard line. UT's defense made the game-winning score, a safety, on the next play. UT won by a whopping two points as Dodd showcased his exceptional abilities.

When UT won its next game, a second unbeaten season seemed possible. A fundraising campaign implored each fan to donate a dollar in order to send the school band to Nashville for the upcoming game against Vanderbilt. Tennessee hadn't conquered this archrival in over a decade, but hopes ran high that this was Tennessee's year. As it was said around Knoxville, "in Dodd we trust."[376]

Life in the city seemed a bit brighter, a little more amazing, when the Vols played well. Certainly, couples got along better after a win than after a loss. And UT did win, beating Vandy 6–0, then tying Kentucky. To finish the season, the team slogged it out against unbeaten University of Florida with Dodd leading the way to a 13–12 victory. A truly phenomenal player, Dodd's final record as UT's starting quarterback would be twenty-seven wins, one tie, and two losses. After his career playing for the Volunteers, he coached for many successful years at Georgia Tech. Marie's football allegiance underwent a seismic shift through the 1928 season as she developed an enduring crush on Bobby Dodd. Clearly smitten, when referring to him she would get misty-eyed and murmur, "that ole razzle dazzle!"

Earl and Marie's courtship raced through the autumn of 1928. She met his family, probably at Sunday dinner. He still lived at Mae and Clarence's house with their children and his mother, Sallie. Mae had lived almost as long in Knoxville as in Sevier County, and Sallie had recently returned from a stint living with daughter Ola in Los Angeles. The family put on no city-inspired airs, however. Marie, Sallie, and Mae were all church-going, country ladies who enjoyed each other's company.

In some ways, Earl and Marie's marriage must have seemed as inevitable as Bobby Dodd's fame. While their personalities varied widely, they were both attractive, intelligent, and ambitious. Having achieved much as individuals, the timing was right for them to combine lives with someone else.

Marie would soon make a decision that ensured this outcome ... and ultimately put it into jeopardy.

CHAPTER 17
Lies and Cuba

As Earl and Marie's relationship progressed, they took a brief but crucial road trip, journeying to the Layman farm in Sevier County. Earl's friend Charlie King, his wife, Maggie, and one of Marie's friends, Carmen, accompanied them. The group motored down Sevierville Pike, a narrow, winding road that traversed Bay's Mountain through Shook's Gap, site of the robbery and slaying of Earl's uncle. After entering Sevier County, they eventually passed English Mountain and Granny's Knob, then went slightly out of their way to see the Harrisburg covered bridge. At this point Marie began taking photographs.

Most Sevier County thoroughfares were dirt tracks. The county rock quarry operated near the Laymans' farm, however, so the road in front of the house had been graveled to accommodate heavy trucks. This upgraded road, unpaved but preferable to a dirt lane, foreshadowed the farm itself. A stream yielded fresh water and embraced a spring house that preserved milk and other perishables. Outbuildings included a barn, smokehouse, chicken coop, and beehives. The farmhouse's two porches provided shade or sun, whichever was currently needed. Inside, one fireplace heated the main living area and another the primary bedroom while a massive wood-burning stove dominated the kitchen. From the house to the smallest shed, the buildings showed determined upkeep.

Earl's family had owned this farm for generations, and they enjoyed a certain prestige because of it. While Sevier County didn't have the extensive sharecropping system that prevailed in Alabama, land ownership still dictated the social and economic hierarchy. Certainly, Marie grasped the ramifications of what she saw that day. Before the advent of electricity, the Laymans would have been considered well-off, and the farm still provided status and a buffer against hard times.

Clearly proud of his family's holdings, Earl assumed that Marie's family enjoyed a similar situation, if not better. Just as her childhood freckles had faded, so had traces of her hardscrabble origins. Stylish and more widely traveled than Earl, she displayed a lively mind and avid interest in the world. In the early twentieth century, however, accomplishments and initiative were commendable, but background and breeding really mattered. As an ambitious man who was aware of pervasive prejudice against Appalachian people, Earl knew that marrying well would increase his social standing. Marie knew her background could thwart her desires as it had with her previous boyfriend. A picture taken during the trip to Sevier County reveals her distress. She sits in front of the group of young people with Earl's arm around her—and looks near tears.[377]

Marie made a fateful choice that day, to remain quiet about her family's poverty. Perhaps she even lied about it. To be sure, Earl also withheld personal information during the months when the two dated. He avoided explaining his liberal stance toward liquor even though his girlfriend surely identified herself as a staunch believer in temperance. But a man hiding his consumption of illegal alcohol from a young lady wasn't considered a failing by society, at least not to the same degree as her being untruthful about her parents' lack of status. In any case, both decisions to remain silent would prove unwise.

* * *

After spending the autumn and early winter in East Tennessee, Marie reluctantly returned to Alabama. She had never intended to reside permanently in Knoxville. Since she and Earl only dated briefly, her departure disrupted the intense, early stage of courting that consumed them both. Communication ensued between Alabama and Tennessee, but it was painstaking. Long-distance telephone calls were expensive and had to be prearranged. The couple mostly kept in touch through letters that took several days to reach their destinations. At Christmas, he sent her a bright orange card that read "Christmas Greetings: Sweetheart." The poem inside is sweet without being cloying:

Somebody hopes that your Christmas
Is a happy one, right from the start,
For you are somebody's Sweetheart,
And dear to somebody's heart.

Not one to be overly emotional, he simply signed the card, "Earl."

This gesture must have pleased her because their separation soon ended. A few weeks after Christmas, he proposed, probably after driving to Gadsden to see her. Earl surely intended to ask Fayette Little for her hand, one courting tradition that still prevailed, but Marie must have dissuaded him. If Earl meet her one-armed father and work-worn mother, her lowly background would be obvious. The deception succeeded, probably because she lived in town while her parents farmed in Southside.

At ages twenty-nine and twenty-five respectively, with him the older, Earl and Marie made a swift decision. Instead of a traditional, family-oriented wedding, they would elope. Considered frivolous and fun, eloping was stylish during the twenties, a decade that celebrated spontaneity. The couple did not slink off in secret, however. An engagement party with almost two dozen guests feted the bride on the evening before her marriage. Its arrangements were hasty; the party's description appeared in the Gadsden paper a few days after the couple's marriage notice. Earl didn't attend, most likely because he was driving from Knoxville after a day's work. The marriage announcement described Marie as popular with "the younger set" and almost certainly overstated by claiming that "quite a number of delightful prenuptial parties were given for the bride."[378] The groom was described as a practicing attorney in Knoxville.

On Sunday, February 17, 1929, Earl and Marie married in Chattanooga, Tennessee, exchanging vows and rings in front of two couples from Gadsden. Reverend John W. Inzer, pastor of the First Baptist Church of Chattanooga, performed the service in his living room.[379] Marie wore a lovely ensemble of navy-blue georgette and tan lace with matching tan shoes and purse. The thin and sleeveless dress, topped by a matching jacket, skimmed her lower knees in the reigning flapper style.

* * *

The newlyweds immediately drove to St. Augustine, Florida, where they spent their first night together. Presumably, they called Earl's family in Knoxville, informing them of the marriage. The next day, the honeymooners motored south through Florida and, upon reaching that state's southernmost tip, turned onto a newly opened highway. This road stretched across long bridges, traversed tiny islands, and included an automobile-carrying ferry, but it allowed Earl and Marie to skip across the Florida Keys to the far-flung isle of Key West.[380] The tiny community of fishermen, sponge divers, and palm trees hadn't yet become famous, but cruise lines advertised it as the most convenient gateway to Cuba. In Key West, Earl and Marie enjoyed warm February weather before boarding a ship to Havana, a winter vacation site for America's wealthy. Luxury hotels in the city included the Astor, Savoy, Plaza, and Sevilla-Biltmore. Earl used a considerable amount of his savings to pay for this honeymoon, especially since he probably shipped his car to and from the island nation.

Glorious weather and clever marketing had made Cuba a glamorous destination for those who could afford it. Brochures cited Christopher Columbus who had described the island as "the most beautiful land that human eyes have ever seen."[381] Judging by the cruise lines' promotional materials, Cuba had only improved since Columbus's endorsement. They praised Havana's shopping, dining, and drinking opportunities. The Prado area catered to a rich, well-dressed clientele, and tours could be arranged to see plantations outside the city. An oceanfront drive dotted with palm trees paralleled the glistening blue Caribbean. Fishing, golfing, and gambling opportunities abounded. For those who indulged in the smoking fad, up to fifty cigars could be brought back to America, duty-free.

Earl and Marie had the great luck to arrive in Havana during the month-long carnival celebration. Entertainment included parades, automobile races, and flower festivals.[382] In the daytime, they frolicked on the beaches and browsed the quaint shops where he bought her a necklace featuring a large, coral flower. At night the couple meandered through narrow, winding streets that radiated with European charm. They dined on exotic dishes at family-owned restaurants. During these travels the couple surely consummated their marriage, binding their lives together in yet another way. If their activities proved as satisfying as the honeymoon's romantic location, all went well.

After a week in Cuba, Earl and Marie returned to the United States, arriving in Miami via the SS *Iroquois* on February 28.[383] Known as the "Nation's Playground," Miami sparkled as an icon of twenties frivolity. Its gorgeous weather allowed tourists to revel in "every amusement, every sport, and every diversion."[384] Colorful art deco hotels lined its beaches and housed the wealthy and famous.

* * *

By the time the newlyweds returned to Knoxville, Earl had been absent for two weeks, quite possibly the longest vacation of his life. Meanwhile, a marriage announcement ran in the *Knoxville News Sentinel* that stated details of the couple's wedding and included a large picture of the bride. It also volunteered that the marriage had come as a surprise. Mae's husband, Clarence, who was employed by the paper, likely typeset the article and seemingly couldn't resist adding this bombshell. Earl's family wasn't accustomed to elopements.

Not long after the couple settled in Knoxville, they had wedding photographs taken. Earl looked dashing and professional in a gray suit and tie. Marie sported shoulder-length hair instead of the fashionable bob she had favored for years. The longer curls gave her a softer beauty. A necklace that ended in a large coral rose complemented her satin blouse and light-green jacket. Sporting a shy smile, she almost glowed. Both she and Earl exuded confidence and contentment.

In a sense, these photographs capture their subjects' experiences during the 1920s. As rural Appalachian transplants, they personify the American ability to be self-made. They had both prospered, largely through their own initiatives. He left comfortable surroundings, in nineteenth century terms, to advance in twentieth-century America. She rose from poverty through determination and her own vision. Coming of age in the innovative twenties profoundly affected both of them as progress in transportation, the standard of living, and societal freedoms flourished. Marie, in particular, identified with her fun-loving, norm-breaking generation. The era's prosperity also benefitted this couple, particularly since he participated in the stock market and they both could afford consumer products.

The good times did not reach everyone, however. Almost a third of American households still required working wives or children in order to survive. Most of the country's poor fell into two broad categories: those living in rural areas, especially in the

South that Earl and Marie knew well, or the cities' day laborers and recent immigrants. Many Americans had become accustomed, even comfortable, with poverty among these groups.[385] Knoxville faced specific challenges during the famous decade. Highways now outperformed the railroads that once sustained its economy, but the city's surrounding mountains made roadbuilding expensive and time-consuming. Regional extraction industries such as mining and lumbering had passed their zenith.[386] Now thoroughly industrialized, the city had a high unemployment rate and the era's typical pollution, as well as long-term crowding in its poorer neighborhoods.

Despite these realities, in February of 1929, when Earl and Marie returned to Knoxville from their honeymoon, they had every reason to foresee a glorious future.

CHAPTER 18
Adjustments

ON OCTOBER 24, 1929, eight months after Earl and Marie married, the stock market took its first dive. This decline didn't cause great panic because analysts had warned that the market couldn't maintain its incredible heights. Warning signs had vibrated throughout the economy. Farmers' profits had stagnated since the end of the Great War, and many veterans still struggled. Sales of automobiles and radios had leveled off once those who could afford them made an initial purchase.[387] Much of the country's consumption had depended on the innovation of buying on credit. This seemingly easy money, combined with the promises of advertising and a genuine desire for the products, had made Americans overindulge. They eagerly bought the refrigerators, ranges, water heaters, and so forth that freed them from time-consuming home labor. These purchases improved lives but obscured the reality that wages had stagnated. Payments on the new possessions challenged many a family budget.

In the days after the market's crash, most Americans believed its losses would be overcome. They remained hopeful about their local economies and the national one. On October 29th, however, key businesses started selling stocks, which caused prices of even the best offerings to plunge and the market to lose about $10 billion in one day.[388] A wide range of shareholders suffered great losses. Earl, with his carefully accumulated portfolio, likely felt the hit. The Great Depression had begun.

The economy slowed even more in the spring of 1930 because of a second disaster: bank failures. Rural communities had long contained small institutions that functioned without protection from the Federal Reserve System. When they collapsed, depositors lost their money, a fact that Americans knew well. Now the market crash had weakened the country's large banks because they had made loans tied to stocks. As this vulnerability became public knowledge, countless individuals tried to protect their savings by withdrawing them, causing bank runs. At first, the affected banks tried to fulfill these requests and offset the panic by distributing their cash on hand. But they couldn't access money tied up in loans, so when additional customers demanded their deposits, the banks ran out of cash. Then they collapsed, and the remaining depositors lost their savings. Every bank failure fed the ongoing crisis. Across America, almost fourteen hundred financial institutions failed in 1930, containing deposits that exceeded $850 million.[389] The next year's losses were even greater. The closing of these banks devastated average Americans, many of whom had escaped direct repercussions from the stock market's fall.

The panic engulfed Knoxville in late 1930 after the Bank of Tennessee failed in Nashville. Ongoing news about that calamity included reports of over $3 million being lost by the state.[390] A few days later, the Holston-Union, which occupied the same building as Earl's office, experienced a run. The bank distributed $725,000 in one day, trying to stave off ruin by placating customers who demanded their funds.[391] Nevertheless, it crashed in a sudden frenzy. The next day, Knoxvillians who ranged from the unemployed to the rich loitered on the sidewalk outside the bank's doors, hoping it would reopen so they could get their money.[392] Not only did the Holston-Union never reopen, but several other financial institutions in the city also struggled and failed, taking the savings of ordinary Tennesseans with them.[393] Remarkably, the Bank of Knoxville would weather both the bank-run crisis and the Great Depression itself.

* * *

As these disturbing events unfolded, Earl and Marie settled into marriage. They lived with his sister Mae and her husband, Clarence Smith, on Parkview Avenue. The Smith children, Margaret, Betty, and Jack, also lived there, as did Earl's mother, Sallie. While living arrangements with extended family were common, the crowded household surely challenged the newlyweds who began saving for their own home. Marie continued to work at Sterchi Brothers Furniture while Earl concentrated on solidifying his law practice with help from E. G. Stooksbury and Ben Winick.

Most of Earl's legal cases drew little attention, but one provided him with lots of publicity—the negative kind. He testified on events that stemmed from his work as an attorney, fueling a citywide scandal. The fiasco began when three men were accused of stealing $1,500 in loot from a tourist's car. After being caught, one of the thieves volunteered that they had used the Knoxville fire captain's personal truck during the crime. Detectives found much of the stolen merchandise in the captain's business office, which resulted in a case against him for concealing stolen property.[394] Since a city employee appeared to be aiding and abetting criminals, the lawsuit generated lots of attention, with its every facet under scrutiny.

Earl got involved when the mother of one of the accused thieves retained him as her son's lawyer. Before hiring him, she had promised the tourist $100 in exchange for him not showing up to testify about the robbery. This practice turned out to be common in town, but the deal fell through because the thief's mother could only raise $50.

The lawsuit about city officials dealing in stolen property soon grew to explore the practice of paying victims in order to convince them to drop charges. A vaguely phrased note proved the tourist's complicity with the mother's offer: "$100—by Jan.

4—for three."[395] Once this situation became public, Earl had to testify in order to explain the note and how it revealed the common but controversial tactic used by Knoxville lawyers. He mentioned discussing the case with Attorney General Bibb who, according to one publicized account, told Earl that if he got the tourist's promise not to prosecute the thieves, then the criminal court case against Earl's client would be dismissed.[396] Of course, having the case dismissed would also have helped the fire captain. Bibb not only denied this accusation but also convinced a judge to issue a warrant for the former robbery victim, a Detroit greeting card salesman. This tourist, who undoubtedly wondered why he chose to visit Knoxville, was charged with accepting a bribe in exchange for fixing a case. Under cross-examination, the prosecuting attorney tried to get Earl to either admit that Knoxville's attorney general was responsible for the payoff scheme or that Earl was "working the game" without the attorney general's knowledge.[397] Earl only admitted that he had talked with the attorney general.

These revelations caused the infuriated trial judge to utter a "scorching statement that the Knox County Bar Association should get busy and clean up."[398] In response, the fire captain's lawyer volunteered in court that a defense lawyer and prosecuting attorney working together was "perfectly ethical."[399] Apparently, this statement made the judge even more irate. He turned the proceedings over to a grand jury "because of the frequent mention" of the attorney general "and the reference to 'fixing' cases by lawyers."[400]

Earl's testimony had helped to reveal questionable activities by political figures, but he tried to downplay his role. This proved difficult, especially when one article referred to his testimony with the subtitle: "Layman is Evasive." Reflecting the political nature of the trial, and the city, Knoxville's other newspaper countered this viewpoint by printing a statement by the fire captain's attorney that clarified his "high esteem for Layman."[401] Earl surely disliked the attention and might have enlisted his brother-in-law, Clarence Smith, to help obscure his part in the drama. Clarence worked as a *News Sentinel* typesetter, and that paper mistakenly referred to

"E. W. Layman" as the attorney noted in the proceedings, not the correct "W. E."

Earl eventually emerged unscathed from the ordeal, but he had just withstood a first swipe from Knoxville's famously volatile political climate.

* * *

During the summer of 1930, Earl and Marie's finances remained solid. They took a vacation, visiting Patsy and Jim in northern Virginia so Patsy could meet her younger sister's husband. The trip seems to have been a success. The newlyweds had their picture made while touring George Washington's home, Mount Vernon. Earl exudes style in his tie and knee-length golfing pants; Marie charms in a white outfit topped by the rose necklace she often wore during these years. They look decidedly happy. That summer, Earl felt so financially secure that he became a small business owner. He and Clarence Smith opened Chilhowee Playgrounds, a Tom Thumb golf course in Park City, a neighborhood just east of Knoxville. Miniature golf courses such as this one enjoyed great popularity in America. The year that Chilhowee Playgrounds opened, there were approximately thirty thousand of them in the US, even though the game had only existed for a few years.[402] Earl and Clarence advertised their venture, promising great fun over eighteen holes.

The next year, Earl and Marie felt confident enough to take an enormous financial step. They purchased a brick bungalow on Burns Road in the East Knoxville community of Burlington.[403] Much of this working-class neighborhood had once been owned by Cal Johnson, the formerly enslaved Black man turned entrepreneur. In fact, an oddly shaped local road, Speedway Circle, had originally been Knoxville's main racetrack, which was owned by the horse-loving Johnson. Burlington contained many conveniences: two drug stores, a small grocery, a hardware store, a funeral home, a chicken hatchery, and a feed and seed store.[404] A streetcar line connected the community with downtown. Streetcars reversed on most city lines, meaning the driver stopped the vehicle, walked to the back, and then started driving forward in the direction the car just came from. In Burlington, however, the tracks "looped," allowing the vehicle to change direction by moving forward around a half-circle. This took more real estate but simplified the streetcar service and helped make Burlington a quality place to live.

Built in the late twenties, the Laymans' house sported Arts and Crafts styling. A short staircase led to the front porch, a partial wrap-around with white banisters. The one-story dwelling had two bedrooms, a fireplace in the living room, and a basement that contained the furnace. When the couple moved in, a picture had to be taken. Earl proudly stands by the porch, shaking paws with a dog. Apparently, he is being congratulated on his purchase by one of his long line of pets. Marie sits behind them, looking enchanted with the exchange. Once they became homeowners, the couple began entertaining. When Charlie Jenkins, the dentist who introduced them, and his wife visited, the foursome played bridge, the era's most popular card game. The new homeowners also stayed close with Mae and Clarence and made friends in the community. When a Burns Street neighbor died, Earl served as a pallbearer.

* * *

During these first years of marriage, Earl and Marie learned each other's habits, talents, and shortcomings, setting the patterns of their marriage.

Similar to changes in cultural attitudes toward finding a life partner, the concept of marriage had also progressed during the twenties, changing in several ways. Women of Marie's generation increasingly viewed matrimony as the joining of two people who had equal status and who found fulfillment in each other.[405] Men still tended to provide financially for the family, but as the number of working women increased and their standing in society improved, so did their status as wives. These women expected more out of marriage than previous generations had. The popular literature they enjoyed, in print, film and on the radio, promoted the idea of romance.[406] They liked that idea, and gradually, the expectations for a good marriage came to include personal happiness and shared pleasure in the bedroom.[407]

These new views of marriage altered the roles of both genders. Adapting to them took time. Men who agreed with the traditional idea that they should be obeyed didn't welcome these changes. Taken aback by a wife who wanted a partnership, they often failed to meet her expectations. In order for the genders to be equal, women also had to abandon some conventional ideas. Their role as the family's moral guidepost, one ethically superior to the husband, had to fade. Jazzy girls who frequented speakeasies probably had little trouble abandoning this view. Marie and many others, however, kept their religious-based, Progressive-era beliefs. She considered saving her husband from any troubling habits to be her moral duty.

Marie and Earl agreed on other points, and both considered marriage to be a lifelong commitment. She kept a booklet titled "Our Marriage Day." Among a dozen Biblical verses referring to holy union, it contained one untitled hymn:

The holiest vow that man can make,
The golden thread in life,
The bond that none may dare to break
That bindeth man and wife
Which blessed by Thee, whate'er betides,
No evil shall destroy,
Through care-worn days each care divides,
And double every joy.

The poem proclaims that marriage is a bond that halves any troubles and doubles happiness. These lines surely spoke to Marie, who often found that poetry expressed her emotions.

As views of marriage grew complicated during the twenties, so did the role of single women. Marie's life experiences reflect their desire to better themselves and to join in the era's playfulness. Some women experimented with sexual freedom. But society pushed back on this last practice, clinging to its traditional beliefs that nice women should be pure. It insisted on different standards for the genders and dealt harshly with women who challenged sexual boundaries. One of Earl's court cases provides a fine example. He defended a Knoxville man accused of the statutory rape of a sixteen-year-old. This legal term refers to consensual sex between one person who is underage and another who is significantly older, usually five to ten years older. Two other men were charged with aiding in the crime which might mean they lied about the man's age to the girl but perhaps referred to more nefarious acts. That Earl accepted this client seems surprising, as he wouldn't enjoy defending anyone guilty of a heinous crime. But two core values of the American legal system are paramount: every accused deserves legal representation and is presumed innocent until proven guilty. Also, situations that are resolved in court often concern the more despicable aspects of human behavior.

Reflecting the times, much of the trial concerned the girl's behavior. On the stand, she "denied she had been delinquent" before having sex with the older man but did admit that her father had threatened to put her in reform school.[408] In other words, her father had previously accused her of being sexually active. This fact essentially decided the case. The court determined that "under the statute, the unsupported testimony of an alleged wronged female is not sufficient to convict if alleged previous derelictions can be established."[409] So, according to the law, an earlier sexual experience negated the sixteen-year-old's testimony on the statutory rape. The man was let off because the girl might not have been a virgin before they had sex, but his sexual background never figured in the case. His two accomplices also went free. This double standard ensured a man's advantage when his testimony differed from a woman's. Essentially, the law penalized a young girl for violating the societal belief that her role was to remain innocent and save men from degeneracy, not contribute to it.

A more famous Knoxville incident of the era involved a single woman who successfully challenged her seducer in court. Ralph Scharringhaus conducted a seventeen-year-long secret affair with Evelyn Hazen by claiming he would marry her as soon as he had the money. She finally tired of waiting and sued him for breach of promise. Amazingly, she won but never saw any of the $80,000 settlement. Even Hazen, who was much more socially prominent than the girl in Earl's lawsuit, lost her job and was rebuked by family members and acquaintances when her sexual status became known. She did, however, find long-term employment with the University of Tennessee's English Department.[410] For all the attention given to fun-loving, cocktail-drinking flappers, large segments of society demanded that women be morally superior to men and punished them harshly if they weren't.

CHAPTER 19

Anxiety and Hope

BEING YOUNG, EMPLOYED, AND RESILIENT, Earl and Marie successfully navigated the early Depression, but they did not remain unscathed. His miniature golf course folded after operating for one summer, and his stock portfolio was decimated. The market plunged again in 1931, falling more than 2 percent. Then it kept falling. When the crash finally ended in 1932, the market had lost almost 90 percent of its value.[411]

At this point, the country's situation plummeted with terrible speed. Job losses increased until over a quarter of American homes lacked even one paid laborer; meanwhile, the employed worked fewer hours and received less pay.[412] Those lucky enough to have jobs curtailed their spending. With fewer products being sold, factories laid off workers who then couldn't buy food or pay their mortgages. The domino effect of a faltering economy became unescapable. Far from isolated regional events, these disasters devastated millions of individuals throughout the country, not just in particular cities or states.

The awfulness of 1932 went beyond closed factories and job losses. Charles Lindbergh's twenty-month-old son was kidnapped from his own bedroom. The Lindberghs paid $50,000 in ransom, but within a few weeks, searchers found the child's lifeless body. A horrified nation contemplated that even a national hero couldn't escape the era's wretchedness.

Another disturbing occurrence involved Great War veterans who remained worse off than most other segments of society. Desperate, they demanded the extra compensation promised to them eight years earlier in the project that Marie had worked on in DC. Each veteran was due approximately $1,000, an enormous sum in the depressed economy. The payments weren't scheduled to begin for over a decade, but these men didn't care. They journeyed across country to the nation's capital, often accompanied by their wives and families. As they traveled, they gained members and publicity.

Called the "Bonus Army," the throng arrived in Washington in May 1932, declaring that they would stay there until paid. Up to twenty thousand veterans and their families crowded into the city,[413] many of them lacking food and housing. They established camps of makeshift shelters, which looked so pitiful that authorities turned unused buildings on lower Pennsylvania Avenue into temporary quarters for the crowds.[414]

Since Congress had arranged the extra compensation, it would decide whether or not to pay it ahead of schedule. President Hoover refused to intervene and said that he would veto the bill if it passed. Thousands of veterans clustered on the Capitol stairs during Congress's debate on the issue. When their request for early payment was denied, most of the former soldiers left Washington peacefully, but several thousand remained. The local police couldn't dislodge them from the camps, so General Douglas MacArthur, army commander for Washington, DC, used six hundred soldiers and a platoon of tanks to remove the men and their followers. His troops invaded the camps on horseback and spread tear gas, killing two infants. After this attack, the veterans set their temporary housing on fire and left the city.[415]

Through newsreel footage, Americans saw these dramatic events as they were replayed in the nation's movie theaters. The episode horrified most viewers who believed American's veterans deserved better treatment. It also contributed to President Hoover's reputation of being uncaring toward the country's traumas. In November, he would lose the presidential election to Franklin Delano Roosevelt (FDR).

* * *

While the Depression affected all areas of the country, attempts to counter it would greatly alter East Tennessee. In 1932, advocates were still struggling to form a national park in the Great Smoky Mountains. After years of fundraising, the states of Tennessee and North Carolina, along with private donors, had raised $5 million for the cause.[416] But during a time of economic hardship, more money was needed. When New York philanthropist John D. Rockefeller matched the $5 million with money of his own, a park became feasible.

Years after the concept of a southeastern national park was first formed, the federal government started acquiring land for it. In North Carolina, Champion Fibre Company, a logging enterprise that provided timber to paper mills, owned over ninety thousand acres that were targeted for the park.[417] The lumber company at first refused to sell, then fought the process by vastly overpricing its holdings. When Champion finally sold its land, the acreage received over three times the price as nearby tracts that became national forests.[418]

East Tennessee organizers faced a different problem. Most of the state's nearly five thousand tracts earmarked for the park belonged to small landowners, with over a thousand of them family farmers.[419] Those living in the Cades Cove area of Blount County, many of whom were descendants of original settlers, became especially noteworthy. Some did not want to sell their farms, and the public disliked making them do so, no matter how fervently it supported the park. Officials resorted to the unpopular practice of condemning land, forcing owners to sell when given a fair price. However, Tennessee laws stated that owners didn't have to move until the death of the agreement's original signer. Some small farmers used this loophole to retain the use of their properties for decades. So did wealthy owners of mountain vacation sites.

Negative publicity over the evictions helps to explain a Depression-era decision that had long-term consequences. The Great Smoky Mountains National Park has never charged an entrance fee. No one definitively knows why the state of Tennessee insisted on this largesse, although two main theories prevail. Free park entrance gave mountain people unlimited access to their former lands, including family cemeteries. In an economic climate that made any fee prohibitive, this decision created goodwill. More prosaically, Tennessee wanted to keep the Newfound Gap Road available for interstate commerce. Since the highway runs from Tennessee to North Carolina, providing access to the park as well as traversing it, an entrance fee was illogical. In any case, the no-fee stipulation was established in the contract that deeded the road to the national government.

The Smokies, as the park became known, opened to the public while still a work in progress. Its infrastructure was created from local materials, namely the smooth rocks that line mountain streams. This gave a rustic appeal to park bridges and buildings, entrance signs, water fountains, and restrooms. One unexpected long-term park benefit was renewed wildlife. Clear-cut logging had so devastated the original habitat that protecting animal life wasn't a primary goal of the park's creators, yet the Smokies eventually gained fame for species that ranged from black bear and trout to lightning bugs. With access to the park completely free, a million tourists visited during its first year.[420]

The Laymans visited often and were typical of Knoxvillians because they entertained out-of-town guests in the park. Earl preferred Sevier County sites, including the highest point in Tennessee which the Cherokee named "Kuwohi" but during Earl's time was called Clingman's Dome.

The Smokies would become America's most visited national park. The lack of an entrance fee became problematic because day visitors toured by car, clogging its narrow roads. Tourists who did venture on foot strained the rest facilities, welcome centers, and shorter hiking trails. When other national parks faced similar problems, they routinely raised their entrance fees to cover increasing costs, but the immensely popular Great Smoky Mountains couldn't charge at all.

* * *

In August of 1932, Earl and Marie defied the Depression's oppressive influence with a rather marvelous event. While the era's birthrate plummeted, they welcomed a child into their family.

Marie had eagerly awaited the birth. While pregnant, she slept fitfully and lay awake contemplating the child's possibilities, what traits the baby would gain from her and from Earl. She considered her eyelashes to be short and stubby, for example, but her husband had long, enviable lashes. As he slept, she would reach out and delicately touch them, praying that the child would inherit this trait from her husband. Sure enough, their son had long, dark eyelashes, along with her distinctive red hair.

At the time, childbirth usually occurred at home with women from the mother's family attending, along with a doctor or midwife. Most Americans viewed hospital deliveries as expensive and unnecessary. Perhaps because her mother and sisters lived in other states, Marie thought differently. She gave birth the modern way, in a medical facility. Her decision foretold a coming trend when doctors would perform births while the mother lay unconscious, taking the process from women and giving it to near-strangers who were usually male. Fathers also bypassed the immediate experience as they dawdled in waiting rooms, unable to see or hear their child's entry into the world.

Soon afterward, Marie filled out the baby's birth certificate. She listed her husband's middle name as "Warren" instead of "William," perhaps revealing how little the two actually knew each other. She gave their son the agreed upon name, Earl, in a tribute to his father. On her own, Marie then followed the Southern tradition of using her maiden name as the child's middle name. The designation

"Earl Little Layman" would cause ill will between mother and son as the boy could not fathom why she thought "Little" to be an appropriate title for a male. She and Earl soon started calling their son "Bobby Earl," a name that he kept throughout childhood.

Having quit her position at Sterchi's Furniture, Marie stayed home as a mother and housewife. The culture exempted fathers from infant care, so she was exclusively responsible for the baby. Determined to be an excellent parent, she did what she thought a modern woman should do: she consulted the experts on how to best raise her child.

Unfortunately, she did so at a time when the popular concepts of child-rearing were rigid and disturbing. Early twentieth-century physicians recommended discipline, even for babies. One popular pamphlet, *Infant Care*, advocated strict feeding schedules and instructed mothers to ignore their infant's cries. It strenuously warned mothers against playing with their babies and encouraged them to expect young children to spend long periods of time sitting in a playpen.[421] Such extreme advice didn't just stem from one writer. A popular book published the year Bobby Earl was born, *The Care and Feeding of Infants* by Frederic Bartlett, advocated toilet training at age one month. It suggested that children could be induced to participate by inserting a "soap stick" into the rectum.[422] Little data exists on how many mothers actually tried this strategy, but its appearance in print gave it chilling authority.

Advice to mothers didn't end there. In the late twenties, John B. Watson, a pioneering behaviorist, had published a work on child-rearing that was based on his belief that environment shaped human behavior instead of emotion or reason. He agreed with the prevailing concepts of strict feeding schedules, early toilet training, and that mothers should ignore a baby's cries.[423] Watson had a dismissive attitude toward mothers' instinctive beliefs and lectured those who wanted to coddle and play with their children. He warned them that "mother love is a dangerous instrument … which may inflict a never-healing wound, a wound which may make infancy unhappy, adolescence a nightmare, an instrument which may wreck your adult son or daughter's vocational future and their chances for marital happiness."[424]

In other words, Watson blamed lifelong problems on intimacy between mother and child, not the lack of it.

Similar views of child-rearing prevailed for years. Dr. Benjamin Spock dominated the childcare advice business for half a century. His first book, published in 1946, admonished mothers about spoiling their *infants* and told them to use "a little hardening of the heart'" in order to withstand a baby's cries.[425] Both Watson and Spock claimed that a mother's being affectionate toward her children could be damaging. The gap between these assertions and women's instincts caused great anxiety for mothers such as Marie who loved their offspring and desperately wanted to raise them well.

* * *

By the end of 1932, usually considered the Depression's worse year, the innovative outlook and general frivolity that prevailed when Marie and Earl came of age had vanished for just about everyone. Americans had to relinquish their expectations of upward mobility and disposable income, as a growing chasm separated life before the economic calamity from life after it. Marie and her entire generation learned that fun times spent dancing the Charleston had forever ended.

After this terrible year, Franklin Delano Roosevelt became president in early 1933, and the federal government began a more aggressive approach to solving the economic crisis. In his acceptance speech for the Democratic presidential nomination, FDR had vowed to create a "new deal for the American people." The phrase would reappear in his economic plan called the New Deal. Roosevelt's inaugural address expressed hopefulness, promising Americans that "the only thing we have to fear is fear itself." The new administration initiated the Federal Emergency Relief Act which included $500 million in relief funds for the poor. A four-day bank closure, called a "holiday," was designed to halt bank failures. Among other innovations, two major organizations were started in order to create jobs for unemployed Americans. Both the Civilian Conservation Corps, which completed much of the Smokies' infrastructure, and the Works Progress Administration hired unemployed men to work on public projects.

In 1933, Roosevelt launched an elaborate and expensive plan that centered on East Tennessee. Even more than the founding of the Great Smoky Mountains National Park, this idea would prove controversial and profoundly alter the region.

Throughout the 1930s, even nature contributed to the nation's woes. Midwestern states experienced a drought so extensive that the accompanying winds blew their topsoil as far as New York City and Washington, DC. In East Tennessee, intermittent flooding had caused property damage and loss of life for years. Debates raged over how to regulate the waterways and who should be in charge. Alabama's Wilson Dam had been built to negate the Muscle Shoals, a particularly hazardous stretch of water, but in order to be truly effective, it needed to be part of a river-wide system. John R. Neal, Tennessee law professor, had long argued that the government should control America's rivers instead of independently owned companies doing so.[426] He believed that the resources these waterways provided belonged to all Tennesseans.

Neal found an ally in Senator George Norris of Nebraska. The two advocated for a series of dams on the Tennessee River that would supplement Wilson Dam. Neal personally helped write the Tennessee Valley Authority (TVA) act that Congress passed in May of 1933.[427] Although details would be hashed out later, the agency aimed to control the region's flooding, create hydroelectric power, and aid the Appalachian poor. Many East Tennesseans agreed with these goals and coveted electricity for its ability to improve their lives. In 1933, only a few residents living outside Knoxville had electrical power, including a meager 3.5 percent of Tennessee Valley agriculturalists.[428]

A contrary opinion valued the free-flowing waters. Knoxville had been founded just below the intersection of the French Broad and Holston Rivers in order to take advantage of the era's river transportation. To some, impeding these powerful waterways seemed fundamentally wrong, but even critics probably didn't realize how much the dam system would alter the aquatic ecosystems. This argument merged with an immensely practical one. TVA's mission depended on taking immense acres of farmland from East Tennesseans. Counties to the southeast of Knoxville, those affected by the national park, would be spared, but vast sections of seven counties north of the city would be fundamentally changed through flooding. The crucial difference between the two projects was that the park had taken acreage to preserve it, but this new enterprise took land and rendered it unusable.

TVA chose Knoxville for its headquarters because the nearby Clinch River would be the first one dammed. As the agency started taking shape, infighting began among its three board members, Arthur Morgan, David Lilienthal, and Harcourt Morgan (no relation). TVA's wide-ranging goals allowed for considerable disagreement over its mission. Arthur Morgan held Progressive-era beliefs about improving the lot of communities while benefitting farmers as well as industry.[429] He lamented the agency's effect on those forced to move, saying that "tens of thousands of cases of land sales to the government" had been taken for granted even though they "involved an important and often tragic human experience."[430] David Lilienthal, on the other hand, wanted to create a regionally dominant electricity producer. The third board member was Harcourt Morgan, the former president of the University of Tennessee who had clashed with John R. Neal. A Southerner who had lived in Knoxville for over twenty-five years, Morgan's fondness for the area was soon considered a liability within the organization.[431]

Despite problems created by these differences, TVA settled into Knoxville. A fire had wiped out much of Market Street and part of Union Avenue in 1930, clearing the way for its headquarters to locate on Union. The city block eventually housed over a hundred agency offices, including those of the three feuding board members and most of the engineers. Once it was no longer needed as a post office, the Custom House provided another location.

Meanwhile, TVA continued to accumulate East Tennessee real estate, often creating hard feelings that were intense and long-lasting.

CHAPTER 20
Town Poverty

IN KNOXVILLE, JUST AS IN MOST OF THE COUNTRY, lower-income residents suffered the brunt of the Depression's hardships. Layoffs of low-wage workers ran through almost every type of employment. East Tennessee's marble business suffered because construction fell nationwide. Area carpenters and bricklayers lost work because the number of local projects dropped by almost two-thirds.[432] Small businesses also failed, as reflected in one of Earl's legal cases. He was named trustee of the People's Fruit and Grocery Company after it went under, closing three stores and leaving its workers unemployed. So many jobs were lost that Knoxvillians went hungry. Charities served free food at a local hospital and along the city's center of business, Gay Street.[433]

Conditions worsened for the exploding number of unemployed who lived in town.[434] Naturally, they lived in the crowded tenements and shantytowns that had further deteriorated over the decades. By 1934, a nationwide study found Knoxville to have inadequate housing when compared to dozens of other cities. Forty percent of homes had no bathing facilities, and almost 30 percent were overcrowded.[435] A new shantytown developed beside the Tennessee River under the Gay Street Bridge. It lacked electricity and a sewer system, and occupants had to row across the river to get fresh water at a spring.[436] These squatters had fashioned shacks made of scavenged materials, cutting and straightening oil barrels to serve as rooftops.[437] Across America, the destitute did what they could to improve their housing, such as reinforcing the walls of their dwellings with cardboard and newspapers.

During these years, the elderly suffered to an extent that is probably understated. Tennessee had no pension for the aged, and struggling family members had fewer means and ability to care for them. In order to eat, poverty-stricken older Americans took what jobs they could get despite their physical limitations. Youngsters also worked, as child labor remained legal in America until 1938. Working-class children experienced great hardship and essentially entered adulthood even earlier than Marie had. In East Tennessee, children scoured the railroad tracks, picking up coal that had fallen off the open train gons. Because it fueled factories and furnaces, coal could be used, traded, or sold.

A particular group of desperate women, prostitutes, garnered lots of attention in Knoxville. A local police officer claimed they had increased 100 percent in six months and were virtually attacking men on the street. Sexually transmitted diseases were said to be running wild, as almost three hundred different women had received treatment for them within one month.[438] Officials touted a workhouse, or jail, for women as a primary solution to the problem, but even this era of double standards did not completely absolve men of their complicity in the women's plight. Citizens claimed that the city ignored its pimps and brothel owners, and that women would not turn to prostitution if business owners paid them fairly for legal work. The young men of the Civilian Conservation Corps were blamed for attracting the working girls into Knoxville and for causing sexual havoc elsewhere. Reports claimed they had impregnated East Tennessee girls to the point that fathers deliberately set fires on the weekends in order to occupy the young men on their days off.[439]

Knoxville's Black citizens found themselves at a severe disadvantage. White residents were often the first to receive any available jobs, plus they gradually took positions previously held by Black Knoxvillians. The proportion of Black laborers working as city pavers, in the telephone industry, as bakers and cooks, and for the railroads all fell drastically during the thirties.[440] The resulting unemployment caused social ills in the Black community that ranged from a high murder rate to school truancy and the resulting lack of literacy.[441]

In many ways, the Depression hit men of both races the hardest. They often identified with their jobs as coalminers, railroad men, or attorneys, and felt adrift when unemployed. Men also served as their families' primary breadwinners. The culture supported these concepts, which put immense pressure on husbands and fathers. Well into the 1930s, instead of considering their unemployment to be caused by a powerful historical event, many men viewed it as a personal failure.[442] Under the stresses of hunger and insecure housing, families disintegrated. Men across America left their homes to look for jobs—or to flee their responsibilities. Slang evolved to distinguish between the many travelers who illegally rode the railroads. "Hobos" moved around in search of work, while "bums" just traveled the rails. Some Americans lacked sympathy for the country's dispossessed, disparaging them as freeloaders who were a drain on society.

The desperation of America's poor showed in letters written to President and Mrs. Roosevelt. Their correspondence was littered with heartbreaking admissions that crime seemed the only way to feed starving children and that suicide might solve family problems. Several writers requested the first couple's used clothing.[443] American women had returned to sewing much of the family's clothes, and they relentlessly reused fabric. Mrs. Roosevelt's discarded dresses could be altered, making them suitable to wear at community events such as church. As better garments became threadbare, they were worn as daily attire and still later during manual labor. Cloth fragments would eventually become part of a quilt, made to keep family members warm at night. Once it became frayed, that quilt might be used to line a coat. Even this money-saving process required resources that not everyone had. One visitor to a Knoxville shantytown emphasized the inhabitants' poverty by describing their grimy clothing, which was noticeably repaired with patches and safety pins.

Both Marie and Earl sympathized with the downtrodden, she because of her childhood poverty and he out of innate compassion. In small ways, they both tried to help Knoxville's chronically unemployed and the transients who briefly stayed in the city and then moved on. These men, as they overwhelmingly were, developed informal networks that told them which areas of town to avoid, where they would be tolerated, and who to ask for help. Before long, a succession of solitary men arrived at the Laymans' doorstep with heartfelt requests for food. Every time, Marie would give the man a cloth and tell him to dust her porch railing while she prepared a meal. She didn't give handouts but also never turned down a hungry man's request. The Laymans' white porch banisters were cleaned so frequently that Earl claimed they glistened more brightly than any others in Burlington.

As Knoxville's poor White population burgeoned, several politicians catered to them. City Councilman Lee Monday had long supported the city's large population of Appalachian migrants. By the Depression, another spokesperson had gained local fame: Caswell (Cas) Walker. While in his early twenties, Cas had opened a small grocery store on Vine Street, becoming so successful that he developed a string of stores. His customers were the city's poor, both Black and White. Knoxville's wealthier businessmen often ignored this clientele, but Cas courted them. He turned grocery store giveaways into festive occasions by throwing fifty live chickens off his store roof or greasing a pig and paying boys to catch it.[444] When Cas began a radio show, the *Farm and Home Hour*, it aired at six o'clock in the morning, when day laborers ate breakfast. Immensely popular, it ran for years and, in the future, would successfully transition to television.

Cas understood his customers because he shared their Appalachian roots. He also shared a background with Earl.

The two men grew up across the ridge from each other in Sevier County, with Earl the older by two years.[445] Cas's father, Thomas, worked as a farm laborer, and his family lived in poverty. At seven years old, Cas had nine siblings, hadn't attended school during the past year, and probably could not read or write.[446] Nevertheless, in the small community, the Laymans and Walkers knew each other well. One of Cas's uncles, Charles Walker, witnessed the last will and testament of Earl's father.[447] Charles Walker owned a country store, most likely the one that sat a half mile from the Layman farm.[448] As a boy, Cas might have worked at that store, learning skills that explain his ability to run a Knoxville grocery as a young man.

At some point in childhood, Cas decided to steal a watermelon from the Layman farm. Possibly the most delicious item that can be grown in East Tennessee, when cooled in a mountain stream, this fruit becomes the ultimate summer treat. Unfortunately, Earl's older brother, Lem, caught Cas in the act and decided to teach him a lesson. Lem told Cas that he knew his family struggled financially, so he would give Cas a watermelon. The young boy excitedly started toward home, carefully balancing his unwieldy prize. Lem watched Cas progress for a few feet, then stopped him. He announced that he would give Cas two melons, then three ... if he could carry them home all at once. Of course, no child could manage such a feat. Lem probably assumed that a lesson had been learned and allowed Cas one melon. In later years, Cas, who enjoyed a good story, would tell this one on himself.[449]

As teenagers, Earl and Cas left Sevier County around the same time, the summer of 1917, but their attitudes differed. Earl entered Knoxville as an ambitious son, determined to succeed through hard work and intellect, while Cas blazed into town like a wild child seeking success through turmoil. If Earl felt ambiguous toward his mountain roots, Cas exaggerated them, developing a hillbilly persona that gained him customers and notoriety. As he gathered wealth and eventually power, Knoxville's elite were not amused.

Many considered him a liability who damaged the city's reputation. Cas, after all, served as a constant reminder of the town's prevailing Appalachian population.

Even though Earl projected rational thought while Cas thrived on hyperbole, the two men got along. They both served clients from the same low-income population, benefitting from their connections to Sevier Countians now living in Knoxville. During private conversations, Cas would often drop his hillbilly act, revealing considerable intelligence.[450] Having known the grocery store owner since childhood, Earl found the other man's showboating to be amusing. In later years, Cas's sensational newspaper, *The Watchdog*, could always be found in the Layman household. Earl would chuckle over the outrageous and completely unproven claims found there while Marie would shake her head and mutter "that Cas."

Cas had a long career that included hosting a radio program, the one that first featured Sevier County's Dolly Parton, and being a television host, a small-newspaper publisher, a city councilman, and a Knoxville mayor. A few of his more disgraceful moments involved a fist fight during a city council meeting, a picture of which appeared in the newspapers, and his stance against adding fluoride to the city water. On this subject he stood proudly, publicly announcing that he had always been against poisoning the water supply. Cas became "part huckster, part spokesman for Knoxville's poor and fearful, and part demagogue" who "set the tone" for the city.[451] His low-income constituents loved him. By the 1950s, when he was a millionaire, the city's poor often wrote him asking for aid that they could not find elsewhere.[452] In this way, he functioned much as FDR had for desperate Americans during the Depression. Cas's demeanor, however, also encouraged an impressive list of foes. It included Knoxville mayor and entrepreneur George Dempster who famously claimed, "If I ordered a whole carload of SOBs and they just sent Cas, I'd sign for the shipment."[453]

* * *

By 1933, all but Prohibition's staunchest supporters believed the experiment had failed. One of Earl's legal cases revealed the typical attitude toward moonshine in Knoxville and provided the local paper with an amusing anecdote. Authorities had charged two men with storing alcohol and a woman with selling it. Earl, who served as attorney to one of the bootleggers, appealed his client's twenty-five-dollar fine. One man's angry wife claimed in court that her husband had bought liquor from the woman and then became enamored with her. The husband denied this accusation but did so while grinning widely. Far from touting the evils of alcohol or the criminal nature of bootlegging, the account presented the episode as lighthearted entertainment.

This struggle between a husband who drank and a wife who found it offensive also played out in Earl and Marie's marriage. He undoubtedly hid any imbibing from her as they courted, and in a classic double standard, probably preferred a teetotaling wife. However, one of Marie's expectations for marriage was a husband who didn't drink booze. His doing so violated her idea of a morally upright man. She believed it her religious duty to convince Earl to change, an attitude that caused friction between them. The stresses of Depression life likely contributed to their impasse. When he received liquor as payment for legal services, she felt that the practice shortchanged their family's needs. Neither Earl nor Marie ever revisited their roles in this ongoing dynamic.

The United States, however, had reconsidered its relationship with alcohol. Even most women agreed that Prohibition had failed. Well over twice as many of them had joined an organization seeking its end than had advocated for it in the powerful Woman's Christian Temperance Union.[454] Congress eventually repealed Prohibition, partly because the government needed money and could get it by taxing liquor. However, East Tennesseans and many other Americans had bought tax-free booze for years and didn't want to pay higher prices, so they continued purchasing the bootleg variety. A battle raged between the tax-evading moonshiners and the government agents who were trying to shut them down in order to secure a revenue stream. Once Prohibition ended, local governments that did allow liquor limited the sales to certain days, hours, and buyer ages. In Knoxville, temperance-influenced legislation banned liquor by the drink in the city and kept liquor stores closed on Sundays for decades.

The same month that Prohibition ended, authorities captured a prominent outlaw from Knoxville. For fifteen years, Ehude Fellows, the man convicted of murdering Earl's uncle, had evaded capture. After escaping from the Knox County jail during the 1919 race riot, Ehude skulked about, then landed in Memphis where he got married.[455] Fellows's wife learned that he was an escaped convict but kept his secret until her death. Later, the felon remarried. His second wife learned about his past and presumably told her mother. That mother-in-law eventually turned Fellows in to the authorities, and he was finally captured, a decade and a half after his escape.[456] For several years, Fellows even stayed in jail. For Earl's family, his recapture surely brightened one of the Depression's most difficult years.

CHAPTER 21
Marie's Forte

FOR MIDDLE AMERICANS SUCH AS EARL and Marie, it was the length of the Depression, year after year of anxiety and subtle deprivation, that took a toll. The threat of ruin pervaded their daily lives. Too often, seemingly secure families faced misfortune with an abruptness that frightened families and neighbors. Earl's sister Mae and her husband, Clarence, experienced this when he was laid off from his typesetting job at the *Knoxville News Sentinel*. When they couldn't keep up with their mortgage payments, the bank repossessed their house, and they endured the dislocation of a forced move. Clarence took odd jobs, trying to earn enough cash to pay the rent. Their experience wasn't unusual. By 1933, two-fifths of American homeowners were in the process of losing their homes.[457] Clarence and Mae were luckier than many others. Produce, eggs, and meat from the Layman farm in Sevier County kept their family fed and healthy.

Middle-class families became determined to avoid any implication of an economic slide, so the concept of keeping up appearances gained huge importance. The state of a man's facial hair, for example, portrayed his financial status. A well-shaven face delineated the better off from those who lived without running water or had to choose between personal hygiene and feeding their families.[458] Hobos didn't shave, but middle- and upper-income men did, daily. As for middle-class women, they had entered the workforce in unprecedented numbers during the twenties, but their working in the thirties implied that their families neared financial ruin. Working women were also seen as taking jobs from men, the ones considered responsible for the family's finances. This idea became so engrained that it helped solidify America's belief that women should stay at home with their children.[459]

Being employed didn't protect workers from hardship, however. As early as 1933, the typical salary in the United States had dropped almost in half.[460] University of Tennessee professors were lucky when they withstood a pay cut of one-fifth.[461] With less money coming into households, middle-class families began spending their savings. They conserved items such as coal and changed their daily habits to avoid spending cash. Knoxville's streetcar use plummeted because ordinary citizens considered it an unnecessary expense.[462] Participation in charity groups declined, as did the number of Knoxvillians who had telephones.[463]

The price of goods fell, hurting those who depended on sales for a living, but no one wanted to pay the full cost. Bartering goods for services became common, which further reduced prices. When Americans defaulted on mortgages or quit paying for items bought on credit, all kinds of commodities and household goods were seized and auctioned. Buying them provided one way to get a cut-rate item. City Councilman Lee Monday became a real estate mogul by purchasing foreclosed properties in Knoxville.

During her years spent working at furniture stores, Marie had developed a taste for fine furnishings. She favored heavy Victorian pieces that conveyed a sense of permanence. Whether she consciously realized it or not, tenant farmers who frequently moved could never have owned such stately items. Since she couldn't afford to pay the salesroom price, she bought a dining set at auction that included a walnut table with several extensions, eight upholstered chairs, and a china cabinet. On auction day, after Marie won the sales lot, its previous owner sought her out. The woman described her love for the furniture and despairingly asked Marie to care for it. This undeniably awkward conversation greatly touched Marie who felt somewhat guilty for profiting from the woman's misfortune.

Even though they could obtain items cheaply or by bartering, middle-class families needed hard currency to pay their mortgages, insurance bills, and automobile loans. Earl struggled in this area, partly because compassion compelled him to represent some clients who obviously wouldn't be able to pay him in cash.[464] Instead, the Laymans would find a basket of eggs or vegetables on their porch steps, often without a note to reveal which of Earl's pro bono clients had left them. Marie, who ran the household on a strict budget, found these gifts of limited use. After all, the family owned chickens, and she knew where to find cheap vegetables. Cash, though, was always needed. Earl searched for paying work as an attorney, but the available cases gradually dried up. During hard times, disgruntled individuals presumably settled disputes in more basic ways than through the legal system.

Earl eventually found a way to support his family during the economic crisis, but it required him to bury his pride. Society's previous fondness for buying on credit had been followed by widespread loss of income, so unpaid bills became common. Having collected debts for Woodruff's Hardware before law school, Earl reentered the field. After the Knoxville trustee's office had gotten what cash it could out of an overdue account, Earl would buy the debt for a fraction of the amount owed, then work to acquire the remainder of the money. This practice became instrumental in getting his law practice, and therefore his family, through the Depression.[465] It wasn't what he had envisioned as a career, but as the saying went, "it paid the bills."

Financial stress probably contributed to Earl's resentment over Marie's prevaricating, if not outright lying, about her family's poverty. By this time, he had discovered the depth of her deception. After several years of marriage, the Laymans had visited Marie's family in Alabama, staying with Grace and her family in Gadsden.

Marie's sister Gladys, who worked in Washington, DC, accompanied them on the trip. An attractive, even glamorous woman, Gladys was a reminder that poverty had never defined Marie's family. In fact, if one believed in a human's ability to better herself, Marie and her sisters exemplified the best of that ideal. Nevertheless, the trip didn't go well. Earl invariably met his in-laws, whose appearance announced their financial state. Fayette's missing arm hallmarked the day laborer's vulnerability while Ninnie's emaciated frame and thinning hair reflected a lifetime of hard work.

If one of Marie's expectations for marriage was a nondrinking husband, one of Earl's was a wife who furthered his aspirations. Feeling cheated and manipulated, whenever he and Marie argued, Earl would disparage her family's poverty, especially their lack of land. Marie, who loved her parents, didn't always accept her husband's criticism without retort. In at least one reply, she derisively called him a "fancy man," referring to his superior attitude and city ways. After this trip, Earl rarely ventured into Alabama. Marie continued to interact with her family, writing long letters to various relatives. She also visited her sisters, especially those closest to her in age.

***

In some ways, no woman was better prepared for the rigors of Depression life than Marie. Her poverty-stricken childhood had given her the ability to economize, even though she had hoped to leave that lifestyle behind. Becoming a housewife did present challenges for her, though. Appliances such as dishwashers and self-cleaning ovens had not yet been invented, so housework depended on the ancient drudgery of scrubbing, along with its companions: sweeping, washing, mopping, polishing, and dusting. Since the concept of taking one's shoes off at the door had not reached America, family members frequently tracked dirt into the house. A machine washed the laundry, but it had to be hung on a clothesline and then ironed. Marie didn't enjoy any of these chores. She also didn't mind if her home contained some of the clutter of daily living such as a pile of newspapers on the couch. In a generation when some women judged each other according to the state of their homes, Marie never considered her worth as a person to be reflected in her ability to clean.

As frugality became a way of life, middle-class wives aimed to save money with every transaction. Electrical appliances were fixed at home or taken to a repairman instead of being replaced. Women typically sewed the family's clothes, and Marie owned a sewing machine, but she disliked the tedious process of measuring the recipient, cutting fabric, sewing the garment, and creating button holes. Zippers remained rare, except in jackets and children's clothing. Homemade shirts and dresses had to withstand repeated use and laundering. Naturally, the flapper's thin, sleeveless dresses went out of style, giving way to heavier fabric and longer skirts that were warmer and more durable. In a change that flattered most women, the twenties' fascination with a boyish figure ended. Waists and curves became fashionable again and were balanced by broader shoulders. Once these changes occurred, fashions worn by middle-class women stagnated. For all but the wealthiest Americans, clothing needed to last, not be discarded for a newer look.

Marie, lackluster maid and disinterested seamstress, did have a forte: cooking. Over the years, she produced an astounding amount of quality meals. Part of her success came from an intuitive understanding of basic food preparation, in particular the need for quality ingredients. In her day, gathering a meal's components took an inordinate amount of time. Taken to her level of expertise, the task required considerable knowledge and multiple relationships.

For many cooks, common dishes and entrées originated in their backyards. Home gardens provided many summer meals, and just about everyone in Burlington kept a flock of chickens for a cheap supply of eggs and fryers, the term for chickens destined for a cast-iron skillet. Having the birds so close, though, meant that turning them into dinner required a backyard slaying. A chicken could easily be killed by picking it up, then slinging it by the head so its own body weight broke its neck. Or one could just chop its head off.

This sometimes caused the bird to briefly scramble around while headless in a display that children found gruesome but fascinating. Marie rejected this chore and always asked a neighbor friend to kill her birds. She couldn't avoid unpleasantry, however. Removing its feathers required scalding the chicken, which created a pungent odor that hung in the air as Marie painstakingly plucked off the wet feathers. Only after these steps were completed could the serious cleaning, butchering, and cooking commence.

Other meats on the Layman table came from Sevier County. Each year, Earl's brother, Lem, raised two hogs that were earmarked for his and Earl's families, and every fall the Knoxville Laymans helped butcher the animals. After the pigs had been shot between the eyes, the adults started the messy job of cleaning and prepping them. Once salted, smoked, or pickled, these hogs provided meat through the winter. Except for the small intestines, no part of the animals went to waste. Bobby Earl was often given a tail, which he considered a treat. Accustomed to living close to his food sources, he happily roasted it over a fire, then gnawed the meat off.

A few food items could be purchased from the comfort of home. Traveling salesmen peddled wares such as Watkins Spice products, going door to door across America. Most families enjoyed these visits, especially those who lived in isolated areas. The men, who were usually personable and polite, provided a welcome distraction from the day's work by passing along news of a local birth or a neighbor's health. They also sold much-loved products.

Shopping in the era's dry-goods stores tended to be time-consuming, even though every neighborhood had one. Stands of crackers or barrels full of Coca-Cola usually clogged the store's middle aisle. Clerks stood behind a counter with shelves of canned vegetables lining the wall beyond them. These employees gathered most of the customers' items, weighing out flour, dried beans, corn meal, and so forth. During busy periods, overly methodical or talkative clerks didn't keep up with demand, so shoppers had long waits for their orders. A more efficient system gradually replaced this flawed one, and modern grocery stores arrived in Knoxville in the midst of the Depression. Piggly Wiggly stores started this revolution by having shoppers chose their own canned goods from shelves.

With housewives reluctant to part with cash, companies devised innovative ways to entice their business. Giving away a free item proved popular. Towels came in boxes of laundry soap, and small toys nestled in boxes of caramelized popcorn called Cracker Jacks. Quaker Oats and other major brands came with glass dishware tucked inside the packaging. This "depression ware" featured a dazzling array of designs and colors, such as pink, yellow, and green. Another marketing technique allowed loyal customers to earn free products. The Jewel Tea Company sold coffee, tea, and other goods. Its customers could receive an entire line of kitchenware if they bought enough merchandise. Marie earned an Autumn Leaf teapot, one of the company's more popular items. The White Stores grocery chain, a Knoxville staple, distributed stamps with each purchase, which were collected and traded for free items. With discretionary income virtually nonexistent, this scheme enthralled everyone in the family. Available products ranged from the practical to the decorative, so perusing the catalogues that pictured these choices provided hours of entertainment.

Whenever possible, Marie shopped in downtown Knoxville rather than Burlington. She enjoyed the city's busy ambience, navigating the sidewalks with astounding swiftness for a petite woman. This habit might have been gained while living in busy DC, but she clearly considered speed-walking to be the proper pace for a midsized Tennessee town as well.

The downtown area reigned as Knoxville's shopping mecca for those who could afford it. One of the city's mainstays and Marie's designated site for splurges, Miller's Department Store, enlarged and updated its Gay Street location during the Depression. In 1937, the S&W Cafeteria evolved into an art deco beauty when it moved next to the Farragut Hotel. Stunningly stylish and complete with a skylight and elaborate staircase, the relocation solidified its place as a Knoxville institution. For Marie, the best trips to town culminated with lunch at the S&W, where she tipped Slim Dickenson for carrying her tray and listened to the organ player while eating.

Most of her excursions featured more prosaic destinations. She bought fresh produce and meats near the Market House, a three-story building situated a block west of Gay Street. A Knoxville staple since the mid-nineteenth century, much of the city's fresh food was purchased there. Local vendors rented stalls inside where they sold country ham, sausage, fish, vegetables, baked goods, and more. A pungent odor permeated the building, caused by the fish and meat offerings. The market overflowed onto nearby streets, which also thrived with street preachers, loiterers, and musicians. What mattered to Marie, though, were the lower prices found outside. Called Watermelon Row, the street east of the Market House was almost as well established as the facility itself. There, farmers sold produce out of their automobiles and trucks, vehicles that had flat tires from not being moved in years.

Marie always bought her meats and sausages from a butcher who had a stand near Watermelon Row. He understood her need for quality ingredients and that she would pay a fair price for the best cuts, but not more. When hamburgers came into style, Marie first refused to serve them because she distrusted the source of the ground beef. Being raised on a farm, she knew all too well about the various parts of a slaughtered cow. She and her butcher devised a solution where she selected a round steak and watched as he ground and packaged it. Then she served exceptional hamburgers to her family, ones that met her culinary standards.

When the vegetable crops came in, Marie and her sister-in-law Mae enacted a long-standing ritual of American women: canning. The practice saved money and provided quality food for the winter. Marie was better off than many in that her chore list did not include tending backyard vegetables, except for a few tomatoes. This lack of a garden visibly reinforced the Laymans' middle-class status. Thus, Marie and Mae traveled to the market and bought bushels of beans, peaches, berries, okra, and cucumbers, then transported them to Marie's home. Over the next few days, they canned the vegetables and made pickles and jams for their two households. During these culinary marathons, the kitchen counters overflowed with produce, regular meals were simplified, and the house overheated because canning requires copious amounts of boiling water. Marie and Mae's friendship solidified during these events. Similar to her brother, Mae tended to be quiet. In the two women, these differences in personality complemented each other.

After all this preparation, the resulting meals embodied Southern cooking at its best. Marie produced large breakfasts with rotating menus of eggs, biscuits, sausage, sausage gravy, fried green tomatoes, country ham with red-eye gravy, and fried chicken. Sunday dinner featured a meat such as pork chops, roast beef, or more fried chicken, homemade yeast rolls, and garden vegetables. The green beans or fried okra, bizarrely enough, often tasted as delicious as the simple dessert. Only one drink was available: sweetened iced tea. This dinner and all holiday meals were served at the traditional Southern time: two o'clock in the afternoon. Supper, the last and simplest meal of the day, often consisted of leftovers.

Marie's family took these elaborate preparations and the meals' tastiness for granted. Her son, Bobby Earl, tended to be a picky eater who never seemed to gain weight. Her husband, Earl, wouldn't eat what he considered to be poor people's food, such as poke, which grew wild in East Tennessee, or turnip greens, which Marie loved. Ironically, he craved cornbread, a staple in many an impoverished mountain household. For all her culinary abilities, per her husband's request, Marie made the simple bread for supper—daily.

CHAPTER 22

Diversions

As EARL, MARIE, AND MANY OTHERS struggled through the Depression, so did the city of Knoxville. The number of unemployed more than tripled from 1930 to 1937.[466] Obvious problems included trash piled on the streets and unmarked roads that confused travelers, while a typical underlying issue was the lack of health services for the poor.[467] Crime increased, with even Earl affected. One evening thieves stole his sedan and took it for a joyride. They wrecked it within ten minutes. He promptly swore out a warrant against the intoxicated driver and his passenger, a hitchhiker from Ohio. This drunken escapade inconvenienced the Laymans, but most crime had far weightier outcomes. As violence proliferated in the city, its murder rate increased to unprecedented levels.[468]

Crime and its companion, social problems, often centered in the city's poverty-stricken neighborhoods that were affected by widespread unemployment. Thus, Knoxville's League of Women Voters considered the eradication of the crowded and unsanitary shantytowns to be a worthwhile goal.[469] Of course, this would evict hundreds of the city's poorest citizens and destroy most of the Bowery. Nevertheless, many Knoxvillians agreed with the middle-class organization's recommendations. In the future, this attitude would lead to widespread urban renewal projects that all but decimated Vine Street with its many Black-owned businesses.

Social disparities already handicapped Knoxville's minority community. The head of the Family Welfare Bureau, Louise Bignall, raged against the inadequacy of the city's facilities for Black children, including the orphanage and detention centers.[470] Knoxville's minority community leaders also spoke out against inequality. A few years earlier, C. A. Cowan had lamented the Black high school's overcrowding. Pointing out that Knoxville's Black population had increased over 50 percent in the previous decade, he stressed the need for a Black junior high to be established and for the high school to add a twelfth grade.[471] "C. A. Cowan" was undoubtedly Carl Cowan, a Knoxville College graduate who had earned a law degree from Howard University and would work throughout his life to improve Black lives. Cowan later challenged segregation in the Knoxville County school system, the University of Tennessee, and elsewhere.

By the late thirties, construction projects provided some employment in Knoxville. The Works Progress Administration built another jail in town, one that included facilities for women. Knoxville businessmen and city leaders spearheaded several local projects that included rebuilding viaducts and bridges. The town paid for one particularly stunning building: a new post office constructed of local pink marble. Less grandiose projects included the University of Tennessee's new concrete grandstand for its football field. On Jackson Avenue, the Bowman Moore Hat Company's building became headquarters for JFG coffee. Brown smog with a bitter odor emanated from the building and hovered over downtown. Due to its location in a valley, Knoxville often lacked the breezes needed to dispel such byproducts of industry.

* * *

In October of 1936, Marie gave birth to a second son, again at Fort Sanders Hospital. This baby also sported lush, attractive eyelashes, a trait that might possibly be traced to Marie's power of prayer.

In an act that he had likely considered for months, Earl christened this child Richard Neal Layman. By Richard's birth, Marie had abandoned the popular child-rearing advice to resist coddling her infant. Perhaps she felt a failure at ignoring the modern standard, but she became a happier mother for it. Although she wanted more children, Richard would be her last. In the future, a cyst would be found on her ovary, and its removal made her infertile. Two or three children were the average for her generation, however. Farming no longer required a large family workforce, and wealthier women had access to some birth control.[472] The Depression, however, was really to blame. Because of its disruptions and hardships, birthrates plummeted to unprecedented lows. During the thirties, America's population growth was less than half that of the previous decade and of the following one.[473] Bobby Earl and Richard belonged to the smallest generation of the twentieth century.

* * *

One industry that flourished during the Depression did so by distracting Americans. Entertainment options ranged from the familiar to those using innovative technologies.

Reading served as a popular and, not coincidently, cheap pastime. Americans bought newspapers on city streets or had them delivered to their front doors, often by children. Knoxville wasn't unusual in having two papers, *The Journal* in the morning and the *News Sentinel* in the afternoon. They contained multiple sections to engage their readers' varied interests. The stark front page highlighted national and international events, while interior articles recounted the city's political scandals and its court cases, especially if they had a salacious bent. Sports sections sprawled across several pages and featured extensive articles accompanied by large pictures of athletic stars. Baseball dominated the sports coverage, but golf, boxing, and of course, college football also appeared. The comics enjoyed great popularity, as did the crossword puzzle. A section designed for women contained somewhat stereotypical material, including gossip columns and descriptions of local social events.

The activities of movie stars and socialites, especially their divorces, continued to make headlines. Serialized novels with cliff-hanging chapter endings enticed readers to buy future papers. Home health remedies and cleaning tips also appeared, along with large ads pushing new appliances that most Americans couldn't afford.

In Knoxville, local columns such as Vic Weals's *Home Folks* and Bert Vincent's *Strolling* centered on humorous events around town. Through these columns, funny stories told on the street in the morning could be found in that evening's newspaper. One typical article by Vincent featured seven-year-old Bobby Earl. Apparently, Marie planned to serve "cured ham" for dinner, the term for ham preserved without using water. After hearing the menu of his next meal, Bobby Earl rebelled. He informed his mother that if the pig had been sick, he didn't want to eat the "cured ham." He became adamant on this point, refusing to dine even "if they did kill it."[474]

The Layman household read more than just newspapers. Comic books became Bobby Earl's favorite. Earl enjoyed true crime magazines and inexpensive paperbacks. Marie, along with many other Americans, tried to read the Bible daily. Nationwide, magazines such as the *Saturday Evening Post* and *Good Housekeeping* enjoyed large circulations, and public libraries served growing numbers. America's Book of the Month Club began in the midthirties. Although the company tended to reject works of the highest literary quality, its ability to supply the same novel throughout America did much to regulate the country's reading tastes and therefore its society.[475]

Americans also escaped the grinding reality of their situation through community gatherings. Free public events proliferated, with many of them revolving around religion. Church potluck dinners and revivals functioned as genuine social occasions, with the latter often taking place every night for a week. Marie attended Bell Avenue Baptist Church, where she taught Sunday school, participated in activities, chaired several committees, and made friends with the other women.

The Roxy Theatre provided Knoxville with the opposite type of entertainment. It and several houses of prostitution were on Union Avenue.[476] In between low-priced movies, the Roxy presented risqué vaudeville shows with four female dancers performing for a mostly male audience.[477] Its presence was well known, and Marie refused to shop with the outdoor vendors who set up west of the Market House because doing so would take her near the infamous locale.

Most diversions fell between these two extremes. Attendance at athletic events almost held steady during the Depression.[478] Professional baseball remained so popular that the teams took exhibition tours. Early in the decade, Babe Ruth, Lou Gehrig, and the rest of the Yankees stayed at the Farragut Hotel while in Knoxville. Teams of all levels played double-headers so that the price of one game provided an afternoon's worth of entertainment. Americans also played sports such as miniature golf and sandlot baseball, the term for a game played on a makeshift field.

Attendance at motion picture shows dropped by a fourth in the early thirties but rebounded because of reasonable rates and the determined efforts of film promoters.[479] In fact, as sound technology continued to improve, movies became the era's premier entertainment. Patrons often saw double features, two films for the price of one, while newsreels updated audiences on current events. Even in black and white, these presentations could be jarringly effective. A newsreel showing Hitler's army prompted Bobby Earl to dream that Nazi troops paraded in front of his house with ominous, synchronized steps. More appropriate offerings for children featured a humorous stage show, usually with a clown, or a serial film, shorts that always ended with the hero in danger. At the Tennessee Theatre, the Wurlitzer organ still rose dramatically out of the orchestra pit while being played.

Feature films countered the era's depressing news with stunning entertainment. Hollywood musicals enchanted audiences when dancers such as Fred Astaire and Ginger Rogers graced the screen. William Powell and Myrna Loy made a series of *Thin Man* movies about a frivolous, heavy-drinking, but somehow solidly married couple who solved crimes. Charlie Chaplin continued to make subtle comedic masterpieces, and the Marx Brothers created low-brow comedy through funny quips and energetic slapping. Claudette Colbert played a sassy heiress and Clark Gable a jaded newspaper writer in *It Happened One Night,* a charming romantic comedy. The decade culminated in one of the greatest years in filmmaking, 1939, which produced the instant hit *Gone with the Wind*, a future classic in *The Wizard of Oz*, and John Ford's *Stagecoach*. The latter foreshadowed the power of directors who filmed on location, while the first two incorporated film's newest technology—color.

Until the late thirties, most motion pictures avoided social commentary, even though the time period provided lots of fodder. Finally, Frank Capra directed several movies showing the struggles of average people against the corrupt and uncaring upper class. When John Ford brought John Steinbeck's masterful novel *The Grapes of Wrath* to the screen, the film personalized the struggles of midwestern America.

Another innovation, the radio, proved even more influential on daily lives than movies did. Commercial radio programs started in earnest in the early twenties when the devices that played them were large pieces of furniture similar to phonograph players. Radios gradually became smaller and cheaper, and by 1934, 60 percent of American homes possessed one.[480] Knoxville's radio stations flourished as the regional music they featured gained followers. Cas Walker's *Farm and Home Hour* on WROL promoted local musicians, while James Sterchi's devotion to the region's music also continued. On Saturday nights, his station, WNOX, broadcast live country music from the Lyric Theater during a popular show called *The Tennessee Barn Dance*.

In the thirties, WNOX started airing the *Mid-day Merry-Go-Round* from the seventeenth floor of the Andrew Johnson Hotel. It featured live "hillbilly" music during the years when the genre of country music was coming into being. Acclaimed artists such as Chet Atkins, Archie Campbell, Kitty Wells, Fountain City fiddler Roy Acuff, and Mother Maybell and the Carter Sisters played the show, many of them early in their careers.[481] This showcase of budding talent wasn't accidental. Lowell Blanchard, who also announced UT's football games, hosted the program and spurred its success. He scoured the hills around Knoxville searching for quality performers. Blanchard's ability to find local talent and promote the *Mid-day Merry-Go-Round* made him one of the founders of country music.[482] While it was popular with radio audiences, the program was especially loved by Knoxvillians because they could watch it live. Crowds of viewers routinely overwhelmed the hotel at noon when it aired. As a result, in 1937, the Andrew Johnson's management insisted that the radio station find different lodgings. The show's lunchtime audience was often rowdy and clogged the elevators to the point that hotel guests couldn't use them.[483]

In addition to music, radio stations entertained Americans by reporting sporting events such as boxing matches and horse races. The Layman family faithfully listened to University of Tennessee football games. Earl favored the news and commentary programs that first developed during the midthirties. H. V. Kaltenborn became one of his favorite newscasters, as did Walter Winchell, who specialized in gossipy news but also berated those who appeased Germany's Nazi Party. Marie devotedly tuned into two weekday shows: *Our Gal Sunday*, about an American orphan who married a British aristocrat, and *Ma Perkins,* which featured a kind-hearted widow who managed a lumber yard while raising three children. Cleaning products often sponsored these dramas and insisted their names be repeated alongside the program's title. This caused the shows, which tended to be popular and long-running, to be dubbed "soap operas."

In order to gain a national audience, these nonmusical radio programs avoided references to America's vast regional differences. Unintentionally, this practice implied that there was one proper American way of life, including a preferred dialect. Thus, the era's entertainment, from its novels to its radio shows, encouraged society to standardize in ways that had been previously unconceivable.[484]

Radios became so important that they evolved into a social and economic marker. No one could keep up appearances without one, but a lack of infrastructure hindered their spread in rural areas such as East Tennessee. The region's hilly terrain and poverty combined to make electricity scarce outside of the cities, so mountain people faced considerable obstacles in owning the radios that allowed others to keep up with news and popular entertainment. Their resulting lack of knowledge made them and other rural Americans seem increasingly ignorant and underprivileged. Actually, their poverty level hadn't changed much, but they were less informed. Thus, Appalachian people lived outside of the standardization that increasingly prevailed across the country.

Rural Americans certainly wanted radios. Early models had run on a car battery instead of electricity and were still being manufactured, so rural consumers bought the older style. Earl's brother, Lem, listened to a battery-powered radio on the Sevier County farm. In December of 1941, Earl, Marie, and their children visited the farm for Sunday dinner. While listening to Lem's radio, they heard that the Japanese had just bombed Pearl Harbor. Later that day, Earl and Bobby Earl took an after-dinner stroll and met a local resident. Still reeling from the news, they informed the man about the attack. To cover his ignorance, the neighbor immediately lied, saying, "Oh, yes, I heard about that last week," and hurried along.[485] Appalachian people knew they weren't keeping up, and some felt shame about it. Being ignorant of current events functioned as one more way they were considered lesser, outside of "normal" society.

CHAPTER 23
Painful Change

THE TENNESSEE VALLEY AUTHORITY, of course, claimed that it could alleviate East Tennessee's poverty and apparent backwardness. The mission to dam area rivers, flooding much of the valley, progressed into the midthirties while generating near-constant controversy. Earl agreed with many in the region who had deeply ambivalent feelings toward TVA. He thought that it significantly raised the quality of life in the Tennessee Valley, especially by bringing electricity. However, he was less sure that the federal government should permanently be in the power business.[486]

While establishing an administration, TVA had leased offices at several sites in Knoxville. Locals anticipated a much-needed hiring spree because the area's middle class needed jobs. TVA had a federal government mindset, though, not a local one. The agency brought hundreds of engineers and middle-management employees to the city from elsewhere, leaving Knoxvillians to feel that their qualified middle-class workers had been overlooked. Thousands of East Tennesseans were employed as laborers to build the dams.

Hiring priorities aside, TVA's mission sparked controversy because it hinged upon massive change. The widespread accumulation of farmland, much of it emotionally significant to the owners, generated ill will. TVA's first project, building Norris Dam, forced over three thousand households to move in order to accommodate the flooding.[487] It created thousands of temporary jobs, but not every East Tennessean considered that a worthwhile trade-off. Cherokee Lake, which mostly backed into Grainger and Jefferson Counties, displaced 875 families.[488] It also nearly obliviated the physical remnants of Grainger County's significant contributions to early regional history. The frontier town of Bean Station, for example, was almost completely flooded. Since many landowners resisted selling their property, the government invoked the right of eminent domain in order to seize the acres it wanted. Cemeteries became a point of contention because many neighborhood churches and family farms contained one. TVA offered to move any graveyard that would be flooded, but some landowners sued, hoping the issue might save their land. A federal judge eventually ruled in the agency's favor, saying that the cemeteries would either be relocated or submerged.[489] TVA did move them, sometimes into inconvenient locations that could only be tended by the agency, not family members.[490]

In order to counter the negative press caused by its land acquisitions, TVA's publicity arm moved into action. It addressed the nation, emphasizing the terrible conditions that the agency would rectify in East Tennessee. Unfortunately, that message often disparaged Appalachian people, portraying them as poverty-stricken and even stupid.[491] This stirred Knoxville's fundamental ambivalence toward its own culture, a situation where the criticism of outsiders rarely helps. Some TVA employees so frequently and publicly disparaged the city that two historical accounts of the era referenced their attitude.[492] The controversy continued into the early 1940s when TVA created a propaganda film called *The Valley of the Tennessee*. It celebrated the agency as the bringer of enlightenment to backward Appalachian people too ignorant to appreciate the gift.[493]

The philosophy of TVA's leadership evolved, and the agency focused on goals such as increasing the power production that aided cities and nearby farms, not mountain communities.[494] Workers completed Norris Dam in July 1936, and other dams soon followed, producing electricity and subduing the region's rivers. Knox County certainly benefitted from TVA's presence. In the late thirties, it won a nationwide competition that measured homeowner advancements. Over 100 homes in the county had added running water, and over 160 had gained electricity,[495] so the victory clearly depended on power generated by TVA. The rate of these gains soon slowed, however, and countless East Tennesseans did not receive electricity until after World War II, including the Sevier County Laymans.

Other advantages in turning rivers into lakes were soon apparent while the drawbacks were more nuanced. Fishermen, recreational boaters and barge companies loved the expanded waterways. Underwater, however, stunted pockets of the original ecosystems struggled to survive. Native river mussels, which live in a running current, prevailed for several decades within the submerged confines of the original rivers. TVA rigidly controlled its lakes, raising and lowering water levels throughout the year. This practice countered the seasonal floods, but it also fueled ongoing animosity between locals and agency officials. For major lakes such as Lake Loudoun, formally called the Tennessee River, the agency artificially elevated the water levels several feet in early summer in an attempt to strand debris on the riverbanks. East Tennesseans complained that this "flushing the lake" deposited as much trash into the water as it did onto the banks, but their opinion went unheeded for years.[496]

* * *

With amazing swiftness, Earl and Marie's sons grew from infants into active children. Because of their parents' financial diligence, they enjoyed some advantages such as learning to swim by taking lessons at the downtown YMCA. The classes only contained boys, which was wise since no participants wore bathing suits.[497] The family's Burlington home reverberated with the sounds of pattering feet and slamming screen doors. The backyard, with its fully grown shrubs and large shade trees, served as the boys' main playground. Bobby Earl and Richard shared that yard with the chickens and a family dog named JoJo. A mixture of retriever and collie, the canine excelled as a watchful, loyal companion. Both boys doted on him.

JoJo did have a destructive habit that caused friction between Earl and Marie. He walked the family chickens to death. The dog would pick out one of the birds and stealthily follow it around the yard until it tired. When the chicken sat down, JoJo gently nosed it, making the bird resume its trek. He continued this game until the chicken collapsed from exhaustion and then died. Because Marie fed the family on a limited budget, the unexpected death of a chicken irritated her. Earl, on the other hand, considered JoJo's game to be amusing. He might have even encouraged it by taking eggs from Marie's stockpile and giving them to the dog as a treat. After this happened several times, Marie started charging her husband for the egg, insisting that its worth be repaid to the family budget. This way she somewhat countered JoJo's dent on the backyard poultry.

Because of strict household budgets, mothers in the thirties took on myriad duties. Even middle-class women such as Marie cared for most of their children's injuries and ailments. Medical insurance was rare, so no one wanted to call a physician or go to a hospital. Hazards abounded though. While playing outside, children encountered threats from nature that ranged from poison ivy to poisonous snakes. Bee stings were treated with home remedies, such as wet tobacco or baking soda. Rashes, bites, and even mild concussions were considered an inconvenient price of living that didn't require a visit to the doctor.

Some health issues couldn't be ignored. Nonbleeding puncture wounds, say from a rusty nail, could cause tetanus, with its facial spasms and possible death. Cuts from sharp objects also presented challenges. With antibiotics unavailable, infections could be fatal. Cleaning a cut was usually accomplished with rubbing alcohol, causing sharp agony to the patient. In fact, during the Depression, Americans routinely tolerated high levels of pain.[498] They could take aspirin, but the government had limited the use of cocaine as a pain-fighter. A product called paregoric, however, contained a significant amount of opium and was given to teething infants.

No vaccinations existed for childhood illnesses, which could be serious or even fatal. Both Bobby Earl and Richard overcame the measles, chicken pox, and mumps. These three diseases, which virtually every child experienced, caused separate concerns. Measles was the deadliest, but chicken pox left scars, and popular opinion held that the mumps could render a boy infertile for life. When children contracted these illnesses, they whimpered miserably as their mothers nursed them through various symptoms such as high fevers, open itchy sores, and heartrending lethargy. As a disease moved through the family, these impromptu health care workers might spend weeks caring for one child and then another.

Having experienced youthful hazards herself that ranged from malaria to almost suffocating in the cotton bin, Marie carefully supervised her sons and any young children in her care. She always knew their locations and would not tolerate any risky behavior. If necessary, she used the yelling ability gained in childhood to enforce safe play. Her sons thought she overreacted and eventually turned this attentiveness against her. When they were about eight and four years old, Marie heard screaming from the backyard. Looking out a window, she saw Bobby Earl holding his brother, head down, while Richard shrieked and struggled to balance on his hands. She dropped her housework and ran outside to rescue her youngest. After saving Richard and admonishing Bobby Earl, she started back inside. Unbelievably, as she rounded the corner of the house, she heard Richard exclaim: "Do it again, Bobby Earl! Do it again!"

Marie took some solace in her sons' affection for each other, but their collaboration threatened her peace of mind.

The responsibility of supervising two active boys combined with low-grade stress over finances sometimes drained Marie's mental reserves. She kept poems, newspaper articles, and church bulletin clippings that she identified with, tucking them between the pages of her Bible. One anonymous poem titled "Nobody Knows But Mother" states that:

Nobody knows of the work it makes,
To keep the home together;
Nobody knows of the steps it takes,
Nobody knows—but mother.[499]

Marie clearly felt underappreciated in ways that unpaid house cleaners and babysitters have throughout time. Her strong maternal instincts helped her through these feelings, however. The poem ends by thanking God for the gift of motherhood.

* * *

During the Depression, the middle class occasionally took vacations, typically visits to relatives who provided free lodging. The Laymans visited Marie's sister Patsy and her family in northern Virginia. While there, they toured the District of Columbia's famous sights, including the zoo and monuments on the National Mall. Marie told Bobby Earl and Richard about her experience working in the district when she helped the Great War veterans sign up for extra compensation. She photographed her sons at the same fountain outside the US Capitol Building where she had been pictured years before.

Such vacations were usually reciprocated, and Patsy visited Tennessee with her daughter, Patricia. Even Grace visited Knoxville, driving up from Gadsden with her husband and children during the summers. Gladys, who remained unmarried until late in the decade, lived too far from Gadsden to go home for the holidays, so she often celebrated Thanksgiving and Christmas with the Laymans. During her sisters' visits, Earl and Marie proudly showed off East Tennessee with visits to Norris Dam and the Smokies. At night, Depression-era families economized by staying at home while the children played unsupervised games of hide and seek, fox and hounds, and kick the can. If not playing outdoors, they enjoyed Scrabble or Monopoly, while bridge remained popular among adults. These indoor games had common traits. They all required a modest purchase price, then provided years of entertainment without any added expense.

Sunday dinner with Earl's family reigned as the family's most valued excursion. Chapman Highway had been built to take visitors to the Sevier County portion of the Smoky Mountains, making such visits possible. Earl, Marie, and the boys visited Sevier County twice a month.

A farm provides great fun for kids who aren't saddled with its many chores. On their visits, Bobby Earl and Richard watered the horses and checked on the pigs, then watched Lem milk the cows. While doing so, he would shoot milk into a cat's mouth, which the boys found fascinating. In the summer, they went fishing or crawdad hunting in the creek. Later, they might splash and cavort in the swimming hole portion of that creek, a forerunner of the backyard pool. After dinner, Earl and his boys usually walked to Bogart's Store. Likely the same facility that Cas Walker's uncle had owned, it sold groceries, overalls, tools, boots, motor oil, ammunition, and even dynamite.[500]

In contrast to the family's twice-monthly visits to Sevier County, trips to see Marie's parents in Alabama occurred rarely, although two of them did take place in Bobby Earl's early childhood. During the second visit, he was astonished to find his grandparents living in a different location than before. The contrast with his Layman relatives and their farm was striking. He hadn't realized that families sometimes moved from house to house. Bobby Earl never became close to Marie's parents. When he was seven and his Grandmother Little visited Knoxville, he didn't recognize her.

Although she often went alone, Marie insisted on one trip to Alabama every year. Each Labor Day weekend, she visited her parents and participated in Decoration Day at the small church where her parents and much of her extended family worshiped. This celebration centered around yard work. Rural churches often had an adjoining cemetery that contained generations of the parishioners' ancestors. When weeds began to flourish during the long Southern growing season, the congregations hosted graveyard-clearing events. Since pulling sprouts and vines from around headstones isn't inherently appealing, these workdays were treated as celebrations. Women brought culinary treats, musicians played lively tunes, and children played tag among the tombstones. Marie rarely missed Decoration Day.

CHAPTER 24
Moving On

BY THE LATE THIRTIES, KNOXVILLE DIDN'T HAVE large numbers of wealthy citizens, but when a Layman relative visited, she brought a spark of glamour to town. The guest was Earl's sister Ola, whom he boarded with as a teenager. Now a celebrated Chicago dress designer, Ola's career began when she apprenticed to a Knoxville dressmaker. She had twice lived in California where she first worked for I Magnin, a luxury department store that sold the creations of Parisian designers. Afterward, Ola owned and ran a dress shop in Pasadena. Now she designed wedding attire for Saks in Chicago, catering to those who could afford satin and luxury. Rather shockingly, she had divorced her husband and went by "Ola Lehman," an alternative spelling of her maiden name. Wealthy socialites wore Ola's designs in gorgeous weddings featuring color schemes that originated in the bridesmaids' dresses and filtered through the decor and refreshments. Most Depression-era brides, who often eloped to save money, could only fantasize about such elaborate ceremonies.

Ola's visit generated lots of publicity. The *Knoxville News Sentinel* claimed that her talents produced "lovely creations that will make spectators gasp" at the bride's beauty. She had recently designed bridesmaid dresses that featured puffed sleeves, tight waists, and "camisole slips of fine ruffled muslin, under the billowy skirts."[501] Such over-the-top designs epitomized glamour. Now far removed from her Sevier County roots, Ola planned to visit New York City after Knoxville. She and Earl weren't close. As the younger brother, he probably failed to appreciate her talents and alteration of the family name, although their Swiss Mennonite ancestors commonly used the Lehman spelling. The dislike seemed to be mutual. While visiting, Ola stayed with their sister Mae, a fact mentioned early in the feature article about her, while her connection to Earl was awkwardly inserted into the piece's ending.

Soon after Ola's visit, another figure from Earl's teenage years gained the spotlight. Ehude Fellows, who killed Earl's uncle during a robbery in 1918, had lived for years on the lam, then been captured and incarcerated five years earlier. Now he seemed desperate to stay in the public eye, probably because he craved early release from prison.

Fellows had written a journalist, T. H. Alexander, spinning fanciful tales of his life. He added lots of drama to his description of time spent in Europe as a young adult. The felon claimed that he had joined and then deserted the US Navy although no proof exists that he did either. He probably did work as a sailor,[502] which was how he got to Belgium. Fellows then ventured into Holland and ended up at a camp housing refugees from the Great War. There, he met several men who he assumed were American spies. Fellows maintained that his "native abilities" impressed the men so much that they enticed him into their ranks. After a year spent practicing espionage, he claimed to have been caught at The Hague and sent to a prison camp. Supposedly, he escaped twice only to be recaptured. Finally, so his story went, he escaped a third time and made his getaway in a rowboat headed toward the open ocean. After surviving a storm in the tiny craft, Fellows said he experienced more great luck when an American ship found him adrift on the North Sea and took him to New York.[503]

Fellows's earlier account of his time in Europe had been notably tamer than this one. He hadn't mentioned spying or any risky rowboat escape from captivity. He did refer to a Belgium refugee camp, then reported visiting an American consul and begging for help in returning to the United States.[504]

Alexander, the reporter, was apparently hoodwinked by Fellows. In an era when records consisted of paper files kept in a single location, Alexander had limited ability to verify details, especially since most of the events that Fellows described had occurred in wartime Europe. The compelling stories also tapped into trends of popular culture. Depression-era true crime magazines enjoyed massive popularity, and some Americans viewed criminals as exciting personalities worthy of being idolized, an attitude that likely stemmed from the era's social disruption and the popularity of bootleg liquor. In this sense, Fellows's criminal past increased his appeal, as did his account of events in Europe that made him sound like a rugged adventurer.

The felon also reinvented his experiences in Knoxville. His version of the two escapes from the Knox County jail absolved him of all complicity. He claimed, for example, to have been sleeping in 1918 when a jail mate discovered a miraculously unlocked cell door and sleeping watchman. When describing the night of the 1919 riot, he failed to mention that several of the men who mobbed the jail then worked for hours in order to free him.

Alexander's sympathetic attitude toward Fellows was reflected in newspaper articles that were published from New Mexico to South Dakota. One claimed that the felon felt such guilt and worry over living as a free man that he had aged prematurely, explaining how he looked years older than he claimed to be. In actuality, Fellows had trimmed several years off his age when arrested for robbery and homicide in Knoxville. Nashville's *The Tennessean* so glamorized the outlaw that it claimed his tale ended sadly—with his recapture. *The Knoxville News Sentinel* all but celebrated the criminal, publishing a long article that compared him to a Roman philosopher and related his version of his "colorful career."[505]

Fellows's conviction for Peter Nichols's murder was mentioned amid a slew of positive details.

Soon, Alexander began campaigning for Fellows's release from prison, and in early 1939, Tennessee Governor Gordon Browning pardoned him for his crimes. Even mild-mannered Earl surely seethed at the injustice of Fellows spending less than seven years in jail for murder, two jail escapes, and years of evading authorities.

He didn't remain free for long though. In March of the same year, Fellows was jailed for public drunkenness. The man who eluded capture for a decade apparently couldn't handle being reincarcerated. He tried to hang himself several times, ultimately succeeding on the third attempt.[506] It took over twenty years, but the Ehude Fellows saga, with its nagging unfinished business for Earl's family, had finally ended.

* * *

By the late 1930s, after working in town for two decades, Earl knew many Knoxvillians. His closest friend was Ben Winick, and the two men still practiced law in the same Hamilton National Bank office suite. Ben had a thriving family and participated in city politics.[507] He also stayed active in the Jewish community. During the twenties when prejudice against Jewish people had intensified, he worked to counter anti-Semitic forces in Knoxville by educating the public, particularly through letters to the newspapers.[508] The friends often lunched together at the S&W Cafeteria where they greeted other local attorneys and businessmen.

A series of lawyers occupied the third room in the attorneys' office suite. For several years Earl practiced with a relative of his mother, Rueben H. Nichols. At one point, he took a law partner named Max Moskowitz. One afternoon as Earl and Max chatted on a city sidewalk, a passerby complimented Moskowitz on his newborn son. The proud papa drew in a breath to reply, which caused a button to pop off his suit and shoot ten feet through the air. This story of a new father's pride amused many in town, especially when they heard that Earl kindly plucked the unruly item off the sidewalk and returned it to its owner.

Another encounter on a Knoxville sidewalk involved Earl, Bobby Earl, and a familiar professor. John R. Neal's law school had been successful throughout the twenties and into the thirties but was struggling by late in the decade. Eventually the enrollment dropped to nothing.[509] Unshaven and disheveled, the brilliant attorney still graced Knoxville's streets. His eccentric behavior continued, such as when he sold TVA some of his land but failed to cash the agency's check. This tardiness eventually disrupted TVA's bookkeeping, just as it had UT's decades earlier. An investigation revealed that Neal hadn't lost the check—it was one of many similar documents that he carried in his pockets.[510] When Bobby Earl was a young teenager, he and his father saw Neal on Gay Street, near the S&W Cafeteria. The counselor wore a trench coat from the Great War era and trousers that were ripped up one leg to the knee. Bobby Earl thought the man looked disreputable and peculiar on the business-oriented street. Earl spoke kindly to his mentor, though, and introduced his son to him. Through his manner, Earl conveyed that Neal deserved respect, no matter his physical appearance.[511]

Now well into a career as an attorney, Earl's legal cases varied in scope. Although they usually involved minor, local matters, some were more far-reaching. One young client from California claimed to have signed a blank sheet of paper so that a bondsman would front the money to get him out of a Knoxville jail. The next time the eighteen-year-old saw that signed paper, it had been filled out as a fifty-dollar bill of sale for his car. While it's unknown whether the boy ultimately retrieved his automobile, Earl made sure that the public learned of this unethical practice.

Earl sometimes traveled, his trips made possible by the passenger trains that ran through Knoxville. They left from one of two railway stations that had been built during the town's wholesaling heyday. The Southern Railway depot sat just north of the city center, while the ornate Louisville and Nashville (L&N) depot presided a few blocks to the west. It contained massive oak furnishings and spectacular stained glass. Trains leaving from these depots ferried the attorney across the country, although one trip to Chicago only proved memorable because Earl lost a fedora to the city's gusty wind.

Another legal matter took Earl and Ben Winick to Arizona where they encountered the era's ongoing prejudice against Appalachian people. An East Tennessee man named A. G. Moore had been struck by a car driven by Jack Leibert of New York.[512] Moore died of his injuries, causing a Grainger County grand jury to indict Leibert for manslaughter. Moore's family also filed a civil suit and won several thousand dollars, which they couldn't collect because Leibert had fled the region. The family retained Earl and Ben to track him down. When the two attorneys discovered Leibert living in Arizona and making good money, they traveled there to arrange his return to East Tennessee.

The Knoxville lawyers soon met with Arizona Governor Bob Jones and Leibert's attorneys to discuss the extradition of Leibert to Tennessee. His legal team launched a passionate argument against this action, based on their perception of the region. Evoking every popular Appalachian stereotype, one of them claimed that "those people in Grainger County, Tennessee, are not much more than varmints. [...] They are feudists—shoot each other down— half civilized."[513]

After thoroughly disparaging Tennesseans, the attorney uttered his coup de grâce: "Why, our man can't get justice in Grainger County courts."

The Arizona governor's reply astounded everyone. He "stiffened his spine, turned red in the face, and hammered his desk with his fist." Then he declared, "Gentlemen, I happen to know more about Grainger County than all of you put together. I was born and raised there. The people are not varmints or feudists. They are highly civilized."

Not surprisingly, Governor Jones ruled that Leibert would indeed be extradited to Tennessee. Leibert then agreed to give the victim's family several thousand dollars. Earl and Ben returned home triumphantly after, as a Knoxville paper put it, "upholding the honor of Grainger County."[514]

In addition to practicing law, Earl tried other moneymaking endeavors. Sometimes his compassion and entrepreneurial tendencies combined, such as when he helped a man whom he discovered building a house trailer. Admiring the guy's initiative, Earl agreed to fund a trailer court that would be built on the South Knoxville bluff near the Gay Street Bridge. Similar occasions, with Earl trying to help the underprivileged, happened fairly often. Unfortunately, the trailer court idea ended as these plans typically did, with Earl losing money.[515] One investment, though, couldn't play on his sympathies. Earl had ventured back into the stock market after the 1929 crash, and playing the market became one of his primary interests. In contrast to his frequent pro bono legal work and inadvertent charities, he actually made money in stocks.

Earl also harbored civic-minded ambitions. Public service was considered a worthy goal during his lifetime, one which his father had participated in. As a young man, Mitchell Layman had represented Sevier County in the Tennessee House of Representatives from 1869 to 1871,[516] a term that began the year extremist Republican Governor Parson Brownlow left office. During Mitchell's tenure, the assembly rearranged several Tennessee counties in order to create new ones and passed laws that regulated rebuilding the state's railroads. Sevier Countians habitually elected Republicans such as Mitchell. They had overwhelmingly supported the Union during the Civil War and traced their political affiliation directly to Abraham Lincoln. Throughout Earl's youth, the local newspaper, the *Sevier County Republican,* periodically celebrated the former president by printing his picture. While not as overwhelmingly one-party as Sevier County, much of Knoxville's political activity took place within factions of the Republican Party, so Earl fit right in.

Marie's beliefs and her husband's ambitions complemented each other. She passionately supported the political process because of her youth spent amid voter restrictions, women's quest for suffrage, and the fight for Prohibition. She voted Republican because the party had aided Alabama's women in those struggles. Always one to follow through with her convictions, Marie volunteered for years as an election official at Chilhowee School. She enjoyed talking about politics and frequently interjected her opinions when Earl discussed issues with a visitor. Her husband considered these interruptions to be unladylike, but that never stopped her. The couple agreed on politics and believed that participating in the process could result in a better society.

In 1938, Earl ran for state senator. Trying to distinguish himself from other candidates, he denounced "sound trucks," vehicles driven around Knoxville's streets for the sole purpose of blaring advertising through loudspeakers. Earl considered this unsophisticated practice to be inappropriate in the noisy city, especially when other types of advertising were available. The League of Women Voters apparently agreed, recommending him and Democrat W. P. Chandler as candidates.[517] Unfortunately, this endorsement failed to get Earl elected.

He wasn't the only former Sevier Countian to enter Knoxville politics around this time. Cas Walker shared many of Earl's political beliefs, although the grocery store owner had more flamboyance and willingness to create enemies than Earl ever would. Within a few years, Cas gained a seat on Knoxville's city council, essentially replacing Lee Monday as opposition leader to the established members. Both Walker and Monday represented the underclass, Knoxville's population of Appalachian in-migrants who had once been denied a political voice. Walker enjoyed conflict and pitched himself into battle as the defender of the poor, both Black and White. His presence stoked the simmering boil that was Knoxville politics.

CHAPTER 25
Surviving the Muck

AFTER YEARS OF GOVERNMENTAL CASH FLOWING into town from TVA, by the late thirties Knoxville's economy began overcoming the Depression.[518] To varying degrees, the situation eased nationwide, but the long downturn had changed Americans, making them more accustomed to hardship. For Bobby Earl and his brother, Richard, being children during the greatest economic disaster of the twentieth century had long-ranging repercussions. Their culture, and parents, approved of youngsters gaining a work ethic, and both boys delivered newspapers on their bicycles. They also learned to value perseverance and did well in school, especially Richard. Both learned wilderness skills in the Boy Scouts.

In keeping with the era's belief in mature, independent children, starting about age twelve, Bobby Earl was allowed to spend his Saturdays alone in Knoxville. On these days he had complete freedom, with one limitation. Going west of the Market House into the city's red-light area was strictly forbidden. Still, he felt a great sense of adventure and often began the day by going to the movies. The Tennessee Theater showed first-run films but charged more than other venues, so Bobby Earl preferred the Strand, which featured westerns, his favorite, at a lower price. Before the movie began, he watched the previews and a short serial whose hero would escape from danger, only to get into another hazardous situation before the episode's abrupt ending. Captain America, Dick Tracy, and Batman all underwent these grueling trials. The plots moved so quickly and so enthralled Bobby Earl that he believed the twenty-minute films lasted five minutes, at the most. After the picture show, the boy browsed the ten-cent stores and bought a hamburger at the Krystal on Gay Street. Then he visited the candy store next door that sold corn dogs and Orange Julius, an iced fruit drink.

Christmas made these excursions even more magical, especially since most gift-buying took place during the week before the holiday. Shoppers who could afford it thronged into the city from its adjoining counties. The Salvation Army and the Mile of Dimes set up tables a half-block long on Gay Street, encouraging the crowds to part with their change. As a result, donors and pedestrians clogged the sidewalks.

Refusing to let the throngs slow him down, Bobby Earl hopped onto the street in order to zip past the gridlock. He did stop to gaze into the windows of Miller's and H. H. George and Son department stores, where elaborate holiday displays showcased the store's toys. In reality, he might receive one Christmas gift, such as a bicycle, that represented months of saving for his parents. The stores employed Santa Claus for young children to visit, although by the time Bobby Earl explored the city on his own, St. Nick's simultaneous appearance in two establishments greatly amused him. The boy valued these days in the city, the ordinary ones as well as the holidays. Because of them, he viewed his hometown as overflowing with joy and promise.

* * *

Earl ensured that he had close relationships with his sons. His own father had suffered from tuberculous for years, then died a few weeks after Earl turned seven. That event changed the boy's life because afterward his mother had to manage the farm with help from his brother, Lem. While Earl had contributed, his distaste for the more heartless aspects of farming disconnected him from the other two. He responded to a fatherless and undoubtedly lonely childhood by becoming a doting parent.

Much of his meager spare time was spent with his sons. Baseball games, if double-headers, could occupy an entire Saturday afternoon. The trio supported the Knoxville Smokies, although the team often lost games because management traded any promising player to another team. They had a better chance of seeing their team win when they attended UT football games because Robert Neyland still excelled as the team's coach. Knoxvillians adored the Volunteers, especially in 1938. That season culminated in the undefeated University of Tennessee Volunteers playing the undefeated University of Oklahoma Sooners in the 1939 Orange Bowl. The defense-heavy game proved mentally and physically challenging. It became so brutal that Coach Neyland sent tailback George Cafego into the game with instructions to help maintain calm. Soon, though, Cafego joined his teammates in roughhousing with the Oklahoma players. Tennessee ultimately prevailed, with Cafego in the lead, winning the university's first national championship and generating elation in the Layman household and throughout the state. The next year's team also excelled, with ten wins and a Southeastern Conference co-championship. In fact, from 1938 to 1940, UT won thirty-one out of thirty-three games. Every win provided a spark of joy during hard times, and the Laymans became multigenerational fans.

Other than following the Volunteers, fishing reigned as the trio's favorite pastime. East Tennessee's rural landscapes provided rich locations for it and hunting. Many a resident depended on the two activities for supper. Although Earl had learned to shoot as a child, he favored fishing, an attitude that his boys soon acquired. As Bobby Earl put it, "Anything Dad loved to do, I loved to do."[519]

The Layman men's fishing trips began as simple excursions. They sat on the bank holding cane poles with fishing line tied onto the ends. Cane plants grew near water and were free for the taking, making them the cheapest fishing tackle. The trio gradually became more ambitious but still had to be frugal. Earl tried designing reels that would fit onto the cane poles, allowing the trio to cast their lines across the water instead of just dropping them in, but this feat proved to be outside his meager mechanical abilities. Eventually, he purchased store-bought rods and reels, and the three learned how to fly fish.

With so many shared activities, Earl and his sons formed a united trio, while Marie supervised the children as they completed daily homework and chores. Her role in the family contrasted with her husband's position as the easy-going father, the doting papa. Instead of expecting Earl to help with discipline, she undertook it alone, including the unpopularity it brought her. Earl became the fun parent, the father he never had. Marie became the busy mother who denied requests and insisted that her sons follow the family rules.

Their marriage persevered, however. Living in a society with no concept of counseling, they dealt with problems on their own. As Earl worked long hours, Marie stayed in touch by calling him at the office every afternoon,[520] perhaps a more intense schedule than he preferred. His refusal to stop drinking remained a source of conflict. When Marie found liquor that her husband had hidden, she promptly poured it out. He retaliated by emptying her bottle of White Shoulders cologne. Undeterred by this impasse, the next Christmas she requested the scent as a gift from her family members. After all the presents had been opened, Marie possessed three new bottles of White Shoulders. When asked what she would do with so much cologne, she replied, "Oh, I might need it."

And then she laughed.

* * *

When her children became school aged, Marie followed her natural inclinations and reentered the workplace. Now that the Depression had eased, keeping up appearances mattered less. She started with a part-time job taking the census in 1940, going door to door in Knox County's Strawberry Plains community. Marie would introduce herself, ask the required questions, and note the replies, making friends along the way. Excited about her experiences, she related them to her family in the evenings. She also worked as a substitute teacher, often finishing the school year for women on maternity leave. Marie flourished as an individual when she could engage with the world, drawing others to her lively personality and lack of pretense. While Knoxville's legal professionals knew Earl, Marie had a wide range of friends and acquaintances, from the neighbors, to her church congregation, to the women at the beauty parlor, to her fellow educators. This last group ranged from the other substitutes to Knox County Superintendent Mildred Doyle.

As Earl's amount of legal work increased, the family's financial state solidified and his previous ambitions returned. Although he had failed in his campaign for state senator, by the late thirties Earl had another political goal: to become a Knox County General Sessions Court judge. After a five-year struggle over the concept, Knoxville began the steps needed to institute a sessions court system, essentially a small-claims court. Earl joined twelve other candidates in vying to be appointed as one of the three judges. Those selected would have an advantage in the next step, election to a two-year post. A second election would decide who won the final, eight-year positions. When he failed to be named one of the original appointees, Earl ran for the two-year term. Neither attempt came to fruition.

Soon afterward, he wrote a letter to the editor of the *Knoxville News Sentinel*, calling out "lawless elements ... making their influence felt in our elections." If more law-abiding citizens didn't vote, Earl claimed, criminals would "eventually dominate us politically and destroy our democracy."

Then he asserted a pastor's right to free speech, stating that ministers could persuade their congregations to vote in order to counter "the efforts of organized law violators."[521] Most likely Marie contributed the idea that ministers could sway the actions of Knoxvillians, but the letter didn't just reveal the couple's disappointment at Earl's loss. The system of vote-rigging prevalent in the city during earlier decades still existed and would extend into the following decade.[522]

Political rivalries had always flourished in Knoxville, but the battles of the 1940s showed remarkable animosity, being "narrow, parochial, visionless—and ugly."[523] The city's different factions hammered each other with much more effort than they spent guiding the city.[524] Earl misjudged the situation if he believed that he could seek political office but not be drawn into the muck. The rivalries burned intensely and never more so than when his Sevier County buddy, Cas Walker, was elected Knoxville mayor. Within the year, Cas was ousted in a brutally contested recall vote.[525] One of Knoxville's most influential politicians of the twentieth century, Cas's methods of countering his enemies lacked all nuance. Earl, of course, was a longtime associate of the grocery store tycoon.

This political turmoil eventually ensnared Earl. The trouble stemmed from his ongoing practice of buying debt and getting what cash he could from the creditors. In this case, two investors funded his purchase of assets from the East Tennessee National Bank, which had collapsed early in the Depression. Earl planned to eke money from the debt, then split the profits with the investors. He didn't realize that some of the claims were ineligible for collection because they had already been foreclosed on or had judgments against them. When Earl tried to collect the debt, he was charged in federal court with four counts of making false claims.[526]

Whether politically motivated, stemming from an error in judgment on Earl's part, or a combination of the two, this lawsuit threatened all his achievements. A guilty verdict would be devastating to his livelihood and reputation. Guilt must be proven, however, and some viewed the lawsuit against Earl with skepticism. At one point during the trial, Judge George C. Taylor questioned the prosecuting US district attorney, asking, "Don't you think this evidence is a little fine-strung to send a man to prison?"[527]

That potential inmate was Earl.

The two-day trial proved exhausting and illuminating. Earl's testimony and the prosecution's cross-examination lasted a grueling three hours. Afterward, his defense attorney called several character witnesses on his behalf. An account of the trial reported that "a cross section of Who's Who in Knoxville" testified to Earl's "good character" and "reputation." United States Senator E. B. Bowles and two sitting judges vouched for him, one from Circuit Court and one from the Juvenile and Domestic Relations Court. These judges knew Earl's professional ethics since his legal cases frequently took him into their courtrooms. In addition, former Knoxville mayor, councilman, and state senator, E. E. Patton,[528] who was known to be one of Cas Walker's supporters,[529] testified to the defendant's upstanding character.

Earl's support ranged beyond legal and political figures. Having been married to him for over a decade, Marie knew her husband. He might refuse payment from a client or lose money in a business deal, but he would never cheat or lie to make a buck. Outraged over the unfairness of the charges and confident of the moral stance she represented, Marie attended every minute of the trial.[530] As much as possible, she ensured that her husband did not face the ordeal alone.

With their futures at risk, waiting while the judge deliberated must have been awful for the couple.

Finally, the verdict was announced. The prosecution was found to have insufficient evidence, which cleared Earl of all charges. Relief flowed through him so intensely that he teared up while standing in the courtroom.[531] This uncharacteristic show of emotion revealed just how grim his experience had been. Marie completely understood. She cried openly in court after the announcement, then hugged her husband for all to see.[532] The couple had met serious adversity with a united front.

Interestingly, the trial caused Earl no long-term career damage. He practiced law in the city for years and eventually fulfilled his ambition of becoming a Knox County General Sessions Court judge. During his career on the bench, Earl showed compassion to the downtrodden and responded to wayward citizens with kindness, perhaps to a greater extent than they deserved. His candidacy announcement had noted that he had been on his own since age sixteen, a slight exaggeration that omitted his family's support. The claim revealed Earl's pride in being self-made, in forging a path in the city which had been unimaginable to him while growing up in East Tennessee's foothills.

EPILOGUE

WITH THE ATTACK ON PEARL HARBOR IN 1941, Knoxville and the rest of the United States barreled from the final years of the Depression straight into World War II. TVA's ability to produce electrical power proved crucial to the war effort. It fueled what became the city of Oak Ridge and the nearby nuclear facilities that played a decisive role in winning the conflict. The agency flourished, bringing more midlevel managers and engineers to Knoxville. Ultimately, the volume and outspokenness of these employees helped to temper the city's character.

Knoxville also changed in physical appearance as urban renewal projects that started in the thirties eventually decimated its shantytowns, wiped out most of the Bowery, and destroyed its Black neighborhoods. Evolving migration patterns also affected the city. When factories in America's Midwest started providing well-paying jobs, rural East Tennesseans moved there instead of nearby cities such as Knoxville. They continued to encounter systemic prejudice, however. Popular entertainment, the era's major force for cultural uniformity, ridiculed those from Appalachia wherever they lived even as these migrants spread out across America.

With so many newcomers arriving from outside the state, less regional influence to counter them, and no desire to exist outside of mainstream American culture, Knoxville's Appalachian character waned.

But the city was still home to decades of mountain transplants. Earl and Marie represent these residents who continued their contributions to the city's culture and economy, debunking the idea that Appalachian people only hindered progress. How much these Knoxvillians appreciated their cultural heritage depended on their character and experiences, with invariable fluctuations throughout their lives. Some came to appear completely urban, identifiable as in-migrants or their descendants only when willing to admit it. Others took pride in their twangy accent or fondness for beans and cornbread. Most tried to balance regional connections against the heavy power of mainstream American culture.

* * *

Earl and Marie eventually moved outside of Knoxville's suburbs to a place in the country. Marie worked as a substitute teacher and served as an election official at a time when few middle-class women worked outside the home. She planted a large garden that she tended herself, forever ensuring the quality of her dinner vegetables. Her eventual grandchildren adored their feisty Momma Layman who so memorably related her travels and adventures.

Earl served as a sessions court judge for more than a decade, ultimately possessing a Gay Street business address for over fifty years. He chose the farm that the couple moved to, with its pristine stream and rolling acres, hiring a man to muck out the barn and milk the cows. Earl named those cows, and many of them came to him when called. So did a gifted herding dog named Major.

Not surprisingly, the farm sat east of Knoxville, near the Sevier County line.

ENDNOTES

Chapter 1

1 "7 Ways to Increase Winter Comfort on the Farm," *Knoxville Journal and Tribune*, January 14, 1918, Newspapers.com, https://www.newspapers.com/image/585520962.

2 William Earl Layman, interview by David Creekmore, 1973, cassette recording owned by the author's family.

3 Mark T. Banker, *Appalachians All: East Tennesseans and the Elusive History of an American Region*, (Knoxville: University of Tennessee Press, 2010), 85.

4 Lucile Deaderick, ed., *Heart of the Valley: A History of Knoxville, Tennessee* (Knoxville: East Tennessee Historical Society, 1976), 146.

5 Throughout this book, descriptions of historic sites are based on past photographs, many of which can be found in the Calvin M. McClung Digital Collection. Some information on existing buildings in Knoxville is from *Historic Downtown Knoxville Walking Tour*, a free pamphlet produced in 2013 by Knox Heritage, which is now also available online.

6 "United States WWI Draft Registration Cards, 1917–1918," digital image s.v. "William Earl Layman," FamilySearch.com, https://www.familysearch.org/ark:/61903/1:1:KZ6K-4K3.

Chapter 2

7 "Alabama News," *Selma Times-Argus*, July 21, 1876, Newspapers.com, https://www.newspapers.com/image/355695913.

8 "1900 United States Federal Census," Blue Eye, Talladega, Alabama, digital image s.v. "J.L. Little," Ancestry.com, accessed on March 8, 2018, https://www.ancestry.com/search/collections/7602. Fayette Little's full name was Jonas Lafayette Little, and his profession was listed as "waterman."

9 1910 United States Federal Census," Phillips, Etowah, Alabama, digital image s.v. "Minnie Little," Ancestry.com, https://www.ancestry.com/search/collections/7884. At this time, Mary Little is five and "Gracie Little" seven. Minnie's full name was Mahulda McGriff Little.

10 Wayne Flint, *Poor But Proud: Alabama's Poor Whites* (Tuscaloosa: University of Alabama Press, 1989), 89.

11 Etowah County Board of Education, "Notes for 1920," Etowah County Board of Education Archives, Gadsden, Alabama; Mary Martha Thomas, *The New Woman in Alabama: Social Reforms and Suffrage, 1890–1920* (Tuscaloosa: The University of Alabama Press, 1992), 61. The board of education notes establish that Marie taught a five month school year in 1920-21. Thomas explains that this term length was standard across the state's rural areas.

12 Flint, *Poor But Proud*, 87.
13 Samuel L. Webb, *Two-Party Politics in the One-Party South* (Tuscaloosa: University of Alabama Press, 1997), 171.
14 Flint, *Poor But Proud*, 193.
15 "A True Friend," *Gadsden Daily Times-News*, January, 17, 1920, Newspapers.com, https://www.newspapers.com/image/322633040.

Chapter 3

16 Russell Harrison, *Progressive Knoxville 1904: A Pictorial Review of the City* (Knoxville: Russell Harrison, 1903), np., quoted in William Bruce Wheeler, *Knoxville, Tennessee: A Mountain City in the New South*, 3rd ed. (Knoxville: University of Tennessee Press, 2020), 1.
17 Clyde Beale and Robert Moorefield, "Drab Shantytown Has No Palaces But 'It's Better Than Up Yonder,'" *The Knoxville Journal*, July 7, 1934, Newspapers.com, https://www.newspapers.com/image/586453300/. Knoxville papers did not furnish detailed descriptions of the city's riverside shantytowns until the mid-1930s.
18 Sonborn Map Company, *Map of Congested District: Knoxville, Tennessee Sections 13, 21 and 22*, 1917, 220 feet per 1 inch scale, 21 by 25 in., Sonborn Map Co.
19 David Creekmore, personal interview with the author, August 1, 2017.
20 William Bruce Wheeler, *Knoxville, Tennessee: A Mountain City in the New South*, 3rd ed. (Knoxville: University of Tennessee Press, 2020), 27; Mark V. Wetherington, "Streetcar City: Knoxville, Tennessee, 1876–1947," *East Tennessee History Society's Publications* 54 and 55 (1982–3), 74.
21 Wetherington, 73–4.
22 Wheeler, *Knoxville, Tennessee*, 27.
23 Banker, *Appalachians All*, 100.
24 Wheeler, Knoxville, Tennessee, 38.
25 Henry D. Shapiro, *Appalachia on Our Mind* (Chapel Hill: University of North Carolina Press, 1978), 18.
26 Mark Twain, *The Adventures of Huckleberry Finn* (New York: Penguin Books, 1884, 2014), 2.
27 Mary Murfree, *In the Tennessee Mountains*, 9th ed. (New York: Houghton Mifflin, 1885). Murfree published as a man, Charles Egbert Craddock, at a time when women writers were denied opportunities. After she became popular, the ruse was discovered and publicized.
28 J. W. Williamson, *Hillbillyland: What the Movies Did to the Mountains & What the Mountains Did to the Movies*, (Chapel Hill: University of North Carolina Press, 1995), 178–9.
29 ——, 180.
30 Cora Ogle, "A Job in the City," *Voices of the Land* (permanent exhibit, East Tennessee History Center, Knoxville, Tennessee).
31 Banker, *Appalachians All*, 14.
32 Wheeler, *Knoxville, Tennessee*, 26.
33 ——, 26.
34 Beulah D. Linn, "Jacob Layman-Revolutionary Soldier," *Sevier County News*, American Bicentennial Section, November 20, 1975, 23, ETHC Verticle File on Sevier County.
35 William Joseph Cummings III, "Community, Violence, and the Nature of Change: Whitecapping in Sevier County, Tennessee, During the 1890s," (master's thesis, University of Tennessee, 1988), 67, https://trace.tennessee.edu/utk_gradthes/8.
36 ——, "Community, Violence," 2.
37 ——, 76–7.
38 ——, 69–70.
39 ——, 1.
40 Wheeler, Knoxville, Tennessee, 2.

Chapter 4

41 Flint, *Poor But Proud*, 207.
42 Thomas, *The New Woman*, 14.
43 ——, 40.
44 ——, 31.
45 ——, 36.
46 Christine S. Pucket and Joe Barnes, *A Panorama of Northeast Alabama and Etowah County* (Gadsden: Starr Publishing, 1992), 69.
47 Etowah County Centennial Committee, *The History of Etowah County, Alabama* (Berwyn Heights: Heritage Publishing Consultants, 1968), 111.
48 Thomas, *The New Woman*, 38.
49 ——, 31.
50 ——, 14.
51 ——, 21.
52 W. L. Deal, "Poor Benny (Come Home, Father)," recorded in Heber Springs, Arkansas, July 16, 1953, MP3 published online by the John Quincy Wolf Folklore Collection, Lyon College, 2002, https://home.lyon.edu/wolfcollection/songs/deallittle1234.html. The unofficial anthem of the Women's Christian Temperance Union, several folklore collections contain variations of this song. The original version, "Come Home, Father" by Henry Clay Work, was published 1864.
53 Flint, *Poor But Proud*, 207.
54 ——, 115, 207–8.

Chapter 5

55 "United States WWI Draft Registration Cards."
56 Reese T. Amis, *Knox County in the World War 1917-1918-1919* (Knoxville: Knoxville Lithographing Company, 1919), https://hdl.handle.net/2027/loc.ark:/13960/t8mc9kc6n.
57 ——.
58 Jack Neely, "Knoxville during the Great War" (lecture, Knox Heritage, Knoxville, TN, February 2018).
59 Louisa Trott, "The Great War in Tennessee's Newspapers" (lecture, East Tennessee History Society, Knoxville, May 16, 2018).
60 "No Prospect of Sex War," *Knoxville Independent*, October 26, 1918, Chronicling America: Historic American Newspapers, Library of Congress, https://chroniclingamerica.loc.gov/lccn/sn85042907/1918-10-26/ed-1/seq-8/.
61 Betsey Beeler Creekmore, *Knoxville!* (Knoxville: East Tennessee Historical Society 1991), 147.
62 ——, 148.
63 Neely, "Great War."
64 Trott, "The Great War."
65 "Must Use Less Sugar, Allied Needs Grow." *Knoxville Independent*, October 12, 1918, Newspapers.com, https://www.newspapers.com/image/352051391.
66 E. L. Bishop quoted in Dave Tabler, "The Great Pandemic of 1918, Part I," AppalachianHistory.net, posted October 9, 2017, https://www.appalachianhistory.net/2017/10/great-pandemic-of-1918-part-1.html.
67 ——.
68 Robert Booker, "Opinion: Flu Epidemic of 1918 Took a Toll in Knoxville," KnoxNews.com, posted March 5, 2018, https://www.knoxnews.com/story/opinion/columnists/robert-booker/2018/03/05/opinion-flu-epidemic-1918-took-toll-knoxville/390038002/.
69 Vincent Gabrielle, "Past Pandemics in Knoxville Have Led to Stark Political Choices – with Deadly Consequences," KnoxNews.com, posted June 2, 2020, https://www.knoxnews.com/story/news/health/2020/06/02/past-pandemics-knoxville-have-led-real-consequences-coronavirus/5089850002/.

70 Neely, "Great War."

71 Gabrielle, "Past Pandemics."

72 Booker, "Flu Epidemic."

73 "Temperance Notes," *Knoxville Independent*, November 16, 1918, Newspapers.com, https://www.newspapers.com/image/352051924/.

74 Creekmore, interview.

75 W. Calvin Dickinson, "Temperance," Tennessee Encyclopedia, last modified March 1, 2018, https://tennesseeencyclopedia.net/entries/temperance/.

76 "Wildcat Booze Flows Freely," *Knoxville Journal and Tribune*, January 10, 1918, Newspapers.com, https://www.newspapers.com/image/585520763.

77 ——.

78 "'Moonshine' has the Call," *Knoxville Journal and Tribune*, January, 10 1918, Newspapers.com, https://www.newspapers.com/image/585520758.

79 Creekmore, interview.

80 William Earl Layman, interview.

81 "To Make Fight on Moonshine," *Knoxville Journal and Tribune*, January 25, 1918, Newspapers.com, https://www.newspapers.com/image/585521390.

82 Wheeler, *Knoxville, Tennessee*, 27.

83 "Court Loses 'Likker,'" *Greeneville Daily Sun*, September 28, 1918, Chronicling America: Historic American Newspapers, Library of Congress, https://chroniclingamerica.loc.gov/lccn/sn97065122/1918-09-28/ed-1/seq-4/.

84 William Earl Layman, interview.

85 "Peter Nichols Near Death Door was Shot Twice by Highwaymen," *Knoxville Journal and Tribune*, February 23, 1918, Newspapers.com, https://www.newspapers.com/image/585522291.

86 William Earl Layman, interview.

87 "3 Arrests in Nichols Case," *Knoxville Journal and Tribune*, February 27, 1918, Newspapers.com, https://www.newspapers.com/image/585522443.

88 ——.

89 "Knoxville Boy Escapes Prison," *Knoxville Journal and Tribune*, November 27, 1917, Newspapers.com, https://www.newspapers.com/image/585415933.

90 "Tells Story of Nichols' Assault," *Knoxville Journal and Tribune*, April 24, 1918, Newspapers.com, https://www.newspapers.com/image/585384062.

91 "Fellows Brothers Deny Shooting Merchant," *Chattanooga News*, April 25, 1918, Chronicling America: Historic American Newspapers, Library of Congress, https://chroniclingamerica.loc.gov/lccn/sn85038531/1918-04-25/ed-1/seq-3/.

92 "Nichols's Friends Aid in Manhunt," *Knoxville Journal and Tribune*, February 25, 1918, Newspapers.com, https://www.newspapers.com/image/585522367.

93 "Lawyer Says Fellows Got New Overcoat in Vain Effort to Escape Conviction," *Knoxville News Sentinel*, December 8, 1934, Newspapers.com, https://www.newspapers.com/image/772619696. There is a slight chance that the coat switch takes place during the retrial.

94 ——.

95 "From all Parts of Tennessee," *Knoxville Independent*, May 4, 1918, Newspapers.com, https://www.newspapers.com/image/352046655.

96 "Five Escape from County Jail; Posse Hunting for Fugitives," *Knoxville Sentinel*, September 14, 1918, Newspapers.com, https://www.newspapers.com/image/586817306.

97 ——.

98 "Ehude Fellows, Whose Life Wrapped Up Secrets of Local and World Violence, Ends It as New 'Break" as Author Begins to Open for Him," *Knoxville News Sentinel*, March 26, 1939, 7, Newspapers.com, https://www.newspapers.com/image/772783909.

99 "Two Prisoners are Recaptured," *Knoxville Journal and Tribune*, September 28, 1918, Newspapers.com, https://www.newspapers.com/image/585523251.
100 "Jury Hard to Get," *Memphis News Scimitar*, April 4, 1919, Chronicling America: Historic American Newspapers, Library of Congress, https://chroniclingamerica.loc.gov/lccn/sn98069867/1919-04-04/ed-1/seq-12/.
101 "Murder in First Degree," *Chattanooga News*, April 5, 1919, Chronicling America: Historic American Newspapers, Library of Congress, https://chroniclingamerica.loc.gov/lccn/sn85038531/1919-04-05/ed-1/seq-5/.

Chapter 6
102 In Marie's newspaper columns, a staggering number of names refer to communities where the Littles lived. This reveals the frequency of family relocations and perhaps Marie's attempt to disguise the number of columns she sent to the Gadsden paper.
103 "Ohatchee R. 1," *Gadsden Daily Times-News*, April 18, 1919, Newspapers.com, https://www.newspapers.com/clip/93454198/horace-freeman-kodaking-near-ohatchee/.
104 "Ohatchee Route 1," *Gadsden Daily Times-News*, May 8, 1919, Newspapers.com, https://www.newspapers.com/image/322712977; and "Gadsden Route 1," *Gadsden Daily Times-News*, May 10, 1919, Newspapers.com, https://www.newspapers.com/image/322713455. The first reference is Marie's article, and the second is Grace's. The author does not document the many similar columns referred to unless they are quoted or contain important information not found elsewhere. They can be found by running name searches on Newspapers.com.
105 "Rural Children Pass Seventh Grade Exams," *Gadsden Daily Times-News*, May 12, 1919, Newspapers.com, https://www.newspapers.com/image/322713480/. Only two of those seventy-three children were Black.
106 Flint, *Poor But Proud*, 193.
107 Marie L. Layman, letter to Sylvia Layman, January 25, 1982.
108 Edwin C. Bridges, *Alabama: The Making of an American State* (Tuscaloosa: University of Alabama press, 2016), 138.
109 Webb, *Two-Party Politics*, 171.
110 —, 171.
111 —, 172–3.
112 —, 172–3.
113 Bridges, *Alabama*, 156, 157.
114 Thomas, *The New Woman*, 40.
115 —, 9.
116 —, 208, 215.
117 Lorraine Gates Schuyler, *The Weight of Their Votes: Southern Women and Political Leverage in the 1920s* (Chapel Hill: University of North Carolina Press, 2006), 8.
118 Doris Anita Little Gerra, *My Little, Steward (Stewart) Ancestors of the Southern States and Allied Lines 1670–1997* (Kensington, MD: self-pub., 1997), 17.
119 —, 17.
120 Bridges, *Alabama*, 174.
121 —, 174.
122 —, 175.
123 —, 175.
124 "South's Women Ask for United Lynching Fight," *Knoxville News-Sentinel*, January 10, 1934, Newspapers.com, https://www.newspapers.com/image/772725145.
125 Flint, *Poor but Proud*, 70.
126 "Rural Children Pass."
127 Bridges, *Alabama*, 172.

128 Paul S. Boyer et al., *The Enduring Vision: A History of the American People*, 7th ed. (Boston: Wadsworth, 2011), 643.
129 ——, 660.
130 Rehagen, "Forgotten Lessons."
131 ——.
132 "The Negro Migration," *Gadsden Daily Times-News*, May 10, 1923, Newspapers.com, https://www.newspapers.com/image/571693879.
133 ——.
134 Bridges, *Alabama*, 172.
135 William J. Collins and Marianne H. Wanamaker, "The Great Migration in Black and White: New Evidence on the Selection and Sorting of Southern Migrants," *The Journal of Economic History* 75, no. 4 (December 2015): 979, https://doi.org/10.1017/S0022050715001527.

Chapter 7

136 John Kyle Thomas, "The Cultural Reconstruction of an Appalachian City: Knoxville, Tennessee, and the Coming of the Movies," *The Journal of East Tennessee History*, no. 65 (1993): 43, https://www.familysearch.org/library/books/records/item/32177-the-journal-of-east-tennessee-history-a-publication-of-the-east-tennessee-historical-society-no-65-1993?offset=6.
137 ——, "Cultural Reconstruction," 43.
138 Sonborn Map, section 13.
139 ——. Shortly before, Charles Street had been renamed from Marble Alley.
140 *Knoxville City Directory* (1924), s.v. "Layman, W. Earl," East Tennessee History Center.
141 *Knoxville City Directory* (1920), s.v. "Layman, Earl, W." East Tennessee History Center.
142 "All Knoxville Is Glorifying over Victory," *Knoxville Sentinel*, November 11, 1918, Newspapers.com, https://www.newspapers.com/image/586774034.
143 ——.
144 "Thousands in Victory Parade," *Knoxville Sentinel*, November 12, 1918, Newspapers.com, https://www.newspapers.com/image/586774261.
145 ——.
146 Neely, "Great War."
147 "Lieut. Wright Cables," November 13, 1918, *Knoxville News Sentinel*, Newspapers.com, https://www.newspapers.com/image/586774502.
148 Amis, *Knox County*.
149 "Tennessee's Valiant Heroes Made History on Battlefield," *Knoxville Sentinel*, March 29, 1919, Newspapers.com, https://www.newspapers.com/image/586653920.
150 Steven Trout, "'Where Do We Go from Here?': Ernest Hemingway's 'Soldier's Home' and American Veterans of World War I (2)," *The Hemingway Review* 20, no.1, (Fall 2000): 3, https://link.gale.com/apps/doc/A68506412/AONE?u=anon~ff3a91d1&sid=googleScholar&xid=26ca4b86.
151 ——, "Where Do We Go," 3.
152 Peter Perl, "Race Riot of 1919 Gave Glimpse of Future Struggles," *Washington Post*, March 1, 1999, https://www.washingtonpost.com/wp-srv/local/2000/raceriot0301.htm.
153 ——, "Race Riot."
154 ——, "Race Riot."
155 Ken Armstrong, "The 1919 Race Riots," *Chicago Tribune*, July 12, 2018, http://trib.in/1TJLF6V.
156 ——, "Race Riots."
157 Boyer et al., *The Enduring Vision*, 691.

158 W.E.B. Du Bois, "Let Us Reason Together," *Crisis* 18, no. 5 (September 1919): 231, https://www.marxists.org/history/usa/workers/civil-rights/crisis/0900-crisis-v18n05-w107.pdf.

159 Wheeler, *Knoxville*, Tennessee, 34.

160 "Thousands in Victory."

Chapter 8

161 Bridges, *Alabama*, 175.

162 Thomas, New Woman, 60.

163 Thomas, *New Woman*, 61.

164 ——, 61.

165 Flint, *Poor but Proud*, 87.

166 Thomas McAdory Owen, *History of Alabama and Dictionary of Alabama Biography* (Chicago: The S. J. Clarke Publishing Company, 1921), quoted in "Calhoun County History," Calhoun County Alabama, May 11, 2022, https://www.calhouncounty.org/history/. This was the case when the school was originally funded in the 1880s.

167 Marie often spoke to the author of attending Jacksonville Normal School. Her activities are not mentioned in the *Gadsden Daily Times-News* from October 1919 to September 1920, just before she begins her first teaching assignment. Thus she undoubtedly attended during that time. No Jacksonville Normal School records or era newspapers from Jacksonville, Alabama, are available.

168 Marie Little Layman, Letter to Sylvia Layman, January 25, 1982.

169 Bridges, *Alabama*, 176.

170 Owen, *History of Alabama*.

171 Layman, Letter to Sylvia.

172 Etowah County Board of Education, "Notes for 1920."

173 Thomas, *New Woman*, 55.

174 ——, 61. On pages 60 and 61, Thomas uses statistics from 1918.

175 Southside High School advanced placement senior English class, "Collection of Old Southside, Alabama," (unpublished manuscript, 1988–1989).

176 Layman, Letter to Sylvia. Details of Marie's mental state, solitary activities, and teaching situation during her first year of teaching are taken from this letter. Morgan's Cross Roads has since been renamed Rainbow City.

177 Etowah County Board of Education, "Notes for 1920."

178 "Etowah Teachers Successful in Examinations," *Gadsden Daily Times-News*, September 16, 1921, Newspapers.com, https://www.newspapers.com/image/322699675.

179 "Morgan's Cross Roads," *Gadsden Daily Times-News*, April 28, 1922, Newspapers.com, https://www.newspapers.com/image/322708683.

Chapter 9

180 William Earl Layman, interview.

181 Matthew Lakin, "'A Dark Night': The Knoxville Race Riot of 1919," *The Journal of East Tennessee History* 72, (2000): 1–29, 2, teachtnhistory.com.

182 Wheeler, *Knoxville, Tennessee*, 34.

183 ——, 34.

184 "Murder in First."

185 William Earl Layman, interview.

186 Lakin, "Dark Night," 8.

187 "Killed in Effort to Escape Negro," *Knoxville Journal and Tribune*, August 31, 1919, Newspapers.com, https://www.newspapers.com/image/585316455.

188 Daniel Okrent, *Last Call: The Rise and Fall of Prohibition* (New York: Scribner, 2011), 212.

189 Lakin, "Dark Night," 6.
190 William Earl Layman, interview Unless otherwise noted, further quotations about the 1919 riot are taken from this interview.
191 Lester C. Lamon, "Tennessee Race Relations and the Knoxville Riot of 1919," *The East Tennessee Historical Society's Publications* 41, (1969): 67–85, 77, teachtnhistory.com. Of the many sources that repeat the rumor about Mays's parentage, Lamon is the only one who provides documentation.
192 Lakin, "Dark Night," 7.
193 William Earl Layman, interview.
194 Lakin, "Dark Night," 17.
195 ——, 14.
196 William Earl Layman, interview.
197 "Damage to Jail May be $15,000," *Knoxville Sentinel*, September 1, 1919, Newspapers. com, https://www.newspapers.com/image/586674844.
198 Lamon, "Tennessee Race," 77.
199 William Earl Layman, interview.
200 Lamon, "Tennessee Race," 78; and "Known Casualties," *Knoxville Journal and Tribune*, September 1, 1919, Newspapers.com, https://www.newspapers.com/image/585317430.
201 "Damage to Jail."
202 Lakin, "Dark Night," 17.
203 "Two Defendants Are Freed in Riot Cases," *Knoxville Journal and Tribune*, October 22, 1919, Newspapers.com, https://www.newspapers.com/image/585393740.
204 "Judge Denounces Actions of Mob in Knoxville Riot," *Memphis News Scimitar*, September 5, 1919, 4th ed., Chronicling America: Historic American Newspapers, Library of Congress, https://chroniclingamerica.loc.gov/lccn/sn98069867/1919-09-05/ed-1/seq-13/.
205 Mary U. Rothrock, ed., *The French-Broad Holston Country* (Knoxville: East Tennessee Historical Society, 1946), 320, https://hdl.handle.net/2027/mdp.39015012076892.
206 William Earl Layman, interview.
207 Lakin, "Dark Night," 18.
208 "Bloody Riots Follow Attack on Jail; Five Known Dead; Many are Wounded," *Knoxville Journal and Tribune*, August 31, 1919, Newspapers.com, https://www.newspapers.com/image/585316455.
209 Lamon, "Tennessee Race," 83.
210 William Earl Layman, interview.
211 "Riot Situation in Knoxville Now Thought to Be Well in Hand," *Greeneville Daily Sun*, September 1, 1919, Chronicling America: Historic American Newspapers, Library of Congress, https://chroniclingamerica.loc.gov/lccn/sn97065122/1919-09-01/ed-1/seq-1/.
212 "Army Officer Is Killed in Race Riot," *Dillon Herald*, September 4, 1919, Newspapers. com, https://www.newspapers.com/image/354162531.
213 ——.
214 "Known Casualties."
215 William Earl Layman, interview; and Lakin, "A Dark Night," 24.
216 "Knoxville in Throes of Serious Race Riots," *Greeneville Daily Sun*, September 1, 1919, Chronicling America: Historic American Newspapers, Library of Congress, https://chroniclingamerica.loc.gov/lccn/sn97065122/1919-09-01/ed-1/seq-1/.
217 "State Guards Turn Machine Guns on Crowd," *Chattanooga News*, September 1, 1919, Chronicling America: Historic American Newspapers, Library of Congress, https://chroniclingamerica.loc.gov/lccn/sn85038531/1919-09-01/ed-1/seq-2/.
218 "Knoxville Has Riot," *Maryville Times*, September 3, 1919, Chronicling America: Historic American Newspapers, Library of Congress, https://chroniclingamerica.loc.gov/lccn/sn89058370/1919-09-03/ed-1/seq-1/.

219 "Knoxville Woman Is Attacked by Negro," *Memphis News Scimitar*, September 25, 1919, 4th ed., Chronicling America: Historic American Newspapers, Library of Congress, https://chroniclingamerica.loc.gov/lccn/sn98069867/1919-09-25/ed-1/seq-15/.

220 Lakin, "Dark Night," 27.

221 William Earl Layman, interview. All of Earl's quotations and opinions on Mays's innocence and trial are taken from the interview.

222 "Hard Blow at Law and Order," *Chattanooga News*, October 25, 1919, Chronicling America: Historic American Newspapers, Library of Congress, https://chroniclingamerica.loc.gov/lccn/sn85038531/1919-10-25/ed-1/seq-8/.

223 Lamon, "Tennessee Race," 84.

Chapter 10

224 "Burns Academy," *Gadsden Daily Times-News*, December 9, 1922, Newspapers.com, https://www.newspapers.com/image/322718314/; and "Cedar Bend High School to Close Thursday," *Gadsden Daily Times-News*, April 28, 1923, Newspapers.com, https://www.newspapers.com/image/571736442/. When Burns Academy was renamed, Marie apparently favored "Cedar Bend," the name of the affiliated church, over "Southside."

225 "There Is No Boy Problem. It Is a Man's Problem," *Gadsden Daily Times-News*, July 2, 1924, Newspapers.com, https://www.newspapers.com/image/571732143.

226 Etowah County Centennial Committee, *The History*, 121.

227 Etowah County Centennial Committee, *The History*, 121.

228 ——.

229 "Brannon Springs," *Gadsden Daily Times-News*, January 5, 1923, Newspapers.com, https://www.newspapers.com/image/571725186. Ninnie's illness is reported on January 19. Marie commented that Faye almost died of influenza, and that her best friend did so.

230 Etowah County Centennial Committee, *The History*, 120.

231 Pucket and Barnes, *A Panorama*, 70.

232 If Patsy and Jim didn't own a car by this time, they did soon afterward. Patricia endured so many drives to Alabama as a child that she remembered them years later. J. L. and Ninnie Little didn't own a radio until well into the 1930s, so it's doubtful that the car belonged to them.

233 Nathan Miller, *New World Coming: The Twenties and the Making of America* (New York: Scribner, 2003), 258.

234 Paul Bergeron, Steven Ash, and Jeanette Keith, *Tennesseans and Their History* (Knoxville: University of Tennessee Press, 1999), 242.

235 "South Side," *Gadsden Daily Times-News*, November 14, 1923, Newspapers.com, https://www.newspapers.com/image/571717911. Etowah County Board of Education records are missing from the 1923–24 school year, but Marie regularly noted her teaching activities in newspaper articles. Her wedding announcement in the *Gadsden Daily Times-News* specifies that she taught at Southside for three years.

236 "West Gadsden Items of News," *Gadsden Daily Times-News*, January 29, 1923, Newspapers.com, https://www.newspapers.com/image/571727087.

237 Marie mentioned the broken relationship caused by the boyfriend's family displeasure with her social status. Several details, including photographs, point to Clifford Johnson as that boyfriend.

Chapter 11

238 "An Old Time Fee-Grabber," *Knoxville Journal and Tribune*, September 27, 1924, Newspapers.com, https://www.newspapers.com/image/586077859.

239 Wetherington, "Streetcar City," 70; and Deaderick, *Heart of the Valley*, 228. While both sources cite a statistic of almost 20 million *riders*, the author has taken the liberty of phrasing the statistic as 20 million individual rides on the streetcar.

240 Wetherington, "Streetcar City," 100.

241 Robert J. Booker, "Knoxville Has Come Long Way from When It Had Just Six Principal Streets," *Knoxville News-Sentinel*, July 30, 2018, https://www.knoxnews.com/story/opinion/columnists/robert-booker/2018/07/30/knoxville-has-come-long-way-when-had-just-six-principal-streets-opinion/810590002/.

242 Sonborn Map Co., sections 21 and 22.

243 *Knoxville City Directory* (1921), s.v. "Layman, Earl," East Tennessee History Center; and *Knoxville City Directory* (1923), s.v. "Layman, W. Earl," East Tennessee History Center.

244 Earl Robert Layman, interview with the author, May 19, 2018.

245 "Story of Logan's Deeds and History of His Life," *Knoxville News-Sentinel*, June 29, 1903, Newspapers.com, https://www.newspapers.com/image/585641492/; and "Butch Cassidy Partner Earned Knoxville Notoriety," *Knoxville News-Sentinel*, August 15, 2001, https://archive.knoxnews.com/news/local/butch-cassidy-partner-earned-knoxville-notoriety-ep-403419960-357608011.html/. The policemen's names are detailed in the second story.

246 "Harvey Logan's Escape," *Knoxville News-Sentinel*, June 29, 1903, Newspapers.com, https://www.newspapers.com/image/585641515.

247 "Butch Cassidey Partner."

248 William Earl Layman, interview.

249 Wheeler, *Knoxville, Tennessee*, 49.

250 Kat Eschner, "The 1919 Black Sox Baseball Scandal Was Just One of Many," *Smithsonian Magazine*, September 1, 2017, https://www.smithsonianmag.com/smart-news/1919-black-sox-baseball-scandal-wasnt-first-180964673/.

251 Thomas, "Cultural Reconstruction," 51.

252 Williamson, *Hillbillyland*, 182.

253 Kevin Brownlow, *Hollywood: The Pioneers* (London: Collins, 1979), 119–20.

254 Thomas, "Cultural Reconstruction," 49.

255 ——, 42.

256 Brownlow, *Hollywood*, 117, 129.

257 Thomas, "Cultural Reconstruction," 38.

258 Creekmore, *Knoxville!*, 146.

259 Matt Lakin, "Crusade & Crash: Twenties Brought Corruption, Cleanup, Calamity," *Knoxville News-Sentinel*, March 25, 2012, https://archive.knoxnews.com/news/local/crusade--crash-twenties-brought-corruption-cleanup-calamity-ep-361042530-357121911.html/.

260 Deaderick, *Heart of the Valley*, 112.

261 Lakin, "Crusade & Crash."

262 Wheeler, *Knoxville, Tennessee*, 41.

Chapter 12

263 Miller, *New World*, 255.

264 Trout, "Where Do We Go," 2.

265 Miller, *New World*, 106.

266 Trout, "Where Do We Go," 2–3.

267   "Knowing the Presidents: Calvin Coolidge," Smithsonian, accessed December 10, 2020, https://si.edu/spotlight/calvin-coolidge.

268   W. M. Cobb, Chief, Personnel Division, Office of the Adjutant General, War Department, Personnel Record to Marie F. Little, June 23, 1924; from the Veteran's Affairs Agency, Personnel Sub-division Records and Files, National Archives at St. Louis, Missouri.

269   W. M. Cobb, Chief, Personnel Division, Office of the Adjutant General, War Department, Personnel Record to Marie F. Little, August 21, 1924; from the Veteran's Affairs Agency, Personnel Sub-division Records and Files, National Archives at St. Louis, Missouri.

270   Tom Lewis, *Washington: A History of Our National City* (New York: Basic Books, 2015), 307.

271   —.

272   United States Veterans Bureau, "Resignation, Marie F. Little," Washington, DC, October 13, 1924, National Archives. This resignation took effect on October 29, 1924.

273   "Little-McDill," *Gadsden Times*, October 27, 1924, Newspapers.com, https://www.newspapers.com/image/571740276. The notice of the sisters' return to Gadsden ran on the same page as Grace and Ed's wedding announcement. Why Grace left Alabama days before her wedding is a mystery.

274   Etowah County Board of Education, "Notes for 1924/1925," Etowah County Board of Education Archives, Gadsden, Alabama.

275   —.

276   Etowah County Heritage Book Committee, *The Heritage of Etowah County, Alabama* (Berwyn Heights: Heritage Publishing Consultants, 1999), 18.

277   "Robertson, Patricia," obituaries, *Washington Post*, November 24, 1976.

278   Lewis, *Washington*, 317.

279   —, 305.

280   Miller, *New World*, 262.

281   Wheeler, *Knoxville, Tennessee*, 55.

Chapter 13

282   Gary Garth, "Deep in the Smokies a Prize Catch," *USA Today*, May 27, 2016, https://pressreader.com/usa/usa-today-us-edition/.20160527/282355448989029.

283   Shelley Smith Mastran, Nan Lowerre, and United States Forest Service, *Mountaineers and Rangers: A History of the Federal Forest Management in the Southern Appalachians, 1900–1981* (Washington, DC: US Department of Agriculture, Forest Service, 1983), 85, https://hdl.handle.net/2027/uva.x001867535.

284   Deaderick, *Heart of the Valley*, 55.

285   Bergeron et al., *Tennesseans*, 239.

286   Vic Weals, "Home Folks," *Knoxville Journal*, September 18, 1955, East Tennessee History Center vertical file.

287   Bobby Eugene Hicks, "The Great Objector: The Life and Public Career of Dr. John R. Neal," *East Tennessee Historical Society Publications* 41, (1969): 35, East Tennessee History Center biography file.

288   Bert Vincent, "Strolling," *Knoxville News-Sentinel*, November 29, 1959, East Tennessee History Center biography file.

289   Hicks, "Great Objector," 41.

290   Luis Ruuska, "The Law Professor Who Rarely Bathed, Got Fired from U.T., and Was Lead Counsel in the Scopes Monkey Trial," University of Tennessee College of Law, January 16, 2016, https://law.utk.edu/2016/01/12/neal/.

291   Wheeler, *Knoxville, Tennessee*, 54.

292 Sarah Cansler, "Stamp Out This Awful Cancer: The Fear of Radicals, Atheists, and Modernism at the University of Tennessee in the 1920s," *Journal of East Tennessee History* 85, (2013): 50.

293 "Law Students Threaten to Quit," *Knoxville News-Sentinel*, July 11, 1923, Newspapers.com, https://www.newspapers.com/image/771843662.

294 "To Continue Fight on Morgan Policy," *Knoxville News-Sentinel*, July 18, 1923, Newspapers.com, https://www.newspapers.com/image/771844128.

295 "Rally around Dr. John R. Neal," *Knoxville News*, July 4, 1923, Newspapers.com, https://www.newspapers.com/image/771842972.

296 "Morgan Policy."

297 Elisabeth Williams, "For Love of the Fight: John R. Neal," *Rhea Notes* 19, no 4. (November 2, 2010): 5, East Tennessee History Center biography file.

298 Barbara Winick Bernstein, telephone interview with the author, 2017.

299 Wendy Lowe Besmann, *A Separate Circle: Jewish Life in Knoxville, Tennessee* (Knoxville: University of Tennessee Press, 2001), 56.

300 Hicks, "The Great Objector," 45

301 Creekmore, interview.

302 Williams, "For Love," 5.

303 Hicks, "Great Objector," 61.

304 Earl Robert Layman, *From the Emmental to Eldee: A History of the Layman Family* (Baltimore: Gateway Press, 2001), 218; and "Judge W. E. Layman," obituaries, *Knoxville News-Sentinel*, October 1974. Mr. Layman, oldest son of William Earl, also recalled his father saying that he tutored with Neal before the law school formally opened.

305 "Judge E. G. Stooksbury, Knox Jurist, Dies at 69," *Knoxville News-Sentinel*, July 9, 1948, East Tennessee History Center vertical file.

306 Bergeron et al., *Tennesseans*, 252.

307 Miller, *New World*, 245.

308 "Dr. Neal, Figure in Trial Dies," *Knoxville News-Sentinel*, November 23, 1959, East Tennessee History Center Bibliography File.

309 Hicks, "Great Objector," 62.

310 ——, 62.

311 ——, 47.

312 "Public Invited to Hear Darrow," *Knoxville News-Sentinel*, June 20, 1925, Newspapers.com, https://www.newspapers.com/image/772674785.

313 Cansler, "Stamp Out," 50.

314 "Public Invited."

315 Williams, "For Love," 5.

316 Hicks, "Great Objector," 45.

317 Ruuska, "Law Professor."

318 Layman, *From the Emmental*, 218.

Chapter 14

319 *Gadsden City Directory* (1927), s.v. "Little, Marie." Her parents continued to live in Southside, as confirmed by Jonas Lafayette Little's 1930 census records.

320 Miller, *New World*, 255.

321 "Gadsden Business Woman Visit Anniston," *Anniston Star*, November 19, 1926, Newspapers.com, https://www.newspapers.com/image/101798998.

322 Ronald Allen Goldberg, *America in the Twenties* (Syracuse: Syracuse University Press, 2003), 165.

323 Miller, *New World*, 255.

324 ——, 258.

325 Goldberg, *America*, 166.
326 Amy McRary, "The 1920s brought Park Dreams, Court Drama and the Theater," *Knoxville News-Sentinel*, February 2, 2017, https://www.knoxnews.com/story/life/arts/2017/02/25/papers-pixels-1920s-brought-park-dreams-court-drama-and-new-theater-knoxville/98211566/.
327 Lyle Saxton, *Fabulous New Orleans* (New York: The Century Company, 1928), 255–66.
328 New Orleans home: ——, 255.
329 Susan Scott Parrish, "The Great Mississippi Flood of 1927 Laid Bare the Divide Between the North and the South," *Smithsonian Magazine*, April 11, 2017, https://www.smithsonianmag.com/history/devastating-mississippi-river-flood-uprooted-americas-faith-progress-180962856/.
330 ——.
331 Saxton, *Fabulous*, 261–2.
332 ——, 264–5.
333 ——, 263.
334 Justin Nystrom, "The Vanished World of the New Orleans Longshoreman," *Southern Spaces*, March 5, 2014, https://southernspaces.org/2014/vanished-world-new-orleans-longshoreman/.

Chapter 15
335 "Bar Examination Passed by Many," *Knoxville Journal*, August 11, 1925, Newspapers.com, https://www.newspapers.com/image/586306608.
336 *Knoxville City Directory* (1926), s.v. "Layman, W. Earl," East Tennessee History Center.
337 Miller, *New World*, 281.
338 Bernstein, interview.
339 Wendy Lowe Besmann, *A Separate Circle: Jewish Life in Knoxville, Tennessee* (Knoxville: University of Tennessee Press, 2001), 45, 56.
340 ——, 59.
341 David Kyvig, *Daily Life in the United States, 1920–1940: How Americans Lived Through the Roaring Twenties and the Great Depression* (Chicago: Ivan R. Dee Publisher, 2004), 214–5.
342 Miller, *New World*, 334.
343 "Your First Move, Johnson City," *Knoxville News*, March 11, 1926, Newspapers.com, https://www.newspapers.com/image/772676095.
344 ——.
345 ——.
346 ——.
347 Bernstein, interview.
348 Miller, *New World*, 101.
349 Okrent, *Last Call*, 211.
350 ——.
351 Malcolm Cowley, *Exile's Return* (New York: Penguin, 1994), quoted in Okrent, 207.
352 Okrent, 207.
353 John Burnham, *Bad Habits* (New York: NYU Press, 1993), 37, quoted in Okrent, 213.
354 Okrent, 213.
355 When Earl bought this car is a matter of conjecture. He owned it by 1931, however, and logically bought it before the stock market crash.
356 Wetherington, "Streetcar City," 101.

PART II
Chapter 16

357 Jack Neely, *From the Shadow Side: and other stories of Knoxville, Tennessee* (Oak Ridge: Tellico Books, 2003), 163.

358 "Come to Make Records," East Tennessee History Center exhibit, September 2016.

359 Kyvig, *Daily Life*, 202.

360 Tim Sharp, *Images of America: Knoxville Music Before Bluegrass* (Charleston: Arcadia Publishing, 2020), 67.

361 "Make Records."

362 Sharp, *Images*, 68.

363 "Make Records."

364 Paul K. Conkin, "Evangelicals, Fugitives and Hillbillies," in *Tennessee History: The Land, the People and the Culture*, ed. Carroll Van West (Knoxville: University of Tennessee Press, 2001), 311.

365 "Make Records."

366 Lynda Childers Shuffridge, "Draughon School of Business (Little Rock)," in *Encyclopedia of Arkansas* (2005), s.v. "Draughon School."

367 *The Draughon Business College*, promotional brochure, circa 1929.

368 Kyvig, *Daily Life*, 133.

369 —.

370 Miller, *New World*, 262.

371 —, 261.

372 Kyvig, *Daily Life*, 96.

373 Deaderick, *Heart*, 469.

374 Jack Neely, *The Tennessee Theatre: A Grand Entertainment Palace* (Knoxville: Historic Tennessee Theatre Foundation, 2015).

375 Deaderick, *Heart*, 469.

376 "Dodd, Bobby," Tennessee Sports Hall of Fame, accessed March 30, 2019, https:www.tshf.net/halloffame/dodd-bobby/.

Chapter 17

377 That Marie lied about her family circumstances during the trip to the Layman farm is conjecture. Certainly she did so around this time, however. The author bases much of this scene on photographs.

378 "News of Society," *Gadsden Daily Times-News*, undated hard copy clipping, 6. An internet search reveals that a line of text on the back is from a February 19, 1929, wire service article. This wedding announcement specifies that the couple drove to Key West. How the car arrived in Miami remains a mystery, but it could have been shipped to Cuba and then back to the mainland.

379 "W.E. Layman Weds," *Knoxville News-Sentinel*, February 24, 1929, NewsBank.

380 "News of Society."

381 *Cuba*, Peninsular and Occidental Steamship Company flyer, USA, 1929, 14. While Marie often mentioned that her honeymoon took place in Cuba, she rarely gave details. Except for the necklace, the description reflects those in era promotional materials.

382 —, 10.

383 "Florida, US, Arriving and Departing Passenger and Crew Lists, 1898–1963," digital image s.v., "Warren Layman" traveling, February 28, 1929, Ancestry.com, https://www.ancestry.com/search/collections/8842. "Warren," used as Earl's middle name, will show up again on a birth certificate.

384 *Cuba*, 6.

385 Kyvig, *Daily Life*, 211–2.

386 Deaderick, *Heart*, 60.

Chapter 18

387 ——.
388 ——, 372-73.
389 Kyvig, *Daily Life*, 218.
390 "Inventory Is Made of Bank of Tennessee," *Knoxville News-Sentinel*, November 12, 1930, NewsBank.
391 Wheeler, *Knoxville, Tennessee*, 57.
392 "Depositors Crowd about Closed Bank," *Knoxville News-Sentinel*, November 12, 1930, NewsBank.
393 Wheeler, *Knoxville, Tennessee*, 57.
394 "Charges Hurled as Robbery Is Aired," *Knoxville News-Sentinel*, January 15, 1930, NewsBank.
395 "Miller Out on Own Word in 'Fixing Case,'" *Knoxville News-Sentinel*, January 18, 1930, NewsBank.
396 "Charges Hurled."
397 "Miller Out."
398 "Charges Hurled."
399 "Fire Captain Is Bound Over," *Knoxville Journal*, January 16, 1930, NewsBank.
400 "Miller Out."
401 "Fire Captain." William Earl Layman was the only attorney in Knoxville at the time with the last name of "Layman."
402 Kyvig, *Daily Life*, 161.
403 *Knoxville City Directory* (1932), s.v. "Layman, W. Earl," East Tennessee History Center.
404 Earl Robert Layman, interview.
405 Miller, *New World*, 263.
406 ——, 263-4.
407 Kyvig, *Daily Life*, 136.
408 "Girl's Admission Frees 3 Youths," *Knoxville News-Sentinel*, September 9, 1934, NewsBank.
409 "Girl's Admission."
410 Laura Still, *A Haunted History of Knoxville* (Asheville: Stony River Media, 2014), 132-3.

Chapter 19

411 Harold Bierman, "The 1929 Stock Market Crash," EH.Net, March 26, 2008, http://eh.net/encyclopedia/the-1929-stock-market-crash/.
412 Kyvig, *Daily Life*, 209.
413 Miller, *New World*, 383.
414 Lewis, *Washington*, 329.
415 ——, 331-2.
416 Creekmore, *Knoxville!*, 148.
417 Mastran and Lowerre, "Mountaineers and Rangers," 117.
418 ——, 118.
419 ——, 117.
420 "History," Great Smoky Mountains National Park, accessed May 7, 2019, https://www.gsmnp.com/great-smoky-mountains-national-park/history/.
421 Nancy Pottishman Weiss, "Mother, the Invention of Necessity: Dr. Benjamin *Spock's Baby and Child Care*," *American Quarterly* 29, no. 5 (Winter 1977): 524-5, https://doi.org/10.2307/2712572.
422 Nicholas Day, "I'm Supposed to Do *What* to Make My Baby Poop? When He's *How* Old," Slate, April 16, 2013, https://slate.com/human-interest/2013/04/history-of-early-toilet-training-advice.html.
423 Weiss, "Mother," 530.

424 Watson in Weiss, 530–1.

425 Spock in Weiss, 352.

426 Ruuska, "The Law Professor."

427 Williams, "For Love," 6.

428 David E. Whisnant, *Modernizing the Mountaineer: People, Power, and Planning in Appalachia* (Knoxville: The University of Tennessee Press, 1994), 47.

429 Aaron D. Purcell, "Suppressed Currents: The 'Fool Report' and the Early Tennessee Valley Authority," *Journal of East Tennessee History* 74, (2002): 73.

430 Morgan in Whisnant, *Modernizing the Mountaineer*, 277.

431 Purcell, "Suppressed Currents," 73, 75.

Chapter 20

432 Wheeler, *Knoxville, Tennessee*, 57.

433 —.

434 "Women Cite 5 Needs of City," *Knoxville News-Sentinel*, May 22, 1936, NewsBank.

435 Wheeler, *Knoxville, Tennessee*, 58.

436 Beale and Moorefield, "Drab Shantytown."

437 "'Please Old Santy, Bring us a Hydrant' Is Plea of Shanty Town," *Knoxville News-Sentinel*, December 13, 1935, NewsBank.

438 "Say Menace of Street Women Grows; Committees Push Workhouse Plan," *Knoxville News-Sentinel*, January 11, 1934, NewsBank.

439 "Says Farmers Fire Woods to Keep CCC Youths Away," *Knoxville News-Sentinel*, March 22, 1934, NewsBank.

440 Wheeler, Knoxville, Tennessee, 58.

441 Wheeler, *Knoxville, Tennessee*, 59–60.

442 Robert S. McElvaine, *The Great Depression: America*, 1929–1941 (New York: Three Rivers Press, 2009), 172.

443 —, 175.

444 Cas Walker, *My Life History* (self-pub., 1993), 120.

445 Earl Robert Layman, interview. Cas told the watermelon story to Robert Earl at William Earl's funeral.

446 "1910 United States Federal Census," Sevier County, Tennessee, Civil District 3, digital image s.v., "Thomas I. Walker," Ancestry.com, https://www.ancestry.com/search/collections/7884. Thomas's 1910 census says he lives on Newport Road, while Sally Layman's 1910 census places her farm in Sevier County, Civil District 3, at the East Fork & Newport Roads. The same census places Charles I. Walker, see two citations further, on East Fork Road in the same county and district.

447 Will of J. M. Layman, February 11, 1908, *Will Book II Sevier Co, Tennessee*, transcribed by Lori Ann McKeehan, (Sevier County Genealogical Society, 2002), 157.

448 "1910 United States Federal Census," Sevier County, Tennessee, Civil District 3, digital image s.v., "Charles I. Walker," Ancestry.com, https://www.ancestry.com/search/collections/7884. The Sevier Country 1880 U.S. Census of John L. Walker proves that Charles and Thomas were brothers. Several Ancestry family trees claim that the "L." in John Walker's name stood for "Layman."

449 Earl Robert Layman, interview.

450 —. In later years, Earl Robert Layman did some of Cas's legal work and often had the chance to speak privately with him.

451 Wheeler, *Knoxville, Tennessee*, 75.

452 Joshua S. Hodge, "Please Don't Broadcast My Name: Cas Walker, Local Celebrity, and the Welfare Gap," Journal of East Tennessee History 90, (2018): 76.

453 Wheeler, *Knoxville, Tennessee*, 73.

454 Kyvig, *Daily Life*, 181.

455 "Ehude Fellows," 7.
456 ——.

Chapter 21

457 Kyvig, *Daily Life*, 218.
458 McElvaine, *The Great Depression*, 172.
459 ——, 184.
460 Kyvig, *Daily Life*, 209.
461 Brad Austin, "'College Would be a Dead Old Dump Without It': Intercollegiate Athletics in East Tennessee During the Depression Era," *Journal of East Tennessee History* 69, (1997): 50.
462 Wetherington, "Streetcar City," 102.
463 Wheeler, *Knoxville, Tennessee*, 57.
464 Layman, *A History*, 218.
465 Earl Robert Layman, interview.

Chapter 22

466 Wheeler, *Knoxville, Tennessee*, 57.
467 "Women Cite."
468 Wheeler, *Knoxville, Tennessee*, 57.
469 "Women Cite."
470 "'Appalling Conditions' Revealed by Survey of Institutions for Negroes," *Knoxville News-Sentinel*, May 22, 1936, NewsBank.
471 "The Forum," *Knoxville News-Sentinel*, January 14, 1934, NewsBank.
472 Miller, *New World*, 264.
473 Kyvig, *Daily Life*, 228.
474 "Cured Ham Was Sick," *Knoxville News-Sentinel*, April 5, 1940, NewsBank.
475 Kyvig, *Daily Life*, 197–9.
476 Neely, *Shadow Side*, 81.
477 ——, 82–3.
478 Kyvig, *Daily Life*, 227.
479 ——, 102.
480 Carole E. Scott, "The History of the Radio Industry in the United States to 1940," EH.net, accessed June 20, 2020, https://eh.net/?s=History+of+the+radio.
481 Ed Hooper, *Images of America: Knoxville's WNOX* (Charleston: Arcadia Publishing, 2009), 15.
482 ——, 16.
483 William E. Hardy, *Historic Photos of Knoxville* (Nashville: Turner Publishing, 2007), 157.
484 Kyvig, *Daily Life*, 104.
485 Layman, *A History*, 122.

Chapter 23

486 Earl Robert Layman, interview.
487 Banker, *Appalachians All*, 180.
488 Stevvi Cook, director of the Grainger County Archives, email message to author, September 22, 2019.
489 Creekmore, *Knoxville!*, 161.
490 Cook, email.
491 Banker, *Appalachians All*, 180.
492 Creekmore, *Knoxville!*, 158; and Deaderick, *Heart*, 62.

493 The author first encountered this film while watching *The Early Show*, a local television program that aired old movies. Even as an adolescent, I noticed that the misrepresentations were striking. Whisnant, 273 mentions the film as well.

494 Banker, *Appalachians All*, 180.

495 Rothrock, *French-Broad*, 209.

496 Earl Robert Layman, interview.

497 ——.

498 Kyvig, *Daily Life*, 142.

499 *New Zealand Tablet*, "Nobody Knows But Mother," April 4, 1912, 61, https://paperspast.natlib.govt.nz/periodicals/NZT19120404.2.90.1.

500 Layman, *A History*, 126.

Chapter 24

501 "Chicago Designer Prefers Originating Trousseaus," *Knoxville News-Sentinel*, August 1, 1938, Newsbank.

502 "US, Applications for Seaman's Protection Certificates, 1916–1940," digital image s.v., "Ehude H. Fellows," Ancestry.com, https://www.ancestry.com/search/collections/61257; and "US, World War I Draft Registration Cards, 1917–1918," digital image s.v., "Ehude Henderson Fellows," Ancestry.com, https://www.ancestry.com/search/collections/6482. Fellows registered for the draft from the Knoxville jail. The author could not find information on military service, including a dishonorable discharge.

503 "Ehude Fellows."

504 "Knoxville Boy."

505 "Ehude Fellows."

506 ——.

507 Besmann, *A Separate Circle*, 108.

508 ——, 57–8.

509 Hicks, "The Great Objector," 46.

510 ——, 61.

511 Earl Robert Layman, interview.

512 Bob Cunningham, "Arizona Folk Discover Their Governor Doesn't 'Take' Remarks about Tennessee," *Knoxville News-Sentinel*, July, 2, 1939, NewsBank.

513 —— All subsequent quotations from the Arizona encounter are from this source.

514 ——.

515 Earl Robert Layman, interview.

516 Linn, "Jacob Layman."

517 "Questionnaire Throws Real Light on Legislative Candidates," *Knoxville News-Sentinel*, July 25, 1938, Newsbank.com.

Chapter 25

518 Banker, *Appalachians All*, 180-181.

519 Earl Robert Layman, interview.

520 Bernstein, interview.

521 "It's Duty of Ministers to Speak on Politics," *Knoxville News-Sentinel*, November 26, 1939, NewsBank.

522 Wheeler, *Knoxville, Tennessee*, 39, 77.

523 ——, 83.

524 ——, 63.

525 ——, 79–83.

526 "W. Earl Layman Heard," *Knoxville Journal*, December 21, 1948, Newspapers.com, https://www.newspapers.com/image/588237667.

527 "Lawyer Free on Charges of False Oath," *Knoxville Journal*, December 22, 1948, Newspapers.com, https://www.newspapers.com/image/588237783/.

528 "W. Earl."

529 Wheeler, *Knoxville, Tennessee*, 78.

530 "W. Earl."

531 "Lawyer Free."

532 ——.

BIBLIOGRAPHY

Ancestry.com. "1900 United States Federal Census." Accessed on March 8, 2018. https://www.ancestry.com/search/collections/7602/.

——. "1910 United States Federal Census." https://www.ancestry.com/search/collections/7884.

——. "Florida, US, Arriving and Departing Passenger and Crew Lists, 1898–1963." https://www.ancestry.com/search/collections/8842.

——. "US, Applications for Seaman's Protection Certificates, 1916–1940." https://www.ancestry.com/search/collections/61257/.

——. "US, World War I Draft Registration Cards, 1917–1918." https://www.ancestry.com/search/collections/6482/.

Anniston Star. "Gadsden Business Woman Visit Anniston." November 19, 1926. Newspapers.com. https://www.newspapers.com/image/101798998.

Armstrong, Ken. "The 1919 Race Riots." *Chicago Tribune.* July 12, 2018. http://www.chicagotribune.com.

Austin, Brad. "'College Would be a Dead Old Dump Without It': Intercollegiate Athletics in East Tennessee During the Depression Era." *Journal of East Tennessee History* 69, (1997): 29–61.

Banker, Mark T. *Appalachians All: East Tennesseans and the Elusive History of an American Region.* Knoxville: University of Tennessee Press, 2010.

Barbara Winick Bernstein. Telephone interview with the author. 2017.

Beale, Clyde and Robert Moorefield. "Drab Shantytown Has No Palaces But 'It's Better Than Up Yonder.'" *The Knoxville Journal.* July 7, 1934. Newspapers.com. https://www.newspapers.com/image/586453300/.

Bergeron, Paul, Steven Ash, and Jeanette Keith. *Tennesseans and Their History.* Knoxville: University of Tennessee Press, 1999.

Besmann, Wendy Lowe. *A Separate Circle: Jewish Life in Knoxville, Tennessee.* Knoxville: University of Tennessee Press, 2001.

Bierman, Harold. "The 1929 Stock Market Crash." EH.Net. March 26, 2008. http://eh.net/encyclopedia/the-1929-stock-market-crash/.

Bishop, E. L. Quoted in Dave Tabler. "The Great Pandemic of 1918, Part I." AppalachianHistory.net. Posted October 9, 2017. https://www.appalachianhistory. net/2017/10/great-pandemic-of-1918-part-1.html.

Booker, Robert J. "Knoxville Has Come Long Way from When It Had Just Six Principal Streets." *Knoxville News-Sentinel.* July 30, 2018. https://www.knoxnews.com/story/ opinion/columnists/robert-booker/2018/07/30/knoxville-has-come-long-way-when-had-just-six-principal-streets-opinion/810590002/.

Booker, Robert. "Opinion: Flu Epidemic of 1918 Took a Toll in Knoxville." KnoxNews. com. Posted March 5, 2018. https://www.knoxnews.com/story/opinion/columnists/robert-booker/2018/03/05/opinion-flu-epidemic-1918-took-toll-knoxville/390038002/.

Boyer, Paul S., Clifford E. Clark Jr., Karen Halttunen, Joseph F. Kett, Neal Salisbury, Harvard Sitkoff, and Nancy Woloch. *The Enduring Vision: A History of the American People.* 7th ed. Boston: Wadsworth, 2011.

Bridges, Edwin C. *Alabama: The Making of an American State.* Tuscaloosa: University of Alabama press, 2016.

Brownlow, Kevin. *Hollywood: The Pioneers.* London: Collins, 1979.

Calhoun County Alabama. "Calhoun County History." May 11, 2022. https://www. calhouncounty.org/history/.

Cansler, Sarah. "Stamp Out This Awful Cancer: The Fear of Radicals, Atheists, and Modernism at the University of Tennessee in the 1920s." *Journal of East Tennessee History* 85, (2013): 50.

Chattanooga News. "Fellows Brothers Deny Shooting Merchant." April 25, 1918. Chronicling America: Historic American Newspapers. Library of Congress. https:// chroniclingamerica.loc.gov/lccn/sn85038531/1918-04-25/ed-1/seq-3/.

——. "Hard Blow at Law and Order." October 25, 1919. Chronicling America: Historic American Newspapers. Library of Congress. https://chroniclingamerica.loc.gov/lccn/ sn85038531/1919-10-25/ed-1/seq-8/.

——. "Murder in First Degree." April 5, 1919. Chronicling America: Historic American Newspapers. Library of Congress. https://chroniclingamerica.loc.gov/lccn/ sn85038531/1919-04-05/ed-1/seq-5/.

——. "State Guards Turn Machine Guns on Crowd." September 1, 1919. Chronicling America: Historic American Newspapers. Library of Congress. https://chroniclingamerica. loc.gov/lccn/sn85038531/1919-09-01/ed-1/seq-2/.

Collins, William J. and Marianne H. Wanamaker. "The Great Migration in Black and White: New Evidence on the Selection and Sorting of Southern Migrants." *The Journal of Economic History* 75, no. 4 (December 2015): 979. https://doi.org/10.1017/S0022050715001527.

"Come to Make Records." East Tennessee History Center exhibit. September 2016.

Conkin, Paul K. "Evangelicals, Fugitives and Hillbillies." In *Tennessee History: The Land, the People and the Culture.* Ed. Carroll Van West. Knoxville: University of Tennessee Press, 2001. 311.

Cook, Stevvi. Email message to author. September 22, 2019.

Creekmore, Betsey Beeler. *Knoxville!* Knoxville: East Tennessee Historical Society 1991.

Creekmore, David. Personal interview with the author. August 1, 2017.

Cuba. Peninsular and Occidental Steamship Company flyer. USA: 1929.

Cummings, William Joseph. "Community, Violence, and the Nature of Change: Whitecapping in Sevier County, Tennessee, During the 1890s." Master's thesis. University of Tennessee, 1988. https://trace.tennessee.edu/utk_gradthes/8.

Cunningham, Bob. "Arizona Folk Discover Their Governor Doesn't 'Take' Remarks about Tennessee." *Knoxville News-Sentinel.* July 2, 1939. NewsBank.

Day, Nicholas. "I'm Supposed to Do What to Make My Baby Poop? When He's *How Old?*" Slate. April 16, 2013. https://slate.com/human-interest/2013/04/history-of-early-toilet-training-advice.html.

Deaderick, Lucile, ed. *Heart of the Valley: A History of Knoxville, Tennessee.* Knoxville: East Tennessee Historical Society, 1976.

Deal, W. L. "Little Benny (Father, Dear Father, Come Home with Me Now)." Recorded in Heber Springs, Arkansas, on July 16, 1953. MP3 published online by the John Quincy Wolf Folklore Collection, Lyon College, 2002. https://home.lyon.edu/wolfcollection/songs/deallittle1234.html.

Dickinson, W. Calvin. "Temperance." Tennessee Encyclopedia. Last modified March 1, 2018. https://tennesseeencyclopedia.net/entries/temperance/.

Dillon Herald. "Army Officer Is Killed in Race Riot." September 4, 1919. Newspapers.com. https://www.newspapers.com/image/354162531.

"Dodd, Bobby." Tennessee Sports Hall of Fame. Accessed March 30, 2019. https:www.tshf.net/halloffame/dodd-bobby/.

Draughon Business College, The. Promotional brochure. Circa, 1929.

Du Bois, W.E.B. "Let Us Reason Together." *Crisis* 18, no. 5 (September 1919): 231–5. https://www.marxists.org/history/usa/workers/civil-rights/crisis/0900-crisis-v18n05-w107.pdf.

Eschner, Kat. "The 1919 Black Sox Baseball Scandal Was Just One of Many." *Smithsonian Magazine.* September 1, 2017. https://www.smithsonianmag.com/smart-news/1919-black-sox-baseball-scandal-wasnt-first-180964673/.

Etowah County Board of Education Archives. Gadsden, Alabama.

Etowah County Centennial Committee. *The History of Etowah County, Alabama.* Berwyn Heights: Heritage Publishing Consultants, 1968.

Etowah County Heritage Book Committee. *Heritage of Etowah County, Alabama, The.* Berwyn Heights: Heritage Publishing Consultants, 1999.

FamilySearch.com. "US WWI Draft Registration Cards 1917–1918." https://www.familysearch.org/ark:/61903/1:1:KZ6K-4K3.

Flint, Wayne. **Poor But Proud: Alabama's Poor Whites**. Tuscaloosa: University of Alabama Press, 1989.

Gabrielle, Vincent. "Past Pandemics in Knoxville Have Led to Stark Political Choices – with Deadly Consequences." KnoxNews.com. Posted June 2, 2020. https://www.knoxnews.com/story/news/health/2020/06/02/past-pandemics-knoxville-have-led-real-consequences-coronavirus/5089850002/.

Gadsden City Directory (1927). Gadsden, Alabama.

Gadsden Daily Times-News. "A True Friend." January, 17, 1920. Newspapers.com. https://www.newspapers.com/image/322633040.

——. "Brannon Springs." January 5, 1923. Newspapers.com. https://www.newspapers.com/image/571725186.

——. "Burns Academy." December 9, 1922. Newspapers.com. https://www.newspapers.com/image/322718314/.

——. "Cedar Bend High School to Close Thursday." April 28, 1923. Newspapers.com. https://www.newspapers.com/image/571736442/.

——. "Etowah Teachers Successful in Examinations." September 16, 1921. Newspapers.com. https://www.newspapers.com/image/322699675.

——. "Gadsden Route 1." May 10, 1919. Newspapers.com. https://www.newspapers.com/image/322713455.

——. "Morgan's Cross Roads." April 28, 1922. Newspapers.com. https://www.newspapers.com/image/322708683.

——. "News of Society." Undated hard copy clipping, 6.

——. "Ohatchee R. 1." April 18, 1919. Newspapers.com. https://www.newspapers.com/clip/93454198/horace-freeman-kodaking-near-ohatchee/.

——. "Ohatchee Route 1." May 8, 1919. Newspapers.com. https://www.newspapers.com/image/322712977.

——. "Rural Children Pass Seventh Grade Exams." May 12, 1919. Newspapers.com. https://www.newspapers.com/image/322713480/.

——. "South Side." November 14, 1923. Newspapers.com. https://www.newspapers.com/image/571717911.

——. "The Negro Migration." May 10, 1923. Newspapers.com. https://www.newspapers.com/image/571693879.

——. "There Is No Boy Problem. It Is a Man's Problem." July 2, 1924. Newspapers.com. https://www.newspapers.com/image/571732143.

——. "West Gadsden Items of News." January 29, 1923. Newspapers.com. https://www.newspapers.com/image/571727087.

Gadsden Times. "Little-McDill." October 12, 1924. Newspapers.com. https://www.newspapers.com/image/571740276.

Garth, Gary. "Deep in the Smokies a Prize Catch." *USA Today.* May 27, 2016. https://pressreader.com/usa/usa-today-us-edition/.20160527/282355448989029.

Gerra, Doris Anita Little. *My Little, Steward (Stewart) Ancestors of the Southern States and Allied Lines 1670–1997.* Kensington: self-published, 1997.

Goldberg, Ronald Allen. *America in the Twenties.* Syracuse: Syracuse University Press, 2003.

Great Smoky Mountains National Park. "History." Accessed May 7, 2019. https://www.gsmnp.com/great-smoky-mountains-national-park/history/.

Greeneville Daily Sun. "Court Loses 'Likker.'" September 28, 1918. Chronicling America: Historic American Newspapers. Library of Congress. https://chroniclingamerica.loc.gov/lccn/sn97065122/1918-09-28/ed-1/seq-4/.

——. "Knoxville in Throes of Serious Race Riots." September 1, 1919. Chronicling America: Historic American Newspapers. Library of Congress, https://chroniclingamerica.loc.gov/lccn/sn97065122/1919-09-01/ed-1/seq-1/.

——. "Riot Situation in Knoxville Now Thought to Be Well in Hand." September 1, 1919. Chronicling America: Historic American Newspapers. Library of Congress. https://chroniclingamerica.loc.gov/lccn/sn97065122/1919-09-01/ed-1/seq-1/.

Hardy, William E. *Historic Photos of Knoxville.* Nashville: Turner Publishing, 2007.

Harrison, Russell. *Progressive Knoxville 1904: A Pictorial Review of the City.* Knoxville: Russell Harrison, 1903.

Hicks, Bobby Eugene. "The Great Objector: The Life and Public Career of Dr. John R. Neal." *East Tennessee Historical Society Publications* 41, (1969): 33–66. East Tennessee History Center biography file.

Historic Downtown Knoxville Walking Tour. Knoxville: Knox Heritage, 2013.

Hodge, Joshua S. "Please Don't Broadcast My Name: Cas Walker, Local Celebrity, and the Welfare Gap." *Journal of East Tennessee History* 90, (2018): 70–83.

Hooper, Ed. *Images of America: Knoxville's WNOX.* Charleston: Arcadia Publishing, 2009.

Knox County in the World War 1917-1918-1919. Knoxville: Knoxville Lithographing Company, 1919. https://hdl.handle.net/2027/loc.ark:/13960/t8mc9kc6n.

Knoxville City Directory (1920). East Tennessee History Center.

Knoxville City Directory (1921). East Tennessee History Center.

Knoxville City Directory (1923). East Tennessee History Center.

Knoxville City Directory (1924). East Tennessee History Center.

Knoxville City Directory (1925). East Tennessee History Center.

Knoxville City Directory (1926). East Tennessee History Center.

Knoxville City Directory (1932). East Tennessee History Center.

Knoxville Independent. "From all Parts of Tennessee." May 4, 1918. Newspapers.com. https://www.newspapers.com/image/352046655.

——. "Must Use Less Sugar, Allied Needs Grow." October 12, 1918. Newspapers.com. https://www.newspapers.com/image/352051391.

——. "No Prospect of Sex War." October 26, 1918. Chronicling America: Historic American Newspapers. Library of Congress. https://chroniclingamerica.loc.gov/lccn/sn85042907/1918-10-26/ed-1/seq-8/.

——. "Temperance Notes." November 16, 1918. Newspapers.com. https://www.newspapers.com/image/352051924/.

Knoxville Journal and Tribune. "3 Arrests in Nichols Case." February 27, 1918. Newspapers.com. https://www.newspapers.com/image/585522443.

——. "7 Ways to Increase Winter Comfort on the Farm." January 14, 1918. Newspapers.com. https://www.newspapers.com/image/585520962.

——. "An Old Time Fee-Grabber." September 27, 1924. Newspapers.com. https://www.newspapers.com/image/586077859.

——. "Bloody Riots Follow Attack on Jail; Five Known Dead; Many are Wounded." August 31, 1919. Newspapers.com. https://www.newspapers.com/image/585316455.

——. "Killed in Effort to Escape Negro." August 31, 1919. Newspapers.com. https://www.newspapers.com/image/585316455.

——. "Known Casualties." September 1, 1919. Newspapers.com. https://www.newspapers.com/image/585317430.

——. "Knoxville Boy Escapes Prison." November 27, 1917. Newspapers.com. https://www.newspapers.com/image/585415933.

——. "Moonshine has the Call." January 10, 1918. Newspapers.com. https://www.newspapers.com/image/585520758.

——. "Nichols' Friends Aid in Manhunt." Newspapers.com. https://www.newspapers.com/image/585522367.

——. "Peter Nichols Near Death Door was Shot Twice by Highwaymen." February 23, 1918. Newspapers.com. https://www.newspapers.com/image/585522291.

——. "Tells Story of Nichols' Assault." April 24, 1918. Newspapers.com. https://www.newspapers.com/image/585384062.

——. "To Make Fight on Moonshine." January 25, 1918. Newspapers.com. https://www.newspapers.com/image/585521390.

——. "Two Defendants Are Freed in Riot Cases." October 22, 1919. Newspapers.com. https://www.newspapers.com/image/585393740.

——. "Two Prisoners Are Recaptured." September 28, 1918. Newspapers.com. https://www.newspapers.com/image/585523251.

——. "Wildcat Booze Flows Freely." January 10, 1918. Newspapers.com. https://www.newspapers.com/image/585520763.

Knoxville Journal. "Bar Examination Passed by Many." August 11, 1925. Newspapers.com. https://www.newspapers.com/image/586306608.

——. "Fire Captain Is Bound Over." January 16, 1930. NewsBank.

——. "Lawyer Free on Charges of False Oath." December 22, 1948. Newspapers.com. https://www.newspapers.com/image/588237783/.

——. "W. Earl Layman Heard." December 21, 1948. Newspapers.com. https://www.newspapers.com/image/588237667.

Knoxville News. "Rally around Dr. John R. Neal." July 4, 1923. Newspapers.com. https://www.newspapers.com/image/771842972.

——. "Your First Move, Johnson City." March 11, 1926. Newspapers.com. https://www.newspapers.com/image/772676095.

Knoxville News-Sentinel. "'Appalling Conditions Revealed by Survey of Institutions for Negroes." May 22, 1936. NewsBank.

——. "Butch Cassidy Partner Earned Knoxville Notoriety." August 15, 2001. https://archive.knoxnews.com/news/local/butch-cassidy-partner-earned-knoxville-notoriety-ep-403419960-357608011.html/.

——. "Charges Hurled as Robbery Is Aired." January 15, 1930. NewsBank.

——. "Chicago Designer Prefers Originating Trousseaus." August 1, 1938. Newsbank.

——. "Cured Ham Was Sick." April 5, 1940. NewsBank.

——. "Depositors Crowd about Closed Bank." November 12, 1930. NewsBank.

——. "Ehude Fellows, Whose Life Wrapped Up Secrets of Local and World Violence, Ends It as New 'Break' as Author Begins To Open for Him." March 26, 1939. Newspapers.com. https://www.newspapers.com/image/772783909.

——. "Girl's Admission Frees 3 Youths." September 9, 1934. NewsBank.

——. "Harvey Logan's Escape." June 29, 1903. Newspapers.com. https://www.newspapers.com/image/585641515.

——. "Inventory Is Made of Bank of Tennessee." November 12, 1930. NewsBank.

——. "It's Duty of Ministers to Speak on Politics." November 26, 1939. NewsBank.

——. "Judge E. G. Stooksbury, Knox Jurist, Dies at 69." July 9, 1948. East Tennessee History Center vertical file.

——. "Law Students Threaten to Quit." July 11, 1923. Newspapers.com. https://www.newspapers.com/image/771843662.

——. "Lawyer Says Fellows Got New Overcoat in Vain Effort to Escape Conviction." December 8, 1934. Newspapers.com. https://www.newspapers.com/image/772619696.

——. "Lieut. Wright Cables." November 13, 1918. Newspapers.com. https://www.newspapers.com/image/586774502.

——. "Miller Out on Own Word in 'Fixing Case.'" January 18, 1930. NewsBank.

——. "'Please Old Santy, Bring us a Hydrant' Is Plea of Shanty Town." December 13, 1935. NewsBank.

——. "Public Invited to Hear Darrow." June 20, 1925. Newspapers.com. https://www.newspapers.com/image/772674785.

——. "Questionnaire Throws Real Light on Legislative Candidates." July 25, 1938. Newsbank.com.

——. "Say Menace of Street Women Grows; Committees Push Workhouse Plan." January 11, 1934. NewsBank.

——. "Says Farmers Fire Woods to Keep CCC Youths Away." March 22, 1934. NewsBank.

——. "South's Women Ask for United Lynching Fight." January 10, 1934. Newspapers.com. https://www.newspapers.com/image/772725145.

——. "Story of Logan's Deeds and History of His Life." June 29, 1903. Newspapers.com. https://www.newspapers.com/image/585641492/.

——. "The Forum." January 14, 1934. NewsBank.

——. "To Continue Fight on Morgan Policy." July 18, 1923. Newspapers.com. https://www.newspapers.com/image/771844128.

——. "W. E. Layman Weds." February 23, 1929. NewsBank.

——. "Women Cite 5 Needs of City." May 22, 1936. NewsBank.

——. Obituaries. "Judge W. E. Layman." October 1974.

Knoxville Sentinel. "All Knoxville Is Glorifying over Victory." November 11, 1918. Newspapers.com. https://www.newspapers.com/image/586774034.

——. "Damage to Jail May be $15,000." September 1, 1919. Newspapers.com. https://www.newspapers.com/image/586674844.

——. "Five Escape from County Jail; Posse Hunting for Fugitives." September 14, 1918. Newspapers.com. https://www.newspapers.com/image/586817306.

——. "Tennessee's Valiant Heroes Made History on Battlefield." March 29, 1919. Newspapers.com. https://www.newspapers.com/image/586653920.

——. "Thousands in Victory Parade." November 12, 1918. Newspapers.com. https://www. newspapers.com/image/586774261.

Kyvig, David. *Daily Life in the United States, 1920–1940: How Americans Lived Through the Roaring Twenties and the Great Depression*. Chicago: Ivan R. Dee Publisher, 2004.

Lakin, Matt. "Crusade and Crash: Twenties Brought Corruption, Cleanup, Calamity." *Knoxville News-Sentinel*. March 25, 2012. https://archive.knoxnews.com/news/local/crusade-crash-twenties-brought-corruption-cleanup-calamity-ep-361042530-357121911.html/.

Lakin, Matthew. "'A Dark Night': The Knoxville Race Riot of 1919." *The Journal of East Tennessee History* 72, (2000): 1–29. teachtnhistory.com.

Lamon, Lester C. "Tennessee Race Relations and the Knoxville Riot of 1919." *The East Tennessee Historical Society's Publications* 41, (1969): 67–85. teachtnhistory.com.

Layman, Earl Robert. *From the Emmental to Eldee: A History of the Layman Family*. Baltimore: Gateway Press, 2001.

——. Interview with the author. May 19, 2018.

Layman, Marie L. Letter to Sylvia Layman. January 25, 1982.

Layman, William Earl. Interview by David Creekmore, 1973. Cassette recording owned by the author's family.

Lewis, Tom. *Washington: A History of Our National City*. New York: Basic Books, 2015.

Linn, Beulah D. "Jacob Layman-Revolutionary Soldier." *Sevier County News*. American Bicentennial Section. November 20, 1975.

Maryville Times. "Knoxville Has Riot." September 3, 1919. Chronicling America: Historic American Newspapers. Library of Congress. https://chroniclingamerica.loc.gov/lccn/sn89058370/1919-09-03/ed-1/seq-1/.

Mastran, Shelley Smith, Nan Lowerre, and United States Forest Service. *Mountaineers and Rangers: A History of the Federal Forest Management in the Southern Appalachians, 1900–1981*. Washington, DC: US Department of Agriculture, Forest Service, 1983. https://hdl.handle.net/2027/uva.x001867535.

McElvaine, Robert S. *The Great Depression: America, 1929–1941*. New York: Three Rivers Press, 2009.

McRary, Amy. "The 1920s brought Park Dreams, Court Drama and the Theater." *Knoxville News-Sentinel*. February 2, 2017. https://www.knoxnews.com/story/life/arts/2017/02/25/papers-pixels-1920s-brought-park-dreams-court-drama-and-new-theater-knoxville/98211566/.

Memphis News Scimitar. "Judge Denounces Actions of Mob in Knoxville Riot." September 5, 1919. 4th ed. Chronicling America: Historic American Newspapers. Library of Congress. https://chroniclingamerica.loc.gov/lccn/sn98069867/1919-09-05/ed-1/seq-13/.

——. "Jury Hard to Get." April 4, 1919. Chronicling America: Historic American Newspapers. Library of Congress. https://chroniclingamerica.loc.gov/lccn/sn98069867/1919-04-04/ed-1/seq-12/.

——. "Knoxville Woman Is Attacked by Negro." September 25, 1919. 4th ed. Chronicling America: Historic American Newspapers, Library of Congress. https://chroniclingamerica. loc.gov/lccn/sn98069867/1919-09-25/ed-1/seq-15/.

Miller, Nathan. *New World Coming: The Twenties and the Making of America.* New York: Scribner, 2003.

Murfree, Mary. *In the Tennessee Mountains.* 9th ed. New York: Houghton Mifflin, 1885.

Neely, Jack. "Knoxville during the Great War." Lecture presented at Knox Heritage in Knoxville, Tennessee. February 2018.

——. *From the Shadow Side: and other stories of Knoxville, Tennessee.* Oak Ridge: Tellico Books, 2003.

——. *The Tennessee Theatre: A Grand Entertainment Palace.* Knoxville: Historic Tennessee Theatre Foundation, 2015.

Nystrom, Justin Nystrom. "The Vanished World of the New Orleans Longshoreman." *Southern Spaces.* March 5, 2014. https://southernspaces.org/2014/vanished-world-new-orleans-longshoreman/.

Ogle, Cora. *Voices of the Land.* Permanent exhibit. East Tennessee History Center. Knoxville, Tennessee.

Okrent, Daniel. *Last Call: The Rise and Fall of Prohibition.* New York: Scribner, 2011.

Owen, Thomas McAdory. *History of Alabama and Dictionary of Alabama Biography.* Chicago: The S. J. Clarke Publishing Company, 1921.

Parrish, Susan Scott. "The Great Mississippi Flood of 1927 Laid Bare the Divide Between the North and the South." *Smithsonian Magazine.* April 11, 2017. https://www. smithsonianmag.com/history/devastating-mississippi-river-flood-uprooted-americas-faith-progress-180962856/.

Perl, Peter. "Race Riot of 1919 Gave Glimpse of Future Struggles." *Washington Post.* March 1, 1999. https://www.washingtonpost.com/wp-srv/local/2000/raceriot0301.htm.

Pucket, Christine S. and Joe Barnes. *A Panorama of Northeast Alabama and Etowah County.* Gadsden: Starr Publishing, 1992.

Purcell, Aaron D. "Suppressed Currents: The 'Fool Report' and the Early Tennessee Valley Authority." *Journal of East Tennessee History* 74, (2002): 69–83.

Rehagen, Tony. "Forgotten Lessons from the 1917 East St. Louis Race Riots." *St. Louis Magazine.* July 2, 2017.

Rothrock, Mary U. Ed. *The French-Broad Holston Country.* Knoxville: East Tennessee Historical Society, 1946. https://hdl.handle.net/2027/mdp.39015012076892.

Ruuska, Luis. "The Law Professor Who Rarely Bathed, Got Fired from U.T. and Was Lead Counsel in the Scopes Monkey Trial." University of Tennessee College of Law. January 16, 2016. https://law.utk.edu/2016/01/12/neal/.

Saxton, Lyle. *Fabulous New Orleans.* New York: The Century Company, 1928.

Schuyler, Lorraine Gates. *The Weight of Their Votes: Southern Women and Political Leverage in the 1920s.* Chapel Hill: University of North Carolina Press, 2006.

Scott, Carole E. "The History of the Radio Industry in the United States to 1940." EH.net. Accessed June 20, 2020. https://eh.net/?s=History+of+the+radio.

Selma Times-Argus. "Alabama News." July 21, 1876. Newspapers.com. https://www. newspapers.com/image/355695913.

Shapiro, Henry D. *Appalachia on Our Mind.* Chapel Hill: University of North Carolina Press, 1978.

Sharp, Tim. *Images of America: Knoxville Music Before Bluegrass.* Charleston: Arcadia Publishing, 2020.

Shuffridge, Lynda Childers. "Draughon School of Business (Little Rock)." In *Encyclopedia of Arkansas,* (2005).

Smithsonian. "Knowing the Presidents: Calvin Coolidge." Accessed December 10, 2020. https://si.edu/spotlight/calvin-coolidge.

Sonborn Map Company. *Map of Congested District: Knoxville, Tennessee Sections 13, 21, and 22.* 1917; 220 feet per 1 inch scale, 21 by 25 in.

Southside High School advanced placement senior English class. "Collection of Old Southside, Alabama." Unpublished manuscript, 1988–1989.

Still, Laura. *A Haunted History of Knoxville.* Asheville: Stony River Media, 2014.

Thomas, John Kyle. "The Cultural Reconstruction of an Appalachian City: Knoxville, Tennessee, and the Coming of the Movies." *The Journal of East Tennessee History,* no. 65 (1993): 40.

Thomas, Mary Martha. *The New Woman in Alabama: Social Reforms and Suffrage, 1890– 1920.* Tuscaloosa: The University of Alabama Press, 1992.

Trott, Louisa. "The Great War in Tennessee's Newspapers." Lecture presented at the East Tennessee History Society in Knoxville, Tennessee. May 16, 2018.

Trout, Seven. "'Where Do We Go from Here?': Ernest Hemingway's 'Soldier's Home' And American Veterans Of World War I (2)." *The Hemingway Review* 20, no. 1 (2000): 5. Gale Academic OneFile. Accessed April 25, 2022. https://link.gale.com/apps/doc/A68506412/ AONE?u=anon~ff3a91d1&sid=googleScholar&xid=26ca4b86.

Twain, Mark. *The Adventures of Huckleberry Finn.* 1884 ed. New York: Penguin Books, 2014.

United States Veterans Bureau. "Resignation, Marie F. Little." October 13, 1924. National Archives.

Vincent, Bert Vincent. "Strolling." *Knoxville News-Sentinel.* November 29, 1959. East Tennessee History Center biography file.

W. M. Cobb, Chief, Personnel Division, Office of the Adjutant General, War Department. Personnel Record to Marie F. Little. June 23, 1924. From the Veteran's Affairs Agency, National Archives.

Walker, Cas. *My Life History.* Self-published, 1993.

Washington Post. Obituaries. "Robertson, Patricia." November 24, 1976.

Weals, Vic. "Home Folks." *Knoxville Journal.* September 18, 1955. East Tennessee History Center vertical file.

Webb, Samuel L. *Two-Party Politics in the One-Party South.* Tuscaloosa: University of Alabama Press, 1997.

Weiss, Nancy Pottishman. "Mother, the Invention of Necessity: *Dr. Benjamin Spock's Baby and Child Care.*" *American Quarterly* 29, no. 5 (Winter 1977): 519–46. https://doi. org/10.2307/2712572

Wetherington, Mark V. "Streetcar City: Knoxville, Tennessee, 1876–1947." *East Tennessee History Society's Publications* 54 and 55, (1982–1983): 74.

Wheeler, William Bruce. *Knoxville, Tennessee: A Mountain City in the New South*. 3rd ed. Knoxville: University of Tennessee Press, 2020.

Whisnant, David E. *Modernizing the Mountaineer: People, Power, and Planning in Appalachia*. Knoxville: The University of Tennessee Press, 1994.

Will Book II Sevier Co, Tennessee. Transcribed by Lori Ann McKeehan. Sevier County Genealogical Society, 2002.

Williams, Elisabeth. "For Love of the Fight: John R. Neal." *Rhea Notes* 19, no 4. (November 2, 2010): 5. East Tennessee History Center biography file.

Williamson, J. W. *Hillbillyland: What the Movies Did to the Mountains and What the Mountains Did to the Movies*. Chapel Hill: University of North Carolina Press, 1995.

ACKNOWLEDGMENTS

This work owes a debt to Dr. Bruce Wheeler beyond the many references to his book Knoxville, Tennessee. As an undergraduate in his American history course at the University of Tennessee, I was astonished to discover that the professor's area of research was my hometown. That knowledge upended my teenaged view of Knoxville as fundamentally dull. I also wish to thank everyone at Warren Publishing for their expertise and patience. I appreciate the early readers of this work who gave pertinent advice with a supportive spirit. Much love and respect go to my dad, Earl Robert Layman, who has a steadfast and contagious love for East Tennessee. Dad willingly shared his parents, including their foibles, with the world. He and my brother, Doug Layman, told me to write Earl and Marie's real story, not a romanticized one. Without that encouragement, this book would not exist. My sons were also supportive, providing feedback in their areas of expertise. And to Gary, my companion in life and an East Tennessean by choice, thank you for your willingness to embrace my part of the world.

www.ingramcontent.com/pod-product-compliance
Lightning Source LLC
Chambersburg PA
CBHW032042080426
42733CB00006B/162